MW01461514

MILITARY CRISIS MANAGEMENT

**Recent Titles in
Contributions in Military Studies**

Democracy under Siege: New Military Power in Latin America
Augusto Varas, editor

Not Shooting and Not Crying: Psychological Inquiry into Moral Disobedience
Ruth Linn

"Seeing the Elephant": Raw Recruits at the Battle of Shiloh
Joseph Allan Frank and George A. Reaves

Civilian Indoctrination and the Military: World War I and Future Implications for the Military-Industrial Complex
Penn Borden

Arms Race Theory: Strategy and Structure of Behavior
Craig Etcheson

Strategic Impasse: Offense, Defense, and Deterrence Theory and Practice
Stephen J. Cimbala

Feeding the Bear: American Aid to the Soviet Union, 1941-1945
Hubert P. van Tuyll

Military Planning for the Defense of the United Kingdom, 1814-1870
Michael Stephen Partridge

The Hollow Army: How the U.S. Army Is Oversold and Undermanned
William Darryl Henderson

Reevaluating Major Naval Combatants of World War II
James J. Sadkovich, editor

The Culture of War: Invention and Early Development
Richard A. Gabriel

Prisoners, Diplomats, and the Great War: A Study in the Diplomacy of Captivity
Richard Berry Speed III

MILITARY CRISIS MANAGEMENT

U.S. Intervention in
the Dominican Republic, 1965

Herbert G. Schoonmaker

Contributions in Military Studies, Number 95

Greenwood Press
New York • Westport, Connecticut • London

Library of Congress Cataloging-in-Publication Data

Schoonmaker, Herbert Garrettson.
  Military crisis management : U.S. intervention in the Dominican Republic, 1965 / Herbert G. Schoonmaker.
    p. cm. — (Contributions in military studies, ISSN 0883-6884 ; no. 95)
  Includes bibliographical references.
  ISBN 0-313-26685-9 (lib. bdg. : alk. paper)
  1. United States—Foreign relations—Dominican Republic.
  2. Dominican Republic—Foreign relations—United States.
  3. Dominican Republic—History—Revolution, 1965. 4. Civil-military relations—United States—History—20th century. 5. Crisis management—United States—History—20th century. I. Title.
  II. Series.
  E183.8.D6S36 1990
  327.7307293—dc20   89-38227

British Library Cataloguing in Publication Data is available.

Copyright © 1990 by Herbert G. Schoonmaker

All rights reserved. No portion of this book may be reproduced, by any process or technique, without the express written consent of the publisher.

Library of Congress Catalog Card Number: 89-38227
ISBN: 0-313-26685-9
ISSN: 0883-6884

First published in 1990

Greenwood Press, 88 Post Road West, Westport, CT 06881
An imprint of Greenwood Publishing Group, Inc.

Printed in the United States of America

∞

The paper used in this book complies with the Permanent Paper Standard issued by the National Information Standards Organization (Z39.48-1984).

10 9 8 7 6 5 4 3 2 1

Copyright Acknowledgment

Maps are reprinted with the permission from *United States Army Unilateral and Coalition Operations in the 1965 Dominican Republic Intervention* by Lawrence M. Greenberg, U.S. Army Center of Military History.

To my wife Jo Ann

Contents

Maps	ix
Abbreviations	xi
Preface	xv
1. Introduction	1
2. Revolt and Response (24-27 April)	19
3. Decisions and Initial Operations (28-29 April)	33
4. Crisis Management	49
5. Air Operations	67
6. Military and Diplomatic Coordination (30 April-5 May)	77
7. Support Operations	97
8. Peace Force and Political Settlement (May 1965-Sept.1966)	109
9. Conclusions	123
Bibliography	135
Index	145

Maps

1. Caribbean Region   2
2. Santo Domingo (1965)   27
3. Santo Domingo-Initial Line of Communication   91

Abbreviations

AFB	Air Force Base
AID	Agency for International Development
ALT	Airlift task force
BCT	battalion combat team
BLT	battalion landing team
CEFA	<u>Centro de Entrenamiento de las Fuerzas Armadas</u> (Armed Forces Training Center
CINCAFLANT	commander in chief, U.S. Air Forces, Atlantic Command
CINCAFSTRIKE	commander in chief, U.S. Air Forces, Strike Command
CINCARLANT	commander in chief, U.S. Army Forces, Atlantic Command
CINCARSTRIKE	commander in chief, U.S. Army Forces, Strike Command
CINCLANT	commander in chief, Atlantic Command
CINCLANTFLT	commander in chief, Atlantic Fleet
CINCSOUTH	commander in chief, U.S. Southern Command
CINCSTRIKE	commander in chief, U.S. Strike Command
CJTF	commander, joint task force
COMCARIBSEAFRON	commander, Caribbean Sea Frontier
CTG	commander, task group
DA	Department of the Army
DCSOPS	Deputy Chief of Staff for Operations and Plans
DEFCON	defense readiness condition
DRF	division ready force

FBI	Federal Bureau of Investigation
GNR	Government of National Reconstruction
HUMINT	human intelligence
IAAF	Inter-American Armed Force
IAF	Inter-American Force
IAPF	Inter-American Peace Force
ISZ	International Security Zone
JACCC	joint air control coordination center
JTF	joint task force
LANTCOM	(see USLANTCOM)
LBJL	Lyndon B. Johnson Library
LOC	lines of communication
LVT	landing vehicle, tracked
MAAG	Military Assistance Advisory Group
MAP	Military Assistance Program
MEB	Marine expeditionary brigade
MEU	Marine expeditionary unit
MI	Military Intelligence
MTT	Mobile training team
NMCC	National Military Command Center
NSC	National Security Council
OAS	Organization of American States
OES	Organizacion de Estados Americanos (Organization of American States)
1J4	14th of June Political Group
OPLAN	operation plan
PR	Partido Reformista (Reform Party)
PRD	Partido Revolucionario Dominicano (Dominican Revolutionary Party)
PRSC	Social Christian Revolutionary Party
PSYWAR	psychological warfare
ROAD	Reorganization Objective Army Divisions
RSD	Radio Santo Domingo
SEAL	sea-air-land team
SOUTHCOM	(see USSOUTHCOM)
STRICOM	(see USSTRICOM)
TAC	Tactical Air Command
TF	task force
TG	task group
TOE	table(s) of organization and equipment
USACGSC	U.S. Army Command and General Staff College
USAF	U.S. Air Force
USCOMDOMREP	commander, U.S. Forces, Dominican Republic
USCONARC	U.S. Continental Army command
USFORDOMREP	U.S. Forces, Dominican Republic
USIA	U.S. Information Agency
USIS	U.S. Information Service

Abbreviations

USLANTCOM	U.S. Atlantic Command (or LANTCOM)	
	USMC	U.S. Marine Corps
USSOUTHCOM	U.S. Southern Command (or SOUTHCOM)	
USSTRICOM	U.S. Strike Command (or STRICOM)	

Preface

This study analyzes the role and management of U.S. military forces in the Dominican crisis of 1965. The Dominican intervention, like other cold war interventions such as Lebanon in 1958, demonstrated the use of rapidly reacting, joint military forces to achieve limited political objectives. Rapid response with overwhelming force enabled American troops to overcome any opposition before it became organized, stabilized the chaotic situation and prevented a communist takeover of the revolution.

I chose to investigate the Dominican action because it represented a good vehicle for the analysis of U.S. civilian-military relationships during a military operation of this kind. At the same time the civil strife continued in Santo Domingo, U.S. military forces engaged in a variety of duties including combat and peacekeeping and did so while OAS, UN and Washington government teams attempted to negotiate a peace settlement. Such a complex environment necessitated tight civilian control of the engaged armed forces and required restraint by the military especially in carrying out their combat duties. Someone pointed out that our failures in Vietnam were due to our incomprehension and inability to cope with the political dimension of the military problem. The reverse was true in the Dominican case where our understanding of the political dimension figured importantly in our military success.

In addition to political-military factors I focused on the joint army-navy-air aspects of the operation. Although I have not attempted to resolve controversies such as the extent of the communist threat, I have concentrated on the uniqueness of the intervention, which made the lessons learned applicable in some circumstances but not in others. A study of the Dominican intervention is important because of its implications for defense needs and structure at a time of tight military budgets. This type of low-intensity conflict may reoccur since many Third World nations, especially in Latin America, are chronically unstable. Also I have attempted to outline the problems associated with quick reacting forces in this action and indicate the absolute necessity for efficient intelligence, communications, logistics and command and control.

My thanks to Lee Kennett, Lester Langley and Earl Ziemke of the University of Georgia History Department for their assistance; to John Lumpkin and Ben Goldman, formerly of the Office of TAC History, for their many helpful suggestions and editorial corrections; to Jean Moenk of the Army Forces Command and Bernard Nalty of the Office of Air Force History who provided my first introduction to the subject; to Lawrence Greenberg, formerly of the Army Center of Military History, who brought me up-to-date on the subject and especially to Lawrence Yates of the Army's Combat Studies Institute who has been very helpful with source materials and has authored an excellent account of the "Power Pack" operation. I also want to thank the staffs of the libraries and research centers of the following institutions for the extensive use of their facilities: the University of Georgia; the Albert F. Simpson Historical Research Center; the Army Military History Institute; the Naval Historical Division; the Marine Corps History and Museum Division; the Army, Navy and Air War Colleges; the Armed Forces Staff College; the library of the U.S. Naval Academy; the Oral History Department of the U.S. Naval Institute; and the Lyndon Baines Johnson Library. Finally, I am grateful for the typing skill and dedication of Rita Cussnick and my word processing expert, Martha Daniel.

MILITARY
CRISIS
MANAGEMENT

1

Introduction

On 24 April 1965 army troops attempted to overthrow the ruling civilian triumvirate in the Dominican Republic. The bloodless coup was successful, but an armed struggle for control of the government broke out between dissident troops and other military forces seeking to establish a military junta. Civilians soon joined the rebellion and the ensuing anarchy in Santo Domingo led to military intervention by the United States. This action occurred at approximately the same time that President Lyndon Johnson made the decision to commit ground troops to the Vietnam War. So just as the United States became involved in conventional warfare in Southeast Asia, U.S. forces carried out a counterinsurgency action in the Caribbean region. The question is, what caused this additional commitment at this time?

One answer to that question lies in the strategic importance to the United States of the Dominican Republic and its critical location in the Caribbean. As practically every U.S. president since Monroe has stated, the region is in our "own backyard." The Dominican Republic shares the island of Hispaniola with Haiti and lies about 600 miles southeast of Miami between Cuba and Puerto Rico, a free commonwealth associated with the United States. Because of its proximity to the continent and Puerto Rico and its strategic position as a gateway to the Caribbean Sea and a guardian of the approaches to the Panama Canal Zone, the Dominican Republic has a long history of military, political, and economic involvement with the United States. The importance of the country to American security interests increased when nearby Cuba became a stepping-stone for the attempted introduction of Soviet offensive missiles into the Western Hemisphere and a base for communist subversion of other Latin American countries (see map 1).[1]

The eastern shore of the Dominican Republic borders the Mona Passage, one of four major choke points of sea lanes in the Caribbean Sea. These are points at which shipping lanes could be severed. The other three major choke points are the Straits of Florida, the Yucatan Channel, and the Windward Passage; all of which border on Cuba. The

Map 1. Caribbean Region

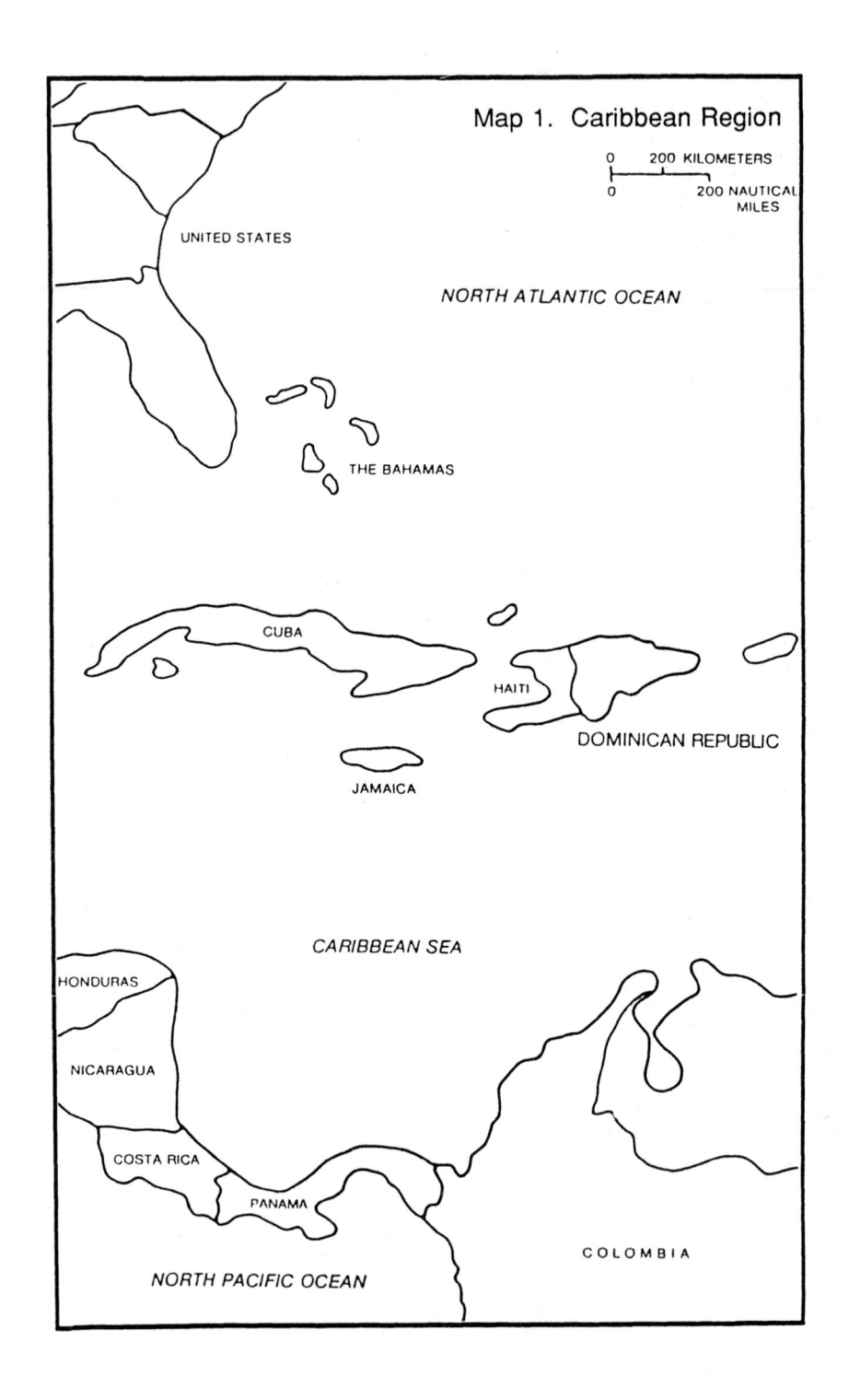

Introduction

vulnerability of the area was well demonstrated during World War II when the Germans sent submarines into the Straits of Florida where they sank a large number of Allied ships. Considerations such as these make the Caribbean area of particular importance to the United States, since over 50 percent of U.S. exports and imports flow through the region. Also, in the event of a conventional war in Europe, roughly fifty percent of supplies for U.S. allies in Europe would pass through the Caribbean. Because of its key location in the region and its over 1,000 miles of coastline with several good harbors, the Dominican Republic has been a country of special interest to the United States throughout its history.[2]

THE UNITED STATES AND THE CARIBBEAN

Broad policies and doctrine associated with Latin America and the Caribbean area have affected the perceptions of Washington officials concerned with Dominican policy. The most well-known and important of such policy statements is the Monroe Doctrine of 1823. This message by President James Monroe set the tone and direction of U.S. reaction to many revolutions throughout Latin America and the Caribbean. One of the principles annunciated by Monroe was that no foreign power should establish a permanent presence or acquire preponderant influence in the Western Hemisphere. At that time Washington officials feared that Europeans such as the French would seek to restore colonial control over Spain's former possessions involved in the Latin American revolutions of 1802-1822. They also feared that Russia might act on its territorial claims along the Pacific coast of North America. The principles of nonintervention by European powers in the Americas became more important after the Spanish-American war of 1898 when the United States became a colonial power itself in the Caribbean. Before that, however, President Ulysses S. Grant took part in an early attempt at the new imperialism when he sought to take over Santo Domingo in 1869.[3]

President Grant, who was noted for his expansionist ideas, became interested in a plan to annex the Dominican Republic in 1869. The country, which was constantly strife-torn and frequently ruled by unscrupulous leaders, had long been an object of U.S. expansionism. The Navy wanted the harbor of Samana Bay for a Caribbean base and businessmen liked the island's timber and minerals and its undeveloped status. An annexation scheme had failed in the 1950s and the attempt of Grant this time also failed. The plan for annexation had been sold to Grant as a business venture but was opposed in Congress. In a special message to Congress in May of 1970, the president warned that if the United States did not take Santo Domingo, some other country would and the Monroe Doctrine would be endangered. The opposition in Congress prevailed, however, and in June the Senate voted 28 to 28 on the treaty of annexation, which was well short of the two-thirds vote needed for ratification.[4]

The fear of foreign intervention in the Caribbean as spelled out by Grant in 1870 did not become acute until after the Spanish-American War of 1898, when the United States acquired control over Cuba and Puerto Rico. The United States also acquired, a few years later, the right to build and control an isthmian canal across Panama. With the new U.S. presence in the Caribbean after the war, Americans began to feel that they had a special responsibility for the region. The strategic importance of the canal and the advent of modern navies led Americans to look at the Caribbean in a new light. The Spanish-American conflict had proved the viability of American domination in the region and Americans thought other countries should recognize U.S. primacy in the area.[5] One of the strongest proponents of these views was President Theodore Roosevelt who established a policy which became know as the Roosevelt Corollary to the Monroe Doctrine.

In his annual message to Congress of December 1904, Roosevelt stated that:

Chronic wrongdoing . . . may in America as elsewhere, ultimately require intervention by some civilized nation, and in the Western Hemisphere the adherence of the United States to the Monroe Doctrine may force the United States, however reluctantly, in flagrant cases of such wrongdoing or impotence, to the exercise of an international police power.[6]

To some this meant that the Monroe Doctrine, originally designed to prevent intervention in the Western Hemisphere by European powers, could now be used to justify intervention by the United States.

The unstable political situation in the Dominican Republic, caused by revolution and the near bankruptcy of the country, occasioned this statement of policy. Roosevelt feared that European nations with Dominican investments might attempt to collect their debts forcibly as they had in Venezuela in 1902. If foreign naval forces came to collect debts, they might stay and acquire bases that would jeopardize the Panama Canal, Cuba, and Puerto Rico. Consequently, in January 1905 Dominican President Carlos Morales and President Roosevelt signed an executive agreement allowing American officials to take over Dominican custom houses. The U.S. Senate approved this agreement in treaty form in 1907. Forty-five percent of the collected customs receipts went to the Dominican government and American officials used the remainder to pay the debts.[7]

During negotiations over the customs agreement two American warships anchored in the harbor of Santo Domingo to influence the discussions, and early in 1904, when an uprising threatened the Morales government, American naval forces not only protected the lives of foreigners in Dominican coastal cities, but intervened in the activities of opponents of Morales. Naval ships prevented the transport of arms to the rebels and, when a group of revolutionists encamped near the capital fired on a launch from an American warship killing one man, U.S. marines landed to dislodge them.[8]

In spite of relatively stable conditions in the Dominican Republic under the customs receivership, in September 1913 another revolution broke out in connection with impending elections. This time American officials arranged an armistice and in 1914 President Woodrow Wilson sent a commission to the Republic to help bring the two sides together in selecting a provisional executive. American warships buttressed the armistice agreements and observers from the United States monitored

Introduction 5

elections in actions foreshadowing those taken later in 1966. These actions did not prevent the eruption of another revolution in 1916; Wilson, convinced of the incapacity of the Dominicans to govern themselves, ordered the occupation of the Dominican Republic. The navy assigned a naval officer, Captain Harry S. Knapp, as military governor, and naval officers and marines took over the ministries and other executive departments, utilizing Dominicans for the lower levels of the government. For eight years American military and civilian personnel ruled the country. In 1924 the marines withdrew after Dominican elections.[9]

The occupation marked a peak in American intervention in Dominican affairs and exemplified Wilson's use of armed force to create stability in Latin American republics. One of a series of interventions more extensive than any under Presidents Theodore Roosevelt or William Taft, Wilson's use of force apparently grew out of his missionary zeal to do good. He wanted to save the peoples of the Caribbean republics from internal anarchy and foreign intervention. American political intervention during this period took the form of denying the right of revolution, placing embargoes on the shipment of arms to insurgents, and mediating between contending factions. U.S. policy aimed chiefly at promoting political stability which, theoretically, would follow from economic development and political reform. During the occupation, Americans improved roads, communications, schools, agriculture, and Dominican administrative and legal systems and organized a national police force. The end of the occupation in 1924, however, did not mean the end of Washington's influence in Dominican affairs.[10]

Even after American renunciation of unilateral intervention in Latin America, the United States maintained fiscal control over Dominican affairs. But, because of the difficulties of disengaging U.S. armed forces from the occupations of the Dominican Republic, Haiti, and Nicaragua, American officials in the late 1920s attempted to reduce American involvement in the Caribbean. During the period of the Rafael Trujillo dictatorship from 1930 to 1960 U.S. entanglement in Dominican affairs decreased, although American customs agents did not leave the country until 1940. In 1960 the Organization of American States (OAS) condemned the Trujillo regime for "acts of aggression and intervention" against Venezuela and the United States broke relations with the Dominican Republic.[11]

Several factors caused this shift in U.S. policy toward the Trujillo dictatorship. In 1959 the United States began to reexamine its Dominican policy because of the increasingly repressive nature of the Trujillo regime and its disruptive effects on Caribbean affairs. Also Washington feared that Fidel Castro's relatively easy removal of Fulgencio Batista in Cuba might be repeated in the Dominican Republic and in other Caribbean countries run by dictators. The United States now began to press for political democracy and economic and social reform throughout Latin America. In March 1961 President John F. Kennedy, who had been critical of former President Dwight D. Eisenhower's policies toward Latin American dictators, announced his Alliance for Progress program and included the Dominican Republic under this ten-year plan for economic, social, and political development in Latin America. President Kennedy took a special interest in the Dominican Republic and American newspapers began referring to the Republic as a "showcase of democracy."[12]

On 30 May 1961 a group of disgruntled army officers assassinated Trujillo. Coups and counter-coups followed and personal hatreds and clashing political philosophies divided the people into factions. After the dictator's death President Kennedy expressed concern for the possibility of the creation of another Cuba in the Caribbean area. U.S. policies toward the Dominican Republic of both the Kennedy and Johnson administrations reflected this concern, which became a major reason for the 1965 intervention. Kennedy saw three possibilities for Dominican political developments in descending order of preference: a democratic regime, a continuation of the Trujillo regime, or a Castro regime. He believed the United States should support a democratic government but should not renounce a continuation of the Trujillo rule until it became clear that a Castro-type regime could be avoided. He saw dangers of an army takeover, which could lead to Castroism. Kennedy's fears were realized when an army revolt triggered the 1965 Dominican civil war, causing the Johnson administration to intervene.[13]

After 1961, in response to Kennedy's strategy for combating communism in Latin America, the United States dropped its support of nonintervention and intervened in Dominican affairs using a wide variety of instruments of influence. American military forces played an important role in many of these activities. Soon after the assassination of Trujillo in May 1961, when it appeared that civil war would break out, a U.S. naval task force arrived in Dominican waters ready to implement a Kennedy-approved contingency plan providing for armed intervention. Then in November 1961, when it appeared that members of the Trujillo family might return to power, Secretary of State Dean Rusk issued a warning that the United States would not remain idle if the Trujillos tried to reassert dictatorial domination. Eight American ships with 1,800 marines backed up this warning by steaming to the Dominican Republic in a show of force for the government of Joaquín Balaguer who had succeeded to the presidency after Trujillo's death. At the same time, U.S. military attachés encouraged key Dominican air force officers to oppose the Trujillos and American navy jets flew over Santo Domingo. These actions played an important part in encouraging the Dominican armed forces to oppose the Trujillos who thereupon fled the country.[14]

In addition to using the threat of armed force the United States employed other measures to further American goals in the Dominican Republic in the post-1961 period. In January 1962, after the formation of a Council of State under Balaguer, the OAS lifted its economic sanctions against the Dominican Republic imposed during the Trujillo regime. In addition to instituting the Alliance for Progress program in the Republic, which channeled economic aid through the Agency for International Development (AID), the United States also supplied police and military advisors to help Dominicans combat insurgency. These advisors trained Dominican police in riot and demonstration control and American Military Assistance Advisory Group (MAAG) personnel taught counterinsurgency techniques to the Dominican army.[15]

Introduction

After the election of Juan Bosch in December 1962 and the formation of a constitutional government, the American ambassador, John Bartlow Martin, actively supported Bosch. The Kennedy administration used the example of the Dominican Republic to test Alliance for Progress goals since the Bosch administration appeared to represent a constitutional and legitimate government dedicated to change and reform. During the relatively short term of the Bosch regime, from February to September 1963, the United States emphasized curbing the communist threat, continuing economic and military assistance at high levels, and reinforcing the Peace Corps program. When the Bosch government became involved in a dispute with Haiti the United States again sent naval forces to the area with plans to intervene if necessary in support of the Dominican government against Haiti.[16]

KENNEDY-JOHNSON NATIONAL SECURITY POLICY

The approach of the Kennedy administration to national strategy and the containment of communism influenced American activities in the Dominican Republic in the early 1960s. Even before 1961, American army officers and some civilian strategists opposed the massive retaliation strategy of the Eisenhower administration. These officers feared that if the United States lost its credibility because of its failure to react with nuclear weapons to low-level communist aggression such as that which had occurred in Korea, the communists might be emboldened to attempt new piecemeal aggression. The theorists believed that the nation needed a new strategy that would meet the challenge of the communists over a wide range of conflict, from insurgency or guerrilla warfare to all-out nuclear war. This new strategy of flexible, controlled response became the basis of Kennedy-Johnson national security policy. It allowed the president an increased number of options in his crisis decisionmaking and provided the rationale for the acquisition of a broad array of military capabilities mainly acquired through building up American nonnuclear forces.[17]

In January 1961 Nikita S. Khrushchev, the Russian premier, made a speech that impressed Kennedy as an authoritative explanation of Soviet intentions. The president discussed it with his staff and read aloud excerpts at a meeting of the National Security Council (NSC). In the eight-hour speech, Khrushchev described three kinds of possible conflicts between the East and the West: nuclear war, conventional war, and wars of national liberation. Khrushchev dismissed nuclear war as too dangerous, conventional war as possibly leading to nuclear war, and wars of national liberation as the most acceptable means of pursuing world communism. His declared faith in victory through rebellion, subversion, and guerrilla warfare prompted Kennedy to reassess American capability to counter this type of warfare.[18]

Kennedy desired to assure full understanding and a common outlook throughout the government concerning wars of national liberation. He suggested preventing or resisting them with a strategy that used all available political, economic, and military resources. This strategy demanded close cooperation among U.S. government departments and agencies in its execution. He believed the internal defense of nations to be a long neglected, political-military policy area and that each appropriate government agency should be made aware of the problem and should elevate its priorities within their organizations. Because of the Kennedy emphasis on internal defense, army officials broadened the mission of the U.S. Army's Special Forces to include both guerrilla warfare and the suppression of insurgencies within friendly countries and increased the number of troops assigned to the Special Forces. In addition Washington officials directed State Department and foreign service officers to receive counterinsurgency training. Also the U.S. military aid program to Latin American countries changed from the supply of weapons and training for hemispheric defense to the supply of military aid for counterinsurgency and internal security.[19]

Kennedy's secretary of defense, Robert S. McNamara, centralized the control of the military and built up American conventional forces in order to meet communist challenges with appropriate force. In March 1961, in a special message to Congress on the defense budget, Kennedy outlined the new doctrine of flexible response. He stated that response to attacks against any part of the free world would be met swiftly and effectively by suitable and selective use of force. Also, American weapons systems would be made usable to civilian authorities in a manner permitting deliberation and discrimination as to timing, scope, and targets.[20]

Some of the principles that evolved from the concepts of flexible response and crisis management applied to the early days of the Dominican intervention such as presidential control of military options, coordination of military action with political-diplomatic action, and tailoring size and composition of forces to specific objectives. These principles required the president and his key military and diplomatic advisors to closely monitor crisis situations. Crisis management and command and control gained in importance under the concept of flexible control, as did the basic idea of liberating diplomacy from adherence to a rigid military strategy such as massive retaliation. Military and diplomatic cooperation became essential and military goals became subordinate to political goals.[21]

Implementation of the flexible response strategy required new organizations, people, and weapons systems. Kennedy officials, in addition to increasing the size and expanding the mission of the Special Forces, built up American ground forces and increased the mobility and airlift capacity of tactical airpower. Washington officials also emphasized command and control systems for the military forces and in 1961 created a new military organization named Strike Command made up of ground and air forces tailored for quick response and augmentation in crisis situations. President Johnson used many of these same forces, organizations, and procedures during the Dominican crisis of 1965.[22]

In October 1963 Kennedy sent a memorandum to the secretary of defense noting that events in the Dominican Republic, referring to the ouster of the Bosch government in September, and other countries in the area might require U.S. military intervention. Kennedy, unsure of American military capabilities for this type of action, asked such questions as "how many troops we could get into the Dominican

Republic in twelve hours, in twenty-four, thirty-six, or forty-eight hours?" He asked similar questions about several other countries in the area that appeared unstable, told McNamara the matter deserved the highest priority, and requested early answers to these questions. In October, when McNamara and the Joint Chiefs of Staff answered Kennedy, they informed him of their plans to increase the readiness of the armed forces by holding mobility exercises during 1964. Preparations such as these helped American forces to respond quickly when needed during the Dominican crisis of 1965.[23]

BACKGROUND TO REVOLT

Instability has characterized Dominican politics for a great part of the history of the country. It became more pronounced after the assassination of Rafael Trujillo in 1961. Since that time, up to the 1966 election, there had been a constant power struggle between various groups of "outs" and "ins" that was more directed toward replacing the government than at forcing it to take specific actions. Students, labor union members, and even businessmen have staged strikes, demonstrated, marched on the National Palace, and clashed with police and army units. Competing Dominican civilian factions and parties have also engaged in conspiracies and subversion and encouraged their military adherents to do likewise. One of the reasons for this political instability has been the Spanish tradition of more individualistic political behavior than that of other cultures. Latin Americans have been more inclined to become devoted to a magnetic leader than to a political platform.[24]

Another deep-rooted Spanish political habit has been the direct participation of the military classes in politics. Until Trujillo established his dictatorship, the elite classes, whose origins were based on ancestry and education, held political and economic power in the Dominican Republic. The dictator, excluded from membership in the elite group by his lower-class origins, assumed control of the armed forces and appointed officers regardless of their class origins. He then used the military to impose his will on the nation and indoctrinated its leaders to believe they were responsible only to him and not to the civilian government. When the dictatorship ended the military refused to subordinate themselves to civilian government and used their monopoly of armed force to perpetuate control of political life. The service commanders tended to function as separate entities and to use their military commands as personal power bases from which they could wield political power. They supported approved governments and overthrew those hostile to military interests, replacing them with military-supported juntas until a favorable civilian regime could be found. For all practical purposes the Dominican military became the real locus of political power.[25]

This approach to political power by the Dominican military contrasted directly with the institutionalization of the U.S. military establishment. In that system military men respond as members of the organization rather than as individual political personalities. The civil-military relations under this corporate system depend not on individuals but on relationships between organizations, and the military establishment, endowed with its own professional functions, is subservient to civilian authority. The Dominican experience has been different. Lines between civil and military authority were tenuous and personal loyalties, rivalries, and opportunism meant more to the military than command responsiveness.[26]

Both the 1963 overthrow of Bosch and the 1965 Dominican revolution may have owed less to ideology than to struggles among competing cliques and to rival civilian efforts to gain the support of various military factions. Lowenthal studied the political roles of twenty-five high-ranking Dominican military officers involved in both of these events. He has concluded that the Dominican officers were not "primarily or even importantly" motivated by ideological considerations. Rather, they showed a chaotic pattern of individual action. For example, six of the twenty-five officers considered on 25 April, a day after the beginning of the 1965 revolution, were trying to set up their own juntas supporting neither the Reid government nor the pro-Bosch coup.[27] This kind of behavior is not that associated with an institutionalized, highly motivated, and professional officer corps.

In addition to the overall causes of political turmoil there were other more immediate causes for the Dominican revolution of 1965. These stemmed from the overthrow of President Bosch in September 1963. Bosch was a controversial figure not only in the Dominican Republic where he had been stigmatized by the army and rightist civilians as pro-communist, but in Washington where government officials considered him a weak, unstable dreamer more prone to writing and poetry than to administering a government. Even progressive democratic Latin leaders such as Betancourt of Venezuela and Muñoz of Puerto Rico warned Dean Rusk, the secretary of state, that Bosch was not capable of organizing and administering a government and would not last long in office. President Johnson, who as vice-president had met and talked to Bosch at Bosch's inauguration in February 1963, summarized his impressions in his memoirs. He believed that Bosch had no solid plans for overcoming the major problems that the country faced and that he did not have the experience, the imagination, or the strength needed to put whatever plans he might have into effect.

Bosch had alienated the upper classes, including the oligarchy made up of Dominican first families and landowners, and had quarreled with senior army officers over corruption. He was opposed also by the rising business-oriented middle class and even by the church. In addition, members of parties he had defeated and rightists in general opposed him. Nor had he won over the poor and lower classes. He had not been able to reduce the high rate of unemployment and his money policies, created to cope with the heavy national debt, had not been well received. Many wondered how Bosch, faced with these problems and opponents, could possibly stay in office.[28]

On 25 September a group of military officers led by General Elías Wessin y Wessin ousted Bosch, the first constitutional president of the post-Trujillo era, forcing him into exile. A civilian triumvirate backed by the military was established. Even before his ouster, however, a loose coalition was formed to back Bosch should a rumored coup by the military succeed. The coalition consisted of members of

Introduction

Bosch's own party, the Dominican Revolutionary Party (PRD); members of the Social Christian Revolutionary Party (PRSC), a number of lawyers interested in the principle of retaining the constitution; and a number of low-ranking military officers from a military academy near San Isidro on the outskirts of Santo Domingo. Also backing Bosch were leaders of the extreme leftist 14th of June Political Group (1J4). Although none of these groups were strong or organized enough to prevent the Wessin coup, soon after the ouster of Bosch they began to take actions against the triumvirate.[29] The triumvirate immediately sought to eliminate or suppress these forces of opposition. On 28 September the junta deported Bosch, who settled in San Juan, Puerto Rico, where he would be near his constituents in the Dominican Republic. The junta also deported about thirty opposition, party members who were mostly members of the PRD and imposed a curfew. In addition the Congress was dissolved and the constitution abrogated. Also in October the triumvirate dismissed eighteen of the young military academy officers known as "academicos," who were known for their constitutionalist sentiments, and assigned their leader a military post in Spain. This group was to play an important part in the military arm of the revolutionary movement in 1965.[30]

These measures taken by the triumvirate were not completely successful in eliminating their opposition, but at least had the effect of weakening their enemies. For example, the PRD, whose members formed the civil arm of the 1965 revolutionary movement, was weakened by the junta's repression. Also, guerrilla action taken by leftist extremists of the 1J4 had opened six guerrilla "focos" in the mountains. These were bases from which small, rural guerrilla bands carried out operations in accordance with the Castro-Guevara strategy of armed struggle that had proved so successful in the war against Batista in Cuba. As a result of the military debacle, in which all the participating members had either been captured or killed, the 1J4 was weakened. The party was outlawed, and its Central Committee no longer existed since two of its members were dead, five were in Cuba, and six were in jail in the Dominican Republic.[31]

During the Bosch tenure from February 1962 to September 1963 the United States officially supported him in spite of a certain lack of confidence in the Bosch government. After the coup President Kennedy adopted a hard line against the triumvirate. He recalled Ambassador Martin, suspended economic and military assistance to the new regime, and withheld official recognition. A few days later there was another military coup, this time in Honduras. The Dominican and Honduran military coups, the fifth and sixth against governments supported by the Alliance for Progress, called into question the workability of that program. The United States tried to pressure the triumvirate to return to at least a semblance of constitutionality but was rebuffed. Washington officials feared that collapse of the triumvirate might bring back a harsh military dictatorship or create an opportunity for a communist takeover. Also, such nations as Great Britain were pressing the Kennedy administration to recognize the triumvirate. Political polarization had begun with the overthrow of Bosch. With extreme leftist opponents caught up in Castro's "mountain fever" and the military hunting them down in the hills it appeared there might be an extended guerrilla war. As a result Washington retreated from its initial position and was prepared to grant recognition to the triumvirate if the regime would establish a timetable for new elections.[32]

When Lyndon Johnson became president after the assassination of Kennedy in November, he sought to maintain continuity in the government by following the policies of the former president. In the process of putting his stamp on the new administration, he made some important adjustments to U.S. foreign policy for Latin America. In December, following the lead of Kennedy, Johnson recognized the triumvirate. He also made a new appointment in the State Department that changed Latin American policy in a more conservative direction. This was done with the appointment of Thomas C. Mann, a foreign service officer from Texas, as assistant secretary of state for interamerican affairs. In addition he appointed Mann special assistant to the president on Latin American affairs and administrator of the Alliance for Progress. The purpose of these multiple assignments was to allow the United States to speak with one voice on matters affecting hemispheric policy.[33]

With policy directives concerning Latin America coming from four different officials including President Kennedy, the administration of Latin American affairs had been chaotic. Mann established some order so that clearances for outgoing cables could be obtained more rapidly and technical issues could be resolved at lower levels. Mann called his ambassadors together and explained a new U.S. policy of: cooperation with Latin American governments no matter how they attained power with the exception of communist- controlled regimes; promotion of economic growth; neutrality on social and political reform; and protection of U.S. private investment. Since Mann became a key adviser to President Johnson many of his ideas were reflected in the U.S. response to the triumvirate and later to the Dominican revolution.[34]

The triumvirate eventually evolved into a two-man regime dominated by the former foreign minister Donald Reid Cabral, a moderate who had been abroad when the military ousted Bosch. Unrest continued under the Reid regime. The nation had inherited deep-seated personal hatreds from the Trujillo era and many Dominicans believed that the authoritarian Reid did not intend to allow free elections in 1965 as promised. Labor problems had increased when the world price of sugar dropped below the cost of Dominican production. Dominican dependence on sugar for foreign exchange forced Reid to take unpopular measures for controlling the economy. He also made himself unpopular with military leaders by reducing the military budget, closing post exchanges, and shutting off lucrative smuggling, a prerogative of high-ranking military officers during the Trujillo years. The junior officers disapproved of the slow pace of the Reid reforms, especially in retiring senior officers left over from the Trujillo regime. Many younger officers and enlisted men favored the progressive policies and social welfare programs advocated by Bosch and disapproved of the return by the military-backed Reid government to the constitution of 1962. They wanted reinstitution of the liberal Bosch constitution of 1963. This split in the military was the immediate cause of the 1965 revolt.[35]

Introduction 13

In addition to the military other groups opposed Reid, including farmers, day laborers, merchants, and small businessmen who looked to the financially insolvent government for relief. Reid tightened credit in order to limit imports and restore the balance of payments. He also accepted major loans from the United States and the International Monetary Fund, steps considered by some to limit Dominican sovereignty. Enmity toward the Reid government came from the political left and right including the two most important parties, Bosch's PRD and Balaguer's Reform Party, each led from abroad by an exiled former Dominican president hoping to regain power. Practically the only support Reid received came from the United States and the Dominican military.[36]

With the Dominican Republic no longer a "showcase for democracy," Washington officials backed Reid who represented a different viewpoint from the democratic left. He was a businessman and member of a powerful oligarchic Dominican family and was adamant against agrarian reform and other progressive programs. The Dominican oligarchy consisted of a relatively small number of families related by blood and marriage who had provided the presidents of the country (with the exception of Trujillo) and dominated its economy and the business community. Their fortunes were based on land, sugar, coffee, trade, and finance. To Washington, Reid represented a right-wing military regime that was considered safe under the new guidelines of the Mann policy for Latin America. Washington heavily supported the triumvirate with economic and military aid and backed the enthusiasm of Reid for U.S.-sponsored civic action projects and his efforts to restore economic stability and end military corruption.[37]

At the embassy level, relations between the U.S. ambassador, William Tapley Bennett, Jr., and Reid were very close. The ambassador considered Reid the best hope for a stable, prosperous, and democratic country. The close relationship, however, offended some Dominican nationalists who nicknamed Reid "el americano" and Bennett "el otro triumviro." Bennett tried to dispel the image of unqualified U.S. support for Reid but was largely unsuccessful. The more Reid tried to bolster his political authority by identifying his regime with the United States the more criticism he received from the nationalists.[38]

General Wessin, who commanded the Armed Forces Training Center (CEFA), was also a major supporter of Reid. His elite group of about two thousand specially trained soldiers, unlike regular Dominican army units, had tanks, recoilless cannon, and artillery. Trujillo, in creating CEFA, had made it an independent organization to serve the head of state as an elite guard and to watch over the armed services. Officers in the army, navy, and air force commanded forces that outnumbered those of CEFA but their troops were scattered throughout the country and, with the exception of three army battalions and a naval frogman unit, were poorly trained and equipped.

The regular military resented the CEFA force and feared the power of Wessin who had been newly promoted to general following his successful role in the coup against Bosch. A factor in the strength of CEFA was the collocation of the unit with a large part of the Dominican air force at the 19th of November air base at San Isidro.

Taken together CEFA and this air force unit concentrated about four thousand armed men, all the tanks, and most of the air power of the country in one location on the outskirts of Santo Domingo. This was three and a half times more military personnel than at any other camp. The concentration of military power so close to the capital city allowed the president considerable leverage in controlling the military if he could depend on the CEFA commander.[39]

Faction-ridden as the Dominican military was, one could guess that this estimate of the unity of the army and air force units at the San Isidro air base might be in error. In January, Colonel Juan de los Santos Céspedes was named air force chief of staff with the temporary rank of general. He was not anti-Wessin but considered the CEFA chief a difficult and dangerous neighbor. Since Wessin controlled San Isidro he was considered the power behind the throne. He saw himself as the guarantor of order and the chief support of the regime against leftists in the country. Wessin answered only to the president and he and his troops were provided with special favors including better housing and food. Reid, however, made the mistake of letting it be known that he regarded his alliance with Wessin as temporary. In spite of this Wessin continued to help the government remove any enemies it uncovered in the military. Since Wessin had been instrumental in removing both Bosch and Balaguer from the presidency, it seemed that if a rumored coup actually occurred, he would support neither Reid nor one of these leaders but an independent military junta.[40]

The rumors of a coup attempt throughout the spring of 1965 had some basis in fact. Ever since Bosch had been exiled to Puerto Rico in 1963 he had conspired to return to the Dominican Republic and resume his presidency. He was the only one who actually knew all the secrets of the conspiracy which was ultimately successful. The conspiracy included civilians from the PRD and military personnel. Bosch believed that the only real power in Santo Domingo was the military and therefore it would be necessary to use force in regaining his position. Lieutenant Colonel Miquel Angel Hernando Ramírez, chief of planning and training on the army staff, emerged as a leader who could unite the various factions involved in the conspiracy.[41]

In November 1964, the PRD revolutionaries and the Hernando Ramírez group combined and worked out a plan for the conspiracy. The plan was based on a number of prerequisites. The military and not the people was to carry out what was called the "countercoup." The conspirators at this time wanted no popular revolt, no anarchy, and no useless bloodshed. There would be order and discipline but the PRDistas were to exhort the masses to demonstrate in the streets in favor of the movement. Hernando Ramírez and his officers foresaw a rapid victory. Victorious, the so-called "constitutionalist" troops would return to their barracks. Bosch, Molina Ureña, and Peña Gómez, who later played important roles in the revolt, and other PRD leaders knew and approved of these plans.

Leaders of the military bureau of the 1J4, who were militant leftist extremists, offered to cooperate with the conspirators but were rebuffed and given the secondary role of mobilizing the 1J4 sympathizers who numbered in the thousands. Under no circumstances did the conspiracy leaders envision military action for the 1J4. The military bureau realized that the movement was "democratic-bourgeois" but hoped to steer the mass mobilization in a more radical direction once the coup had begun.[42] Radicalization of the masses was soon to be realized when the revolt erupted on 24 April.

NOTES

1. Thomas D. Anderson, Geopolitics of the Caribbean (New York: Praeger Publishers, 1984); Thomas E. Weil et al., Area Handbook for the Dominican Republic (Washington, D.C.: U.S.GPO, 1966); Howard J. Wiarda, The Dominican Repubblic: Nation in Transition (New York: Frederick A. Praeger, 1969).

2. Michael Moodie and Alvin J. Cottrell, Geopolitics and Maritime Power (Beverly Hills:Sage Publications, 1981), pp. 48-49.

3. Harold Molineu, U.S. Policy Toward Latin America (Boulder: Westview Press, 1986), p. 16; Thomas A. Bailey, A Diplomatic History of the American People, 9th ed., (Englewood Cliffs, N.J.: Prentice-Hall, Inc., 1974), pp. 184-185; Lester D. Langley, Struggle for the American Mediterranean (Athens,Ga.: University of Georgia Press, 1976), pp. 26-50.

4. Thomas G. Paterson et al., American Foreign Policy: A History to 1914, 2d ed. v. 1, (Lexington, Mass.: D.C. Heath and Company, 1983), pp. 143-144.

5. Langley, Struggle for the American Mediterranean, pp. 166, 186.

6. U.S. Congress, 1904, Theodore Roosevelt's Fourth Annual Message to the Congress, 6 December 1904, 58th cong., 3d sess. Congressional Record, 5 December - 18 January, 1904-1905, p. 19; Molineu, U.S. Policy Toward Latin America, pp. 40-41; Paterson, American Foreign Policy, pp. 229-231.

7. J. Fred Rippy, The Caribbean Danger Zone (New York: G. P. Putnam's Sons, 1940), pp. 161-165.

8. Dexter Perkins, Hands Off: A History of the Monroe Doctrine (Boston: Little Brown and Company, 1948), pp. 238-242; Dana G. Munro, Intervention and Dollar Diplomacy in The Caribbean, 1900-1921 (Princeton: Princeton University Press, 1964), p.94.

9. Sumner Welles, Naboth's Vineyard II, (Boston: Paul P. Appel, 1966), pp. 866-871; Perkins, Hands Off, p. 259; Rippy, The Caribbean Danger Zone, p. 195.

10. Lester D. Langley, The Banana Wars: United States Intervention in the Caribbean 1898-1934 (Chicago: The Dorsey Press, 1985), p. 77; Munro, Intervention and Dollar Diplomacy in the Caribbean, pp. 269-325; G. Pope Atkins and Larman C. Wilson, The United States

and the Trujillo Regime (New Brunswick, N.J.: Rutgers University Press, 1972), pp. 43-44.

11. Perkins, Hands Off, pp. 373-374; Atkins and Wilson, The United States and the Trujillo Regime, p. 12; Bryce Wood, The Makings of the Good Neighbor Policy (New York: Columbia University Press, 1961).

12. Robert D. Crossweller, Trujillo: The Life and Times of a Caribbean Dictator (New York: The Macmillan Company, 1966), pp. 421-431; Atkins and Wilson, The United States and the Trujillo Regime, pp. 15, 99-125, 137.

13. Arthur M. Schlesinger,Jr., A Thousand Days: John F. Kennedy in the White House (Boston: Houghton Mifflin Company, 1965), pp. 769-771. For a discussion of the Dominican armed forces see Howard J. Wiarda, "The Politics of Civil-Military Relations in the Dominican Republic," Journal of Inter-American Studies, no. 4 (October 1965), pp. 465-484.

14. Abraham F. Lowenthal, The Dominican Intervention (Cambridge, Mass.: Harvard University Press, 1972), pp. 11, 26; Atkins and Wilson, The United States and the Trujillo Regime, pp. 131, 132, 137; Center for Strategic Studies, Dominican Action-1965: Intervention or Cooperation (Washington, D.C.: Center for Strategic Studies, 1966), p.2.

15. John B. Martin, Overtaken by Events: The Dominican Crisis from the Fall of Trujillo to the Civil War (New York: Doubleday and Co., 1966), pp. 5-9, 144, 646. For an interesting comparison between the Alliance for Progress and the more successful Marshall plan see Dexter Perkins, The Diplomacy of a New Age (Bloomington, Ind.: Indiana University Press, 1967), pp. 152-153.

16. Martin, Overtaken by Events, pp. 347, 425; Atkins and Wilson, The United States and the Trujillo Regime, pp. 140-141.

17. Schlesinger, A Thousand Days, p. 310; Maxwell D. Taylor, The Uncertain Trumpet (New York: Harper and Row, 1960), p. 116; Alexander L. George et al., The Limits of Coercive Diplomacy (Boston: Little, Brown and Company, 1971), p.7; Lawrence A. Yates, Power Pack: U.S. Intervention in the Dominican Republic, 1965-1966 (Fort Leavenworth, Kans.: Combat Studies Institute, 1988), p. 35; Russell F. Weigley, The American Way of War: A History of United States Military Strategy and Policy (Bloomington, Ind.: Indiana University Press, 1973), pp. 411, 445, 474.

18. Louise FitzSimons, The Kennedy Doctrine (New York: Random House, 1972), pp. 8-10, 175; Morton H. Halperin, Limited War in the Nuclear Age (New York: John Wiley and Sons, 1963), pp. 16-17; Keith C. Clark and Lawrence J. Legere (eds.), The President

and Management of National Security (New York: Frederick A. Praeger, 1968) pp. 237-238.

19. Martin, Overtaken by Events, p. 141; Schlesinger, A Thousand Days, 341; Stephen E. Ambrose, Rise to Globalism (Baltimore: Penguin Books Inc., 1971), pp. 297-298.

20. George, The Limits of Coercive Diplomacy, p. 7; FitzSimons, The Kennedy Doctrine pp. 12, 173; Walter LaFeber, Inevitable Revolutions: The United States in Central America (New York: W.W. Norton, 1984), pp. 150-151.

21. George, The Limits of Coercive Diplomacy, pp. 9-11; Gordon A. Craig and Alexander L. George, Force and Statecraft: Diplomatic Problems of Our Time (New York: Oxford University Press, 1983) pp. 206-208. The term crisis management as used by George and others involves control of a crisis by measures such as bargaining between two opponents as happened during the Cuban missile crisis. The Dominican intervention did not fit this pattern as there was no clearly defined opponent to the United States. Some of the principles of crisis management did apply to the Dominican intervention and have been analyzed in this study. The term crisis management as used in Chapter 4 refers to resource management, which includes such factors as goal definition and planning that may be independent of a conflict situation. In other words, crisis management and its elements in this study have been used as a structure for analysis irrespective of the conflict situation.

22. Clyde Box, "United States Strike Command Stateside and Global," Air University Review (September-October 1964), pp. 2-10, 12-14; Bruce Palmer, The 25-Year War: America's Military Role in Vietnam (Lexington, Ky.: The University Press of Kentucky, 1984), p. 137.

23. Lyndon B. Johnson, The Vantage Point (New York: Holt, Rinehart and Winston, 1971), p. 197; Ambrose, Rise to Globalism, p. 322.

24. Lowenthal, The Dominican Intervention, pp. 33-34.

25. Weil, Area Handbook for the Dominican Republic, pp. 4-6; Quinten A. Kelso, "The Dominican Crisis of 1965: A New Appraisal." (Ph.D. dissertation, University of Colorado, 1982), p. 28.

26. G. Pope Atkins, Arms and Politics in the Dominican Republic (Boulder: Westview Press, 1981), p.2.

27. Abraham F. Lowenthal and J. Samuel Fitch (eds.), Armies and Politics in Latin America (New York: Holmes and Meier, 1986), pp. 199-203.

28. Martin, Overtaken by Events, pp. 547-590; Johnson, The Vantage Point, pp. 188-189; Thomas J. Schoenbaum, Waging Peace and War: Dean Rusk in the Truman, Kennedy, and Johnson Years (New York: Simon and Schuster, 1988), p. 447.

29. Lowenthal, The Dominican Intervention, pp. 35-36; Piero Gleijeses, The Dominican Crisis: The 1965 Constitutionalist Revolt and American Intervention (Baltimore: Johns Hopkins Press, 1978), p. 103; Martin, Overtaken by Events, p. 675.

30. Gleijeses, The Dominican Crisis, pp. 107, 146; Kelso, "The Dominican Crisis of 1965," pp. 47, 48.

31. Gleijeses, The Dominican Crisis, pp. 110-114.

32. Kelso, "The Dominican Crisis of 1965," pp. 29-30; Martin, Overtaken by Events, p. 545; John B. Martin, U.S. Policy in the Caribbean (Boulder: Westview Press, 1978), pp. 78-81.

33. Martin, U.S. Policy in the Caribbean, p. 91; I. M. Destler et al., Our Own Worst Enemy: The Unmaking of American Foreign Policy (New York: Simon and Schuster, 1984) p. 196.

34. Martin, U.S. Policy in the Caribbean, p. 92.

35. Martin, Overtaken by Events, pp. 637-638; Weil et al., Area Handbook for the Dominican Republic, pp. 4, 6; Lowenthal, The Dominican Intervention, pp. 38-44.

36. Martin, Overtaken by Events, p. 638; Lowenthal, The Dominican Intervention, pp. 38-44.

37. Martin, Overtaken by Events, pp. 114, 133; Yates, Power Pack, p. 21; Gleijeses, The Dominican Crisis, pp. 124-125.

38. Yates, Power Pack, pp. 21, 22.

39. Ibid.; Gleijeses, The Dominican Crisis pp. 126-130.

40. Gleijeses, The Dominican Crisis, p. 130; Yates, Power Pack, pp. 22-23.

41. Gleijeses, The Dominican Crisis, pp. 145-155; Martin, Overtaken by Events, p. 644.

42. Gleijeses, The Dominican Crisis, pp. 156-157.

2

Revolt and Response (24-27 April)

A group of young officers and leaders of the revolutionary party of Bosch combined to initiate the 24 April coup that toppled the Reid government and led to an armed uprising. As the revolt spread and both the embassy and Washington became aware that a crisis was developing in the Dominican Republic, government officials activated the U.S. system for crisis response. They reviewed contingency plans, initiated increased intelligence information collection, activated operations centers, alerted appropriate military forces, and notified key personnel who were absent to return to their posts. On Sunday President Johnson returned to Washington from Camp David ready to take personal command and control of crisis preparations. By the time the situation had become really serious a naval task force was in Dominican waters ready for the evacuation of U.S. and foreign personnel. In the meantime Washington and embassy officials were active in attempting to find a formula for bringing the warring parties together and ending the bloodshed.

REVOLT

Central Intelligence Agency (CIA) reporting concerned with clandestine Dominican groups opposing Reid was fairly accurate. As early as 11 and 12 April, the CIA reported that the PRD was plotting with military officers, led by Hernando Ramírez, to overthrow the Reid government. This group was working through retired and active junior officers. The CIA also reported the activities of other groups such as the San Cristobal group, which was made up of high-ranking officers who backed Balaguer for president. The embassy confirmed at least some of these reports but believed that the Reid regime had the various conspiracies under surveillance and control.[1]

In the third week of April, Dominican officials transferred or dismissed several junior officers of the pro-Bosch cadre. This warning caused the leadership of the ultimately successful conspiracy under

Hernando Ramírez to set a D-day of 26 April for their attempted coup. They decided, however, that if the triumvirate arrested or cashiered any more "constitutionalist" officers, the "countercoup" would begin at once. On 24 April, learning of four more officers who had been discovered plotting against the government, Reid sent his army chief of staff, General Rivera Cuesta, to army headquarters to dismiss the officers involved. When the general arrived the conspirators arrested him and the coup against the Reid government began. Reid, U.S., and Dominican officials were all apparently caught by surprise at the size of the pro-Bosch conspiracy within the Dominican military.[2]

Most of the conspirators were likewise surprised at the sudden turn of events two days ahead of the planned date for the coup. It took some time for the leaders to notify their fellow plotters, but they were able to use the radio to good effect in rallying the people of Santo Domingo to the cause. After the insurgents seized Rivera Cuesta they announced the fall of the Reid regime over local radio stations. The government radio station denied these reports, but a group of pro-Bosch leaders and soldiers barricaded themselves in a studio of the government station long enough to announce that a movement of "young and honest" officers dedicated to constitutional government had overthrown Reid. They called on the people to go into the streets and celebrate the Bosch revolution. Several other rebel-manned radio stations joined in the demand for the return of Bosch and constitutionality.[3]

As the revolt spread an element of chance slowed down the American response to the crisis. Unfortunately the revolt occurred at an inopportune time for the United States because many key personnel in the State and Defense Departments were either not available during the initial phases of the crisis or were new to their jobs. Ambassador Bennett left the Dominican Republic on 23 April to return to Washington for consultation. He was visiting his sick mother in Georgia when he heard of the revolt. He had occupied the post in Santo Domingo for the relatively short time of thirteen months. Other senior officials assigned to the embassy had served in the Dominican Republic for shorter times. President Johnson assigned an entirely new country team to Santo Domingo when he restored diplomatic relations with the Dominican Republic in December 1963. Although many of the Dominican embassy staff including Ambassador Bennett had previously served in Latin America, most were newly appointed to the Dominican Republic. William Connett, Jr., the deputy chief of mission and in charge during the crisis until the return of Bennett, had served in Santo Domingo for only five and a half months. Benjamin Ruyle, the political section chief, had been in the country for just over a year. Only some of the CIA station personnel had a long tenure in Santo Domingo, as they had remained after the break in diplomatic relations in 1963. Eleven of the thirteen members of the military advisory group assigned to the Dominican Republic had left to attend a conference in Panama on the same day as the ambassador had left for Washington. These military personnel maintained close contacts with Dominican junior officers and other lower-echelon military personnel and so would have been useful especially during the early phases of the revolt.[4]

Important changes in government leadership in Washington and the unavailability of key individuals also slowed initial American reactions to the crisis and led to charges of American unpreparedness. On 28 April the directors of the CIA changed and Admiral William Raborn took over the job from John McCone. Also, assistant secretary of state for inter-american affairs, Jack H. Vaughn, newly appointed to his post, was attending a conference in Mexico. His deputy, Robert B. Sayre, Jr., had assumed his job only a week before. Some key military personnel were also new to their jobs. Lieutenant General Bruce Palmer, Jr., assigned command of the American ground forces in the Dominican operation, had been the army deputy chief of staff for operations in Washington. Also, Admiral Thomas M. Moorer relieved Admiral H. Page Smith on 30 April, a week after the Dominican crisis began and as theater commander and commander in chief, Atlantic Command (CINCLANT), assumed overall command of the American forces committed to the Dominican operation.[5]

The embassy began reporting events concerned with the revolt early Saturday afternoon on 24 April. Reports flowed into the State Department Operations Center, the Pentagon National Military Control Center, and the White House Situation Room. Operations Center watch officers notified the appropriate officials in the State Department and Thomas C. Mann, earlier appointed by President Johnson to coordinate U.S. activities in Latin America, called President Johnson. He informed the president at Camp David that the State Department had received a cable from the embassy concerning rumors of a coup in Santo Domingo and rioting in the streets. The National Police had dispersed a crowd of about a thousand persons at the palace, recaptured the government radio station, and dispersed crowds in downtown Santo Domingo. Although rebellious officers and soldiers controlled army headquarters at the 27th of February Camp outside of Santo Domingo, American military attachés reported the uprising confined to some junior and noncommissioned army officers.[6]

Early information concerning events in Santo Domingo depended on reports of CIA personnel and American military attachés, many of whom were friends of Dominican military officers committed to the anti-Bosch forces. Attaché reporting reflected an accurate appraisal of the actions and motivations of the anti-Bosch forces but tended to be sketchy concerning the activities and goals of the pro-Bosch movement. CIA reporting stressed the activities of extreme leftists and Communists. Although collecting intelligence information constituted their primary mission, the attachés performed other functions such as liaison between the embassy and the Reid government, between the anti-Bosch forces and the embassy, and even between Reid and the anti-Bosch forces. Early in the revolt when Reid attempted to sound out his support, he asked the U.S. air attaché to find out if the Dominican air force would comply with an order to act against the rebels. The attaché passed Reid's question to the Dominican Air Force Chief of Staff who told him that the air force officer corps had met and decided not to accept any such order based on their desire to avoid bloodshed. Through their contacts and in some cases close personal friendships with Dominican military personnel, the attachés influenced the Dominican loyalist military officers at critical junctures in the revolt.[7]

The naval attaché, Lieutenant Colonel Ralph Heywood, maintained a close relationship with one of the key Dominican political figures, General Antonio Imbert Barrera, who later during the crisis formed a temporary loyalist government. When the revolt began on Saturday, 24 April, Heywood and Imbert were hunting together. As soon as he heard of the outbreak Imbert called Reid who told him to visit the provincial army garrisons at La Vega and Santiago to ensure their loyalty. Accompanied by Heywood, Imbert visited the installations, urging the troops to remain calm and loyal. The relationship between the military attachés and other embassy officials and the anti-Bosch forces, as demonstrated by the Heywood-Imbert friendship, became a controversial issue and partially accounted for the charge that U.S. policy sided with the anti-Bosch forces. Actually, as this study will indicate, during the full eighteen months of American troop involvement, U.S. policy changed from one of pro-junta to a neutral stance, and then to a policy of what some considered pro-leftist.[8]

By Saturday night 24 April Santo Domingo was relatively calm and the Reid government had retained control of the situation. Early Sunday morning, however, the embassy received reports that rebel soldiers had entered the city and trucked in large quantities of arms, and that Reid's minister of the interior and police had joined the rebels. Control of the situation by the Reid government seemed to be deteriorating. On Sunday the State Department formed a task force at the Operations Center to coordinate the U.S. response to the crisis. This task force remained in operation until 5 June. Early Sunday morning Washington officials briefed key personnel including the president and secretary of state and ordered Jack Vaughn, the assistant secretary of state for inter-American affairs, to return to Washington from Mexico.[9]

On Sunday morning Reid, lacking the support of his military commanders and of the U.S. Embassy, resigned. Shortly before 1100 hours a group of approximately fifty rebel officers and soldiers led by Lieutenant Colonel Francisco Caamaño Deñó, who ultimately became the rebel leader, entered the palace, arrested Reid, and proclaimed the intent of the so-called "constitutionalists" to restore Bosch to the presidency. Pro-Bosch forces again took over the government-controlled radio station, called on the public to gather at the palace, and announced before noon that Dr. Molina Ureña, the highest-ranking member of the 1963 Bosch government then on Dominican soil, would be sworn in as provisional constitutional president pending the return of Bosch.

The acting Dominican military chiefs, air force Chief of Staff General Juan De Los Santos Céspedes, navy Chief Commodore Francisco J. Rivera Caminero and General Elías Wessin y Wessin, the senior military officer and commander of the Armed Forces Training Center, had stood aside and let Reid fall. Now Wessin y Wessin began to take an active part in actions against the pro-Bosch forces. He had led the anti-Bosch coup in 1963 and when it became clear that the revolutionists intended to restore Bosch to power, he decided to fight the movement. On Sunday Dominican air force planes strafed and Dominican naval vessels shelled the palace, apparently in an effort to prevent Molina Ureña from being sworn in as provisional president.

The strafing galvanized the constitutionalists to action and polarized the positions of both rebels and loyalists with the result that meetings in the palace of military and civilian leaders attempting to establish a government to replace the Reid regime broke up. What began as a coup to overthrow the Reid government now became a fight between pro-Bosch and anti-Bosch forces in Santo Domingo, a city of about 300,000 persons.[10]

RESPONSE AND EVACUATION

Washington received CIA reports on Sunday morning of the participation of known extreme leftists among the pro-Bosch groups in downtown Santo Domingo. The chargé d'affairs of the embassy, Connett, reported that the rebels had distributed rifles, machine guns, grenades, and bazookas indiscriminately and these had fallen into the hands of extremists and hoodlums. The rioters had killed a number of police and others had disappeared. Connett warned Washington that the growing disorder would lead to heavy bloodshed. Because of these reports, in midmorning the president ordered the Joint Chiefs to notify Atlantic Fleet headquarters to stand by for possible evacuation of about 1,200 American citizens and others who might wish to leave Santo Domingo. Later Sunday, Washington directed the embassy to tell authorities on both sides of the conflict of American evacuation plans and to request a cease-fire and the cooperation of both loyalists and rebels in helping American forces carry out the evacuation peacefully. The president hoped that a cease-fire would bring the warring parties together to begin negotiating a settlement. Washington ordered ships assigned to evacuation operations to remain out of sight of land but to stand by in the vicinity of Santo Domingo.[11]

At about 1000 hours on Sunday Captain James A. Dare, U.S. Navy, the commanding officer of the Caribbean Amphibious Ready Group, received the order to get underway for the Santo Domingo area from the command post of CINCLANT in Norfolk. The Ready Group, one of a series of such units that deployed quarterly to the Caribbean for exercises and to support contingency operations, was anchored south of Vieques Islands, Puerto Rico, 264 miles east of Santo Domingo. It consisted of six U.S. naval vessels; the Boxer, an amphibious assault ship equipped with helicopters;, the Raleigh, an amphibious transport accommodating helicopters, landing craft, tanks, and assault troops; the Ruchamkin, a high-speed troop transport; the Fort Snelling, a landing ship carrying helicopters, landing craft, and tanks; the Rankin, an attack cargo ship; and the Wood County, a tank landing ship.[12]

Aboard these vessels was the 6th Marine Expeditionary Unit, consisting of a battalion landing team from the 3rd Battalion of the 6th Marine Regiment, 2nd Marine Division; a marine helicopter squadron; a provisional marine air group; and tanks and artillery from the Fleet Marine Force and the 2nd Marine Division. Personnel aboard the Ready Group numbered 131 officers and 1,571 marines assigned to the 6th Marine Expeditionary Unit and 214 officers and 2,737 enlisted navy men assigned to the ships. The Ready Group, on station nearly a month, had reached a high state of readiness having completed two exercise landings and reembarkations in the Puerto Rican area. This force had the capacity to evacuate about three thousand persons either via landing craft, helicopter, or both.[13]

After leaving Vieques, Puerto Rico, about noon on Sunday for Santo Domingo, the ships received information on the progress of the coup, changing conditions ashore, and the bombing and strafing of the presidential palace. Captain Dare and Colonel George W. Daughtry, the marine landing force commander, decided that to accomplish their evacuation mission it would be necessary to land a control element to assure the orderly loading of ships and helicopters. Although the marines of the control element would be unarmed and in fatigue dress with no helmets and no pistol belts, a company of armed marines wearing body armor would back them up. The latter would remain aboard ship ready to go in by helicopter if needed. These preparations by on-the-scene commanders exemplified the type of detailed planning required to meet the requirements of the local situation and supplemented the considerable contingency planning already accomplished by senior headquarters staffs. Its evacuation plans complete, the Ready Group arrived on station about thirty miles off the Dominican coast at about 0200 hours on Monday, 26 April. By then the estimated number of persons to be evacuated had risen to 3,600. The ships stayed out of sight of land Monday, but remained ready to oppose air or surface attack.[14]

On Sunday the State Department began formulating U.S. policy to cope with the chaotic political situation in the Dominican Republic. In midmorning the department told Connett it assumed he had urged the leaders of the Dominican armed forces to form some type of provisional government capable of restoring order and preventing a possible Communist takeover. Thus officials of the State Department as early as Sunday showed anxiety for American lives, concern for a possible Communist takeover, and support for the formation of a military junta. At this early stage of the crisis Washington did not authorize any active embassy involvement to promote compromise among the contending Dominican factions. On Sunday the defense attachés contacted Dominican military officers to explore formation of a military junta.[15]

Sunday afternoon, officials in Washington focused increased attention on the Dominican situation. Undersecretary Mann assumed the key responsibility for directing the governmental response to the crisis from the Operations Center, and center watch officers briefed Secretary of State Dean Rusk. The secretary considered the revolt part of a global communist conspiracy and therefore a factor affecting the U.S. position everywhere in the world including Vietnam. He viewed the civil strife as a potential second Cuba and his questions focused on the strength of the communist representation in the group attempting to gain power in Santo Domingo.[16]

Sunday evening, power was in the streets. Thousands of armed and unarmed students, laborers, urban poor, and middle class in Santo Domingo with varying motives and loyalties had joined the pro-Bosch movement against the Dominican armed forces represented by General Wessin y Wessin, who now became the focal point for popular opposition. By evening Dominican military officials had still not resolved the crisis. Commodore Rivera of the navy, apparently convinced that the pro-Bosch movement would succeed, went to the palace to put his forces at the disposition of the Molina Ureña regime but was dissuaded by the American naval attaché. Since American ships conducting evacuation operations would mingle with Dominican corvettes and gunboats close to shore, it was important for the United States to retain the friendship of the Dominican navy. This incident underscored the importance of the military attachés during the initial phase of the revolt.[17]

By Monday morning, 26 April, mobs and agitators ran riot in the city, and trained teams, many led by communists, organized commando and paramilitary groups. Armed civilians outnumbered the rebel soldiers and it was difficult to determine who controlled the revolt, if anyone. The embassy reported to Washington that the anti-rebel military forces had weakened and that there was a serious threat of a communist takeover with little time left to prevent it. Embassy officials denied a request by Generals Wessin y Wessin and De Los Santos for U.S. troop support.[18]

During the day strident rebel and loyalist broadcasts competed and rebel partisans urged the people to go into the streets, to sack the homes of the Dominican Air Force pilots strafing the city, and to defend the palace. Public services stopped in many areas making power, light, and water unavailable. Lawlessness and violence mounted as civil authority broke down completely and the police disappeared. Atrocity stories circulated and it became increasingly impossible for any force to restore order. Anarchy had become the dominating force. Under these conditions President Johnson met with Ambassador Bennett in Washington at noon on Monday and urged him to work for an immediate cease-fire and the establishment of a junta, emphasizing the unacceptability of another Cuba.[19]

By Monday night both embassy and State Department officials realized that a cease-fire would not be achieved easily and implemented evacuation procedures. American consular officials began registering Americans and other nationals who wished to leave. These authorities designated the Embajador Hotel as an assembly area and the port of Haina, about seven miles west of Santo Domingo, as the point of departure. They then notified American residents desiring to leave to begin gathering at the hotel at 0600 hours Tuesday morning for processing. Early Tuesday morning the Ready Group closed to within twenty miles of the coast and the embarked marines assumed a fifteen-minute alert. At the same time the Joint Chiefs of Staff activated the alerting system to prepare American forces for possible use in the Dominican Republic.[20]

During the late evening of Monday and early morning of Tuesday the Joint Chiefs alerted the two unified commands committed to the Dominican contingency plan, the Strike and Atlantic Commands. The Strike Command alerted and prepared the army and air force forces used to augment the Atlantic Command, whose commander assumed operational control of the deploying units. The two unified commands, then alerted subordinate organizations such as the Tactical Air Command (TAC) headquartered in the Norfolk area. This major air force command then placed the airlift, fighter, and reconnaissance units committed to the Dominican contingency plan in an advanced state of alert and directed these units to remain at their home bases pending further developments. The headquarters of the Continental Army Command, also located in the Norfolk area, alerted the army units committed to the Dominican operation plan, including one two-battalion brigade of about two thousand men of the 82nd Airborne Division at Fort Bragg, North Carolina. In addition, the Atlantic Command alerted several battalions of marines from the 2nd Marine Division at Camp Lejeune, North Carolina, a marine fighter squadron at Roosevelt Roads, Puerto Rico, and the necessary fleet units to support the operation.[21]

At 0400 hours on Tuesday, Major General Robert H. York, commanding general of the 82nd Airborne Division, briefed his troops on the details of the contingency plan, which called for an airborne assault to secure the San Isidro air base in Santo Domingo followed by occupation of positions on the Duarte Bridge leading to the city (see map 2). This alert of the forces that might become involved in the military operation did not reflect Johnson administration thinking so much as accomplishment of a standard procedure used by the Joint Chiefs to ready forces for any eventuality. Between the time of first alert and the time of actual deployment certain actions such as personnel augmentation and logistical support must take place in order to enable the forces to be fully ready on short notice.[22]

The military attachés played an important role in events in Santo Domingo on Tuesday. Early Tuesday, 27 April, Colonel Heywood informed Connett that the anti-Bosch forces had decided to issue an early morning ultimatum to the Molina Ureña regime and then strafe the city to compel agreement. After a series of air attacks on the palace, the Duarte Bridge area, and sections of downtown Santo Domingo, the Wessin y Wessin forces planned to enter the city. Convinced that diplomatic pressures would not succeed in forcing negotiations, the embassy apparently approved of the Dominican military leaders' proposal. The chief embassy concern (expressed by a military attaché over an unsecured radio circuit monitored by pro-Bosch sympathizers) was that the projected military measures should not threaten the areas to be used for the planned evacuation of American citizens nor interfere with the scheduled return of Ambassador Bennett.[23]

Not only were military attachés involved in transmitting the plans of the anti-Bosch forces to the embassy, but they actively took part in facilitating communications between the warring sides. Pro-Bosch military leaders went to the military attaché section of the embassy on Tuesday morning to seek U.S. assistance in arranging negotiations with the Wessin y Wessin forces. The embassy persuaded the Dominican Air Force to postpone the planned air attack and permitted the pro-Bosch personnel to use attaché radio facilities in unsuccessful negotiations with the San Isidro forces since telephone contact was impossible.[24]

On Tuesday morning 27 April the Ready Group closed to within ten miles of Santo Domingo in preparation for the evacuation rescheduled from 0600 to 1200 hours. While these preparations continued Ambassador Bennett arrived at the International Airport about fifteen miles east of Santo Domingo. Driving from the airport

Map 2. Santo Domingo (1965)

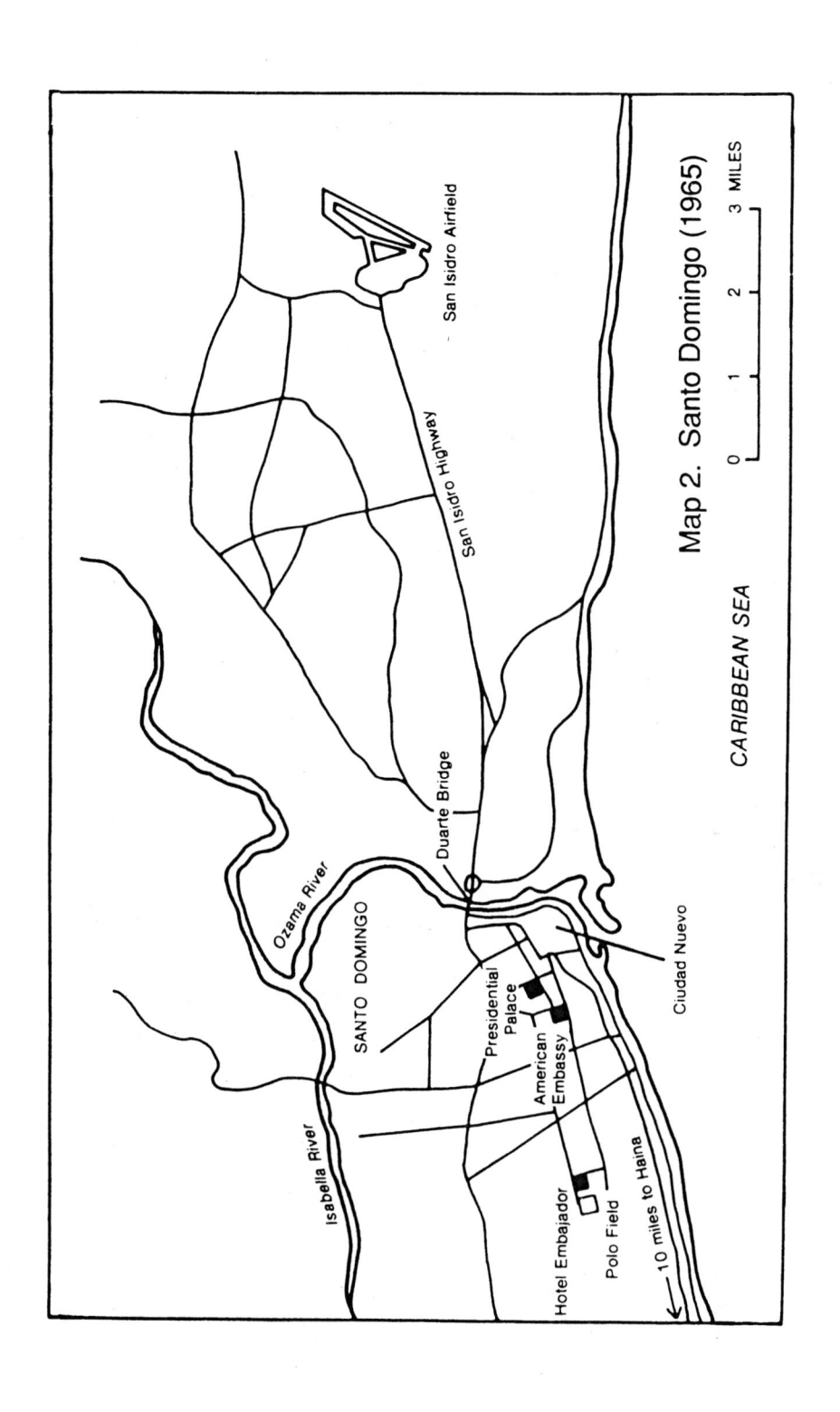

to the embassy would require crossing the Ozama River via the Duarte Bridge, a heavily contested area between Bosch and the Wessin y Wessin forces. To avoid this drive the Boxer sent two observation helicopters to pick up the ambassador at the airport. Since the airport control tower was unmanned the helicopter pilots contacted the arriving ambassador's aircraft by radio and cleared it to land. After a successful landing, the helicopters transported the ambassador to the flagship without further incident. The landing force commander, Colonel Daughtry, accompanied the helicopters on the trip to meet Ambassador Bennett, and a lasting friendship, formed at this time between these two Georgians, created the cooperation between embassy and Ready Group officials necessary for the following successful evacuation and landing operations. After a briefing aboard the Boxer a helicopter transported the ambassador to the port of Haina, west of Santo Domingo, where the evacuation would begin.[25]

Earlier on Tuesday a band of rebels broke into the Embajador Hotel where Americans had gathered for evacuation and fired at random into the walls of the building. This incident raised doubts among embassy officials of rebel sincerity in promising to guarantee American lives and property during the evacuation. The Ready Group now closed to five miles off the coast and the Wood County and Ruchamkin proceeded to Haina to await the arrival of the evacuees. Bennett requested the Boxer and Raleigh to move within easy visual range of downtown Santo Domingo to show the Dominican people that the planes strafing the city were not from American aircraft carriers. These ships operated among Dominican corvettes and gunboats steaming one to three miles offshore.[26]

Marine helicopters from the Boxer flew to the polo grounds adjoining the hotel to help in the evacuation, bringing ashore communications equipment. Marines installed this equipment at the American embassy and at the San Isidro airbase, General Wessin y Wessin's headquarters. Helicopters also brought in pathfinder teams of marines to Haina. These unarmed marines landed near the pier area, controlled the embarkation of evacuees aboard the Ruchamkin--the first ship to arrive alongside the pier--and established control of the pier and access areas. The marine pathfinders also marked out a landing zone for helicopter evacuation operations in the pier area.[27]

By noon Tuesday over a thousand persons had gathered on the hotel grounds awaiting evacuation, and one hour later a motor convoy of busses and trucks began to move the evacuees to Haina. While the evacuation proceeded, a fierce battle raged in the eastern part of the city where Dominican air force planes strafed and navy ships bombarded rebel positions in the Duarte Bridge area. General Wessin y Wessin's tanks, artillery, and infantry crossed the bridge and advanced several blocks into the city against stiff rebel resistance. The force consisted of powerful units from the Armed Forces Training Center and aviation personnel, infantry, and armored forces from the San Isidro air base. In the battle at the Duarte Bridge hundreds of persons, mostly civilians, were killed or wounded in one of the bloodiest single battles in Dominican history. This battle and the arrival of a loyalist force of about one thousand men from San Christobal on the western edge of the city disheartened the rebels and led them to negotiate.[28]

The provisional president, Molina Ureña, and eighteen rebel officers including Colonel Caamaño arrived at the embassy about 1700 and asked Ambassador Bennett to mediate between them and the San Isidro forces. Bennett told them that he had no authority to mediate and that the matter should be settled by Dominicans talking to Dominicans. Faced with an apparently hopeless situation, the Molina Ureña government collapsed and Ureña and several of his aides took refuge in the Columbian Embassy. Colonel Caamaño and other constitutional leaders continued to fight.[29]

The evacuation continued and by Tuesday evening over six hundred Americans had, at the Haina piers, boarded the two ships departing for San Juan, Puerto Rico. Marine helicopters flew an additional 250 passengers to the Raleigh and about three hundred to the Boxer from the polo grounds. On Tuesday the marine helicopter squadron logged about sixty flying hours in 102 sorties using twenty helicopters. Tuesday night seven of the helicopters remained overnight at the polo grounds to take care of any emergency evacuation or liaison problems.[30]

With the collapse of the Molina Ureña government, embassy officials assumed that the rebellion had collapsed. Bennett conferred with the police chief, Hernán Despradel, who predicted that the streets of Santo Domingo would be cleared of opposition that night. The ambassador informed Washington that a mopping-up operation probably would be accomplished soon and that he expected the anti-Bosch forces to prevail. In summarizing the country team's analysis of the confused situation to Washington Tuesday night, Bennett reported that embassy officials had not attempted to impose a solution but rather had sought to arrange a cease-fire and promote talks between the two sides. He reported that the Molina Ureña regime had admitted that it was unable to control the rebels and also pointed out the Castroite flavor of the radio and television broadcasts from the rebel side. This report included information that known communist groups, well-armed and organized, had moved rapidly to take advantage of the uncertain situation in downtown Santo Domingo. The sense of crisis in Washington now began to subside and the State Department, in a briefing paper prepared for the White House Tuesday afternoon, predicted that General Wessin y Wessin would soon control Santo Domingo. Tuesday night the president and the director of the CIA, John McCone, conferred briefly on the Dominican situation and agreed that, although the threat of another Castro emerging in the Dominican Republic would bear watching, U.S. intervention would not be necessary. By Wednesday the situation had changed completely and the president made the first of a series of decisions to commit American forces to the intervention.[31]

NOTES

1. Center for Strategic Studies, Dominican Action--1965, pp. 8-9; Atkins and Wilson, The United States and the Trujillo Regime, p. 142; Martin, Overtaken by Events, p. 645.

2. Gleijeses, The Dominican Crisis, p. 158; Yates, Power Pack, pp. 24-25.

3. Martin, Overtaken by Events, p. 646; Lowenthal, The Dominican Intervention, pp. 64-65; Center for Strategic Studies, Dominican Action--1965, pp. 11-12.

4. Tad Szulc, Dominican Diary (New York: Delacorte Press, 1965), pp. 67-68; Jules D. Yates, "The Dominican Crisis," Mitre Working Paper (Bedford, MA: Mitre Corporation, 1973), p. 8. Key personnel such as senior foreign service officers, military attachés, and military advisory group personnel make up the country team that advises the ambassador of important developments in the assigned country. Since the team members develop expertise in the problems of their assigned countries and must be capable of coordinating U.S. activities and agencies in the country, continuity in country team personnel assignments is important.

5. Lowenthal, The Dominican Intervention, pp. 63-64.

6. Ibid., p. 65; Johnson, The Vantage Point, p. 187; Center for Strategic Studies, Dominican Action--1965, p. 12; Martin, Overtaken by Events, p. 645.

7. Lowenthal, The Dominican Intervention, pp. 55, 69; Martin, Overtaken by Events, p. 645; Center for Strategic Studies, Dominican Action--1965, p. 8. For the importance of the military attachés as policy advisers and as members of his "crisis" crowd see Martin, Overtaken by Events, pp. 148, 115.

8. Lowenthal, The Dominican Intervention, pp. 63, 67.

9. Ibid., 68-70; Schlesinger, A Thousand Days, pp. 420-421; Jerome Slater, Intervention and Negotiation: The United States and the Dominican Revolution (New York: Harper and Row, 1970), p. 22; Martin, Overtaken by Events, p. 647. Martin and Slater agree that the passing out of arms on Saturday night and Sunday morning to thousands of civilians (estimates range from 2,500 to ten thousand according to Slater) in order to broaden the base of the movement and counter any reaction from the bulk of the armed forces, changed the nature of the revolt and prepared the way for the violence that followed. Martin wrote that an American police adviser asked Caamaño, whom he knew well, why the rebels had given guns to so many communists. Caamaño replied, "I know we've given the communists plenty of guns, but we had to do it to win and get rid of Reid. When we get in power, we will pick up all the guns." (See Martin, Overtaken by Events, p. 650).

10. Lowenthal, The Dominican Intervention, pp. 69, 74-78; Center for Strategic Studies, Dominican Action--1965, pp. 19-21; Atkins and Wilson, The United States and the Trujillo Regime, p. 143. Times in

this study are local times unless otherwise designated and are based on the customary military usage of a twenty-four hour clock.

11. Center for Strategic Studies, Dominican Action--1965, pp. 14-16; Johnson, The Vantage Point, p. 190; Lowenthal, The Dominican Intervention, p. 85.

12. Raymond V. B. Blackman (ed.), Jane's Fighting Ships (New York: McGraw-Hill, 1964) pp. 324, 382, 391, 395; James A. Dare, "Dominican Diary," U.S. Naval Institute Proceedings (December 1965), p. 37; U.S. Navy, Atlantic Fleet Amphibious Force, Report of Participation in Dominican Republic Operations for Period 25 April to 6 June 1965, 11 June 1965, encl. 1, p. 1, hereafter referred to as Phiblant, Report of Participation. In this study the title U.S.S. designating a U.S. warship has been omitted.

13. Dare, "Dominican Diary," pp. 37-38; R. McC. Tompkins, "Ubique," Marine Corps Gazette (September 1965), p. 37; Jack K. Ringler and Henry I. Shaw, U.S. Marine Corps Operations in the Dominican Republic, April-June 1965 (Washington, D.C.: Historical Division, HQ U.S.M.C., 1970), pp. 14, 20.

14. Dare, "Dominican Diary," p. 38; Tompkins, "Ubique," p. 34; Center for Strategic Studies, Dominican Action--1965, p. 22; Phiblant, Report of Participation, encl. 1, p. 1.

15. Lowenthal, The Dominican Intervention, pp. 72-73; Atkins and Wilson, The United States and the Trijillo Regime, p. 142.

16. Philip Geyelin, Lyndon B. Johnson and the World (New York: Frederick A. Praeger, 1966), p. 254.

17. Lowenthal, The Dominican Intervention, pp. 82, 84; John W. Ault, "Dominican Republic Crisis: Causes, Intervention, Lessons Learned," Research study, Air Command and Staff College, Air University, Maxwell AFB, Alabama, 1970; Slater, Intervention and Negotiation, p. 23.

18. Lowenthal, The Dominican Intervention, pp. 84-88; Center for Strategic Studies, Dominican Action--1965, pp. 23-24; Kelso, "The Dominican Crisis of 1965," pp. 70-71.

19. Lowenthal, The Dominican Intervention, pp. 84-88; Center for Strategic Studies, Dominican Action--1965, pp. 23-24.

20. Center for Strategic Studies, Dominican Action-1965, p. 24. Dare, "Dominican Diary," p. 40; Phiblant, Report of Participation, encl. 1, p. 1; U.S. Air Force, "The Dominican Republic Crisis of 1965: The Air Force Role," Aerospace Studies Institute, Project no. AU-434-66-ASI (Maxwell AFB: Air University, 1966), p. 9 (hereafter cited as ASI, "Air Force Role"). Standard alerting doctrine called for directing assigned units to come up to certain pre-defined readiness

conditions termed DEFCONS identified by numbers. DEFCON 3, for example, ordered the recall of personnel assigned to the operation, DEFCON 2 directed movement of units to the staging area, and DEFCON 1 authorized loading the troops aboard aircraft or ships. Units alerted had been previously earmarked for Dominican operations in contingency plans, such as Atlantic Command Operation Plan 310/2, developed at all levels of command (see Ringler and Shaw, U.S. Marine Corps Operations in the Dominican Republic, April-June 1965).

21. ASI, "Air Force Role," 17.

22. Yates, Power Pack, p. 32; Lowenthal, The Dominican Intervention, pp. 88-89; "Airborne Ready Forces," Airborne Quarterly (June-August 1965), p. 11; Bruce Palmer, "The Army in the Dominican Republic," Army (November 1965), p. 43.

23. Lowenthal, The Dominican Intervention, pp. 89-90.

24. Ibid., p. 91.

25. Dare, "Dominican Diary, p. 41; Martin, Overtaken by Events, p. 651.

26. Lowenthal, The Dominican Intervention, pp. 90-92. Center for Strategic Studies, Dominican Action--1965, p. 26; Phiblant, Report of Participation, encl. 1, p. 1.

27. Dare, "Dominican Diary," p. 41; Ringler and Shaw, U.S. Marine Corps Operations in the Dominican Republic, April-June 1965, pp. 23-24.

28. Lowenthal, The Dominican Intervention, p. 93; Tompkins, "Ubique," p. 34; Ault, "Dominican Republic Crisis," p. 27; Rowland Evans and Robert Novak, Lyndon B. Johnson: The Exercise of Power (New York: New American Library, 1966), p. 515.

29. Center for Strategic Studies, Dominican Action-1965, p. 29; Kelso, "The Dominican Crisis of 1965," pp. 80-82.

30. Dare, "Dominican Diary," p. 42; Tompkins, "Ubique," pp. 34-35; Ringler and Shaw, U.S. Marine Corps Operations in the Dominican Republic, p. 23.

31. Kelso, "The Dominican Crisis of 1965," pp. 83-84; Lowenthal, The Dominican Intervention, p. 95; Charles Roberts, LBJ's Inner Circle (New York: Delacorte Press, 1965), p. 203.

3

Decisions and Initial Operations (28-29 April)

Crises such as the initial days of Dominican revolt require presidential decisions under the pressures of limited time, high stakes, and incomplete information. Such factors affected the series of decisions made by President Johnson committing American forces to the Dominican action. On Wednesday 28 April the president authorized the landing of a limited number of marines to protect U.S. citizens and property in Santo Domingo. On the following day he authorized increased troop landings to prevent a communist takeover. The president made these controversial decisions on the basis of incomplete information but with the unanimous agreement of his advisers both at the Washington and embassy levels.

Information important to the presidential decisions included the degree of communist participation in the rebel movement and the extent of disorder in Santo Domingo. During the first days of the revolt before U.S. troops landed, the principle sources for this information were military attaché, CIA, and other embassy staff reports. A large number of information reports included descriptions of the activities and plans of the Dominican Communist leadership, warnings that the Caamaño faction had lost control of the revolt, constitutionalist propaganda and rhetoric frequently Castroite in tone, and evidence of a major communist role in the arming, training, and leadership of guerrilla warfare commando units in the rebel zone. The Dominican communists lacked mass appeal, an organizational network, and inspired leadership, but their presence among the revolutionaries led to repeated warnings by Bennett and the embassy staff of a possible communist takeover. Although initial intelligence agency and embassy reports magnified the participation of communists in the revolt, there was considerable evidence of their involvement. What remained in doubt was the degree of communist control of the revolt.[1]

Embassy staff, CIA personnel, and on-the-scene observers tended to accept as fact rumors of rebel atrocities current in the early days of the revolt. Such rumors are characteristic of a chaotic situation in which communications break down, police control is nonexistent, and power moves to the streets. Intelligence collection personnel and analysts failed to cross check rumors that embassy briefers presented as facts and that even appeared in presidential speeches. Such inaccurate reporting was largely responsible for the bad domestic press that the Johnson administration received during and after the intervention.[2]

Information linking communists to disorder in Santo Domingo heavily influenced the president and his advisers in deciding to intervene. They believed the Communists, although few in number, had no effective opposition and in the chaotic situation prevailing in Santo Domingo might prevail over a much larger, unorganized rebel group without effective leadership. They also believed that reports of disorder showed that American lives and property were in danger and required protection not available from Dominican sources.[3]

DECISION TO LAND MARINES

Tuesday night and early Wednesday morning, 27-28 April, the rebels regrouped their forces, resupplied their troops with arms and abandoned tanks, and consolidated their positions in the city. They turned the downtown business district in Santo Domingo, known as Ciudad Nueva, into a stronghold and installed machine guns on the roofs of buildings, including Santa Maria Cathedral, site of the tomb of Christopher Columbus. Armed rebel bands patrolled the downtown area and many observers believed that it was at this time that the communists played their most important role in the revolt by assisting the rebel leader, Caamaño, in regrouping his forces.[4]

By Wednesday morning the Wessin y Wessin forces had lost the momentum gained on Tuesday. Caamaño led a mixed force of military men and civilians in a successful attack on a police station near the Palace of Justice, capturing additional arms and ammunition. The loyalist troops of General Salvador Augusto Montás Guerrero, entering the city from the west, split into small uncoordinated groups, and Wessin y Wessin's troops on the east remained stalled in the Duarte Bridge area. The loyalist forces did not fight effectively together and lacked communications equipment for coordinating the operations of their scattered groups. The American military advisory group chief told Bennett that the San Isidro officers were discouraged and disorganized and that their troops might not be able to hold the Duarte bridgehead much less advance into the city for mop-up operations.[5]

Wednesday morning a three-man military junta led by Colonel Pedro Bartolome Benoit, a Dominican Air Force colonel, was formed to rally anti-Bosch support. Washington and embassy officials had recommended its formation to reunite the fragmented military forces and restore order. This self-proclaimed government represented some semblance of authority in the Dominican Republic after the collapse of the Molina group, and with police support controlled most of the country except for the rebel-held areas of downtown Santo Domingo.[6]

About noon on Wednesday 28 April, Bennett asked Washington to supply the Benoit junta with fifty walkie-talkies, which the loyalists had requested previously. These would help the Wessin y Wessin forces in contacting their isolated pockets of troops. Bennett

Decisions and Initial Operations

stressed that denying the junta this equipment might lead to a rebel victory. Although he regretted relying on a military solution to a political problem, Bennett believed that the battle now was between "Castro-type elements and their opponents," and that if the junta forces lost he might be forced to ask for marines to protect U.S. citizens "and possibly for other purposes." "Which would Washington prefer?" Bennett asked.[7]

At noon on Wednesday CINCLANT activated the command headquarters of Joint Task Force 122 and Vice-Admiral Kleber S. Masterson, commander of the Second Fleet, proceeded to the Dominican area to assume command. His early departure from Norfolk, Virginia, preceded by over twenty-four hours President Johnson's decision to commit a large force to the Dominican action. Admiral Masterson's assignment to the area and activation of the joint task force indicated the Atlantic Command's concern for the gravity of the situation in Santo Domingo and early preparations for a major operation.[8]

By Wednesday afternoon it was clear that the Dominican armed forces could not restore order. Bennett reported to Washington that the police could no longer guarantee the lives of American citizens in Santo Domingo. About 1500 hours Benoit asked the embassy to land American marines to restore order. Bennett reported this oral request to Washington and added that he thought Washington should be planning for their possible use. When the White House received Bennett's cable, McGeorge Bundy, special assistant to the president for national security affairs, arranged for a conference of the president's major advisers on the Dominican situation. Thus the crisis now began more actively to involve key officials.[9]

In addition to evacuating American citizens on Tuesday and Wednesday, U.S. naval forces in the Dominican area engaged in another humanitarian operation. The need for blood substitutes, antibiotics, and medical supplies for treating wounds was urgent and the ships of the Ready Group made available all that could be spared, amounting to supplies for about two hundred wounded. The Ready Group turned over these supplies to marines ashore for distribution to Peace Corps representatives, the Dominican Red Cross, and hospitals downtown. American forces continued to keep medical supplies flowing throughout the Dominican action for the benefit of both the U.S. wounded and the Dominicans.[10]

At about 1600 hours on Wednesday, 28 April, Benoit sent a written request for American military support to the embassy that was relayed by CRITIC cable to Washington. He asked the United States to give "unlimited and immediate military assistance" to the junta to put down the rebellion, which, Benoit declared, armed communists directed in order to "convert the country into another Cuba." Benoit said nothing about protecting American lives and Washington denied the request. The embassy told Benoit that the United States would not intervene unless he declared his forces could not protect American citizens in the Dominican Republic.[11]

Wednesday afternoon Bennett telephoned the landing force commander several times concerning sending in marines to guard the evacuation point at the polo grounds and to augment the marine force at the embassy. He requested evacuation operations be transferred from Haina to the Embajador Hotel because the national police could no longer provide protection along the road between these two locations. As a result, by 1700 hours military authorities had placed the Ready Group marines aboard the <u>Boxer</u> on five minutes notice to land. At Bennett's request the landing force furnished unarmed pathfinders, military police, and helicopter support teams to establish a landing zone at the polo grounds next to the hotel and to assist in the evacuation. Shortly after the arrival of the first helicopters, civilian evacuees began to be flown out to the ships of the task force. After debarking the first evacuees, the helicopters transferred ashore an armed platoon of marines reinforced by two squads in order to augment the marine guard at the embassy. These troops had already landed by the time President Johnson received Bennett's request for military support.[12]

At about 1700 hours Bennett sent a CRITIC message to Washington reporting a deteriorating situation in Santo Domingo. He reported that the country team unanimously agreed that "now that we have a request from the military junta for assistance, the time has come to land the marines." American lives were in danger, he added, and the chief of police had stated the police could no longer protect the road over which the evacuees were moving to Haina. In Washington President Johnson was conferring with Rusk, McNamara, Bundy, Undersecretary of State George Ball, and Special Assistant Bill Moyers when he received Bennett's request to land the marines. Johnson and his advisers believed that they had no choice but to grant Bennett's request for a marine landing. If local authorities could not provide protection to American citizens the United States must and each minute lost might mean a life lost. The president and his advisers discussed the Dominican situation for about one-half hour and telephoned Mann at the State Department and Senator Richard Russell of Georgia. Russell, chairman of the Armed Services Committee, remembered that their discussion concerned the possibility of a Communist takeover.[13]

Johnson and his advisers decided on prompt and decisive action based, as he testified later, 99 percent on the desire to protect American lives and the lives of other nationals. All of Johnson's advisers at the decision-making conference except Moyers were veterans of the Cuban missile crisis and that experience reinforced their belief that the United States should respond to the crisis boldly. The president's senior advisers probably had been selected for their supportive roles so that they tended to agree unanimously with Johnson. Since the president did not solicit hostile or differing opinions, decisions during the intervention tended to be unanimous and to reflect the president's views and assumptions. General Earl Wheeler, chairman of the Joint Chiefs of Staff, did not attend the decision-making conference, but McNamara advised the president that the armed forces had been alerted and were in position to move quickly. Without further consultation the president authorized the landing of five hundred marines but limited their actions to defensive operations during which they could fire only in self-defense.[14]

INITIAL OPERATIONS

At about 1800 hours on Wednesday Captain Dare received the order to land the marines if requested by the ambassador. Bennett and Colonel Daughtry, the landing force commander, briefly discussed the situation and authorized a vertical envelopment by two marine rifle companies and the battalion headquarters. Helicopters transported the marines to the polo grounds without opposition during the hours of darkness and by 2000 hours 536 marines of the 6th Marine Expeditionary Unit from the Boxer had landed. Each helicopter unloaded marines then loaded women and children evacuees for transport back to the ship. By the last flight at midnight 684 civilians had been evacuated. Although alarms occurred during the night, the marines guarding the polo grounds saw no action. Those at the embassy, however, exchanged fire with snipers throughout the night.[15]

During the night of 28-29 April, administration officials informed the public, the Latin American ambassadors, and members of the OAS of the marine landings. The failure of American officials to inform the OAS sooner became another controversial issue during the crisis. Washington authorities believed, however, that the regional organization would have taken too long to decide on appropriate action to meet the crisis, resulting in the loss of American lives. This reflected the urgency Johnson and his advisers attached to the decision to land the marines. On Tuesday the United States had called for a meeting of the OAS Peace Committee to discuss the crisis. At this meeting the committee concluded that it was not empowered to take action and the State Department requested the OAS to convene a special meeting of its council for Wednesday. The council finally convened Thursday evening.[16]

The president met with congressional leaders, the vice-president, and other top officials at 1930 hours Wednesday to brief them on the Dominican situation. At this meeting McNamara outlined the military contingency plans then being put into effect. Later Wednesday evening Johnson addressed the American people on television concerning the crisis and publicly urged both factions to agree to a cease-fire. The president did not mention during this television broadcast the fear of a communist takeover but described the need to protect the lives of Americans and others seeking U.S. help. Presidential critics have claimed that Johnson failed fully to inform the public. The administration's credibility gap became another controversial subject connected with the intervention. Most journalists covering the revolt, however, including some who later criticized the actions of the Johnson administration, believed the 28 April marine landings were justified on humanitarian grounds.[17]

Bennett continued to report a deteriorating situation Wednesday evening, 28 April. Americans in Santo Domingo warned him that they lacked protection in the residential areas. Bennett, seeing a complete breakdown in government authority, recommended that "serious thought be given in Washington to armed intervention which would go beyond the mere protection of Americans and seek to establish order in this strife-ridden country." He added that if the anti-rebel forces failed, then power would be assumed by groups clearly identified with the Communist Party. If that occurred, the United States should intervene to prevent another Cuba. Johnson decided that before intervening in force he should know the reactions of Latin American countries. These he thought might be revealed at the OAS meeting scheduled for the next morning. He also wanted to know if the Dominicans could settle their differences without outside interference and if there was any alternative to more American intervention. Bennett's Wednesday evening cable recommending armed intervention resulted from a secure teletype conference between Bennett, Ball, Mann, and others about the proposed presidential announcement of the marine landings. This conversation included Bennett's recommendation that additional military units be dispatched to the Dominican Republic since the Caribbean Ready Group did not have sufficient forces to perform the intervention mission.[18]

Wednesday evening the Joint Chiefs increased the readiness status of army and air force units already alerted early the day before. Airlift units departed their home bases for Pope Air Force Base, where teams loaded equipment aboard aircraft and 82d Airborne Division paratroopers assembled near the planes they would board. The advanced alert status resulted from an estimate by the Joint Chiefs of the increased possibility of force employment. Washington's control at each step of the alerting and force commitment process, including cancellation of movements already underway, allowed the president a full range of options in the use of the intervening force.[19]

During the night of 28-29 April, Bennett rejected a suggestion by American naval officers for an aerial show of force and declined to consider any additional troop landings until the morning. He also turned down a request by Admiral Masterson for permission to land at the San Isidro airbase, arguing that landing the admiral's aircraft there would look like intervention. By Thursday morning the junta troops, suffering from exhaustion, low morale, hunger, and poor communications, had not entered the city as planned. Continued defections lowered the estimated strength of junta forces to less than two thousand men. By comparison rebel morale was high and the constitutionalists even considered attacking the San Isidro base.[20]

Meanwhile the Ready Group logistically supported the marines already ashore, stood by to provide any needed naval gunfire support, and planned for possible additional commitments of marines and heavy equipment. Thursday morning, marine helicopters flew reconnaissance for the troops ashore, landed more headquarters personnel and supplies, and evacuated additional personnel to the Boxer, bringing the total aboard that ship to 704. By Thursday the Caribbean Sea Frontier headquartered in San Juan, had reinforced the Ready Group with four destroyers, a tanker, and a squadron of marine fighter aircraft to fly combat air patrol over the task force.

On Thursday morning the Wood County returned from San Juan with medical supplies and members of the press. The journalists transferred to the Boxer for a briefing by Captain Dare, the task force commander. At this briefing, when asked how long the marines would remain in Santo Domingo, Dare replied that they would stay as long as necessary to "keep this a non-communist government." Briefings such as this fed media charges that administration officials covered up

Decisions and Initial Operations

the truth by not mentioning fear of a communist takeover as a reason for American intervention.[21]

At the same briefing Dare stated that the marines could return fire only if fired upon first. Although such rules of engagement restricting military behavior are characteristic of operations carried out for political purposes, it seemed to military officials that the State Department had over-reacted in controlling operations in the Dominican Republic. The department, for example, sent a cable Thursday morning to Ambassador Bennett restricting American troop movements to the perimeter of the evacuation areas already held and requiring troop offensive operations to be authorized by the president. Bennett replied that he already had instructed Dare to restrict all troops to the Embajador Hotel area pending further orders.[22]

President Johnson met with McNamara and Mann on Thursday afternoon to go over the latest Dominican crisis reports. They noted that the police force had been decimated and that rebel forces might break out of their strongholds in the center of Santo Domingo. Johnson considered the marine force already ashore too small "for the many tasks we were giving it" (including the securing of an international security zone then under discussion in Washington). He therefore instructed McNamara to order the remainder of the Ready Group marines ashore and to deploy two battalion combat teams from the 82d Airborne to Ramey Air Force Base (AFB) in Puerto Rico as backup. Washington informed the embassy immediately of this decision and several minutes later asked Bennett whether or not direct intervention by U.S. forces was absolutely necessary. This last message also stated that: "We can not afford to permit the situation to deteriorate to the point where a Communist takeover occurs."[23]

The troop commanders, military advisory personnel, and embassy staff reported Thursday morning that the situation had not deteriorated and that there had been no increase in incidents. A Red Cross report described the dead being buried where they fell, rebel looting, and the erection of increased numbers of barricades in the streets. Faced with this confusing situation, the task and landing force commanders visited the embassy for more information. They arrived at about 1430 hours and joined the staff in a briefing and assessment of the crisis. The conferees decided that the rebels had expanded their operation, the junta forces remained stalled, and the police had become ineffective.[24]

In a report to the State Department concerning this meeting Bennett said that he had told Dare to bring the ships carrying marines and heavy equipment closer to shore in preparation for a landing. Twenty minutes later he told Washington that he had just instructed Dare to prepare to land the remaining 1,500 marines of the 6th Marine Expeditionary Unit (MEU). In response to a request by the State Department for an estimate of the situation, Bennett stated, concerning the rebels, that "our best guesswork" indicated that about 1,500 were under Communist leadership, fewer than one thousand were military regulars, and from one to four thousand were "hangers-on." He estimated junta forces to number about 1,700 scattered in various locations throughout the city with the bulk at San Isidro. In addition, he discussed establishing a security zone from the Embajador Hotel to the presidential palace, an area incorporating most American residences and foreign missions. He also mentioned that, on instructions from Mann, he intended to have the three U.S. air force MAAG officers, already at San Isidro helping the loyalists with communications, join with an army MAAG officer in advising the junta on operational planning.[25]

By the time the two officers from the Ready Group, who had met with Bennett, returned to the Boxer, Admiral Masterson had arrived and operation Barrel Bottom--landing the remaining marines--began. Since rebels held the dock area, heavy vehicles for the troops ashore were landed over the beach. During the Haina evacuation operation the beachmaster had observed a landing beach near the port. An underwater demolition team from the Ruchamkin conducted a limited survey of the area and found the beach suitable for landings. Admiral Masterson, having received his orders from the Joint Chiefs via the CINCLANT confirmed the landing decision. He assumed responsibility for the operation as commander of Joint Task Force 122. Captain Dare now became commander, Task Force 124, consisting of all naval units committed to the Dominican operation. Since the task force commander had set H-hour for operation Barrel Bottom at 1730 hours, the Raleigh, Rankin, Fort Snelling, and Wood County proceeded to their unloading stations seven to ten miles offshore at 1500 hours. The first wave of ten tracked landing vehicles proceeded ashore unopposed with the remaining waves following as scheduled. Once ashore the tanks and armored vehicles formed a column and moved down the main highway to the polo grounds where they joined the other marine elements already ashore. By 1830 hours the reinforced battalion landing team of about two thousand men had become an entity again under Colonel Daughtry, the landing force commander.[26]

DECISION TO INTERVENE IN FORCE

Late Thursday afternoon 29 April, Rusk, McNamara, Ball, Wheeler, and others in Washington held a telephone conference with Bennett and members of his staff in Santo Domingo. The Washington officials asked Bennett if he agreed with them that a rebel victory might lead to a pro-communist government. Bennett said he thought it would, adding that the rebels might install Bosch but then quickly discard him. Washington also asked Bennett if the Dominican loyalist forces could prevent a rebel victory. He pointed out the inefficiency and indecisiveness of the San Isidro generals. General Wessin y Wessin, for example, had "done little or nothing for the last three days." Washington officials stated that the administration wished to avoid military action as long as there was a reasonable chance that orderly forces could prevail. Bennett replied he hoped that the additional marines would encourage the San Isidro forces. The administration leaders also asked about the situation in the remainder of the country and were assured that the revolt was confined to Santo Domingo. Also, the conferees discussed administration plans for using the marines to establish an international security zone that would include the residential area and extend from the Embajador Hotel to the American Embassy and then to the sea.

Decisions and Initial Operations

In addition those present discussed a plan for interposing U.S. troops between the rebel and junta forces by sealing off the rebel stronghold in downtown Santo Domingo, thereby forcing the opposed factions to conclude a cease-fire. After the cease-fire the United States would request the OAS to negotiate a political settlement. When asked what he would recommend Washington do in the next six to twelve hours, Bennett replied that the most important action would be to commit sufficient troops to "do the job here rapidly and effectively." He also urged Washington to supply food, medicines, and other supplies for Santo Domingo disaster relief. This conference formed the background for a meeting Thursday evening beginning at 1930 hours during which the president decided on rapid U.S. military intervention in strength primarily to prevent a communist takeover. Johnson firmly believed that the rioting civilians had become dependent on the Communists for arms and ammunition and for leadership of the commando units. He also believed that, with most of the moderate leaders in hiding or asylum, the communists held the keys to power in the Dominican Republic.[27]

The president and his advisers determined the size of forces used based on the need to commit sufficient troops to form an international security zone and to separate the rebel and loyalist forces. McNamara reportedly urged deployment of the entire 82d Airborne Division and agreed with General Wheeler that the number of marines ashore was insufficient for the tasks assigned. A number of military officers disagreed with the size of the military commitment, which eventually reached a peak strength of over 23,500 troops by the middle of May. Washington officials committed a large force for several reasons in addition to the immediate needs of securing a safety zone and accomplishing a de facto cease-fire. Defense of the thirty-mile perimeter required troop increases and military officers in Santo Domingo continued to call for reinforcements. For example, a marine officer told a correspondent on Friday, after snipers had killed the first marine, that because of the difficult terrain in the security zone and the intense sniper fire he needed more troops.[28]

President Johnson and his advisers wanted to avoid the danger of acting too little and too late, which they believed had caused United States reverses in the Bay of Pigs crisis and in Vietnam. The "domino theory" prevalent in 1965 also concerned them since they reasoned that a communist victory in the American sphere of influence in the Caribbean might add to Soviet prestige decisively and cast doubt on U.S. resolve elsewhere in the world. Johnson's comment to John Bartlow Martin, a former American ambassador to the Dominican Republic, "What can we do in Vietnam if we can't clean up the Dominican Republic?" was indicative of this reasoning. As a first step in preventing a communist takeover, President Johnson ordered diversion to San Isidro of the advance elements of the 82d Airborne, which were then en route to Ramey AFB.[29]

At the Thursday evening conference President Johnson and his advisers also discussed the legality of the military action and the diplomatic moves to be taken concurrently. Rusk stated that in cases concerned with the security of the whole hemisphere U.S. actions should not be immobilized by the thirty-year-old Good Neighbor policy, with its emphasis on nonintervention, written before the communists developed the techniques of taking over peoples' revolutions. All agreed that it would be easier to prevent a Communist takeover than to dislodge a Communist government once established, and that the military buildup should be paralleled by diplomatic efforts to obtain a cease-fire, to bring the two factions together in some kind of interim government, and to schedule free elections at a later date. Since Bennett was not on good terms with the rebel leader, Caamaño, another American spokesman should be assigned to deal with the rebel forces. Washington officials assigned this job to Martin. Later Thursday night, following another meeting between Johnson and his advisers to work out the details of the military operation, the Joint Chiefs directed CINCLANT to plan for the establishment of an international security zone. The council of the OAS passed a resolution early Friday approving the immediate establishment of such a zone.[30]

A series of orders approved by the White House over the next few days implemented the president's Thursday decision to commit substantial forces to the Dominican operation. The troop increases resulted not from a single decision to commit a certain number of troops to the operation but from a series of decisions based on calls for more support from the deployed forces and expanding troop missions. From five hundred marines landed to protect the embassy and civilian evacuation on Wednesday, the intervening force increased to about two thousand marines on Thursday to secure an international safety zone, and then by another two thousand army paratroopers on Friday, 30 April. On 2 May the president ordered another two thousand troops to the Dominican Republic and directed McNamara and Wheeler to land an additional 4,500 troops as soon as possible. Justification for these troops was to establish a line of communications between U.S. troops and the need for distribution of food, providing security for Americans and foreign nationals, and helping in evacuation operations.

The president and his advisers at first presented the intervention as a humanitarian effort and played down the political aspects of the action. There is ample evidence, nevertheless, that the president and his advisers were very much concerned by the possibility of a Castro-type communist takeover in the Dominican Republic and the troubles of dislodging the communists once in power. The analogy with Cuba seems to have limited the choices of the decision-makers, as did the president's tendency to rely on unanimous agreement of a small number of key advisers. Johnson did not want the establishment of another communist base in the Caribbean from which revolutionary activity could be launched against friendly Latin American nations. Nor did he desire history and public opinion to blame him for permitting formation of such a base.[31]

NOTES

1. The degree of the communist threat was the first, and probably the most, controversial subject concerned with the intervention. Many American correspondents and observers believed that the Johnson administration grossly overestimated the communist threat in the Dominican Republic. A review of declassified government documents

Decisions and Initial Operations

including State Department and Dominican embassy messages shows that there was ample evidence of communist influence, if not control, especially during the early days of the revolt. Interviews with former rebels or constitutionalists seem to confirm this belief. Also, reports from U.S. intelligence agents who penetrated the rebel movement, and from an interrogation center set up by the U.S. military in the Dominican Republic tended to confirm a communist influence. In addition, incriminating documents indicating communist participation were captured by U.S. troops. The potential for a takeover of the revolt by Castroite communists was a clear danger. My purpose in writing this study, however, is not to analyze the degree of the communist threat but to analyze the decisions of the president and his advisers based on the information available to them at the time and their perceptions of the crisis situation.

For a discussion of the exaggeration of the threat of communism and the inaccuracies present in lists of communists provided the press by governmental spokesmen see Szulc, Dominican Diary, pp. 68-71; Theodore Draper, The Dominican Revolt: A Case Study in American Policy (New York: Commentary, 1968), pp. 167, 169, 201; Thomas Halper, Foreign Policy Crisis: Appearance and Reality in Decision Making, (Columbus, Ohio: Charles E. Merrill Publishing Company, 1971), pp. 66-68. For a discussion of the communist influence based on a review of Dominican embassy and State Department message traffic see Kelso, "The Dominican Crisis of 1965." For an interview with a former rebel who sat in on communist meetings in the Dominican Republic at the time of the revolt and who claimed that, with the disappearance of the PRD leaders, the communists controlled the revolt, see Kenneth O. Gilmore, "The Truth about Santo Domingo," Reader's Digest (May 1966), pp. 93-98. Both Kelso and Gilmore point to the caution of the Johnson administration in publishing the evidence of the communist influence in the revolt and suggest that perhaps Washington was waiting for evidence comparable to the overhead photography available at the time of the Cuban missile crisis. For the case of a CIA agent who was reporting developments from inside the rebel zone from a house which had two hundred rifles buried under the concrete floor of its cellar, see David A. Phillips, The Night Watch (New York: Atheneum, 1977), pp. 170-171.

2. Halper, Foreign Policy Crisis, pp. 47-48, 50. Information collection faced several problems beside the scarcity of reports during the early days of the revolt. Reports from military attachés and CIA station personnel contained the usual preliminary evaluation in the field consisting of an estimate of the source's reliability and the veracity of the information. Unfortunately collection personnel too often used the standard code indicating that neither the reliability of the source nor the accuracy of the information could be determined. Apparently such raw information reports reached the decision-makers without further analysis. Also intelligence collection personnel concentrated on reporting the activities of Communists and omitted reporting on the composition and leadership of the rebel movement (see Lowenthal, The Dominican Intervention, pp. 88, 204). Similarly, political reporting by embassy foreign service officers emphasized the leadership and activities of not only the communists but of the

loyalists who were well known to embassy personnel. There were few embassy staff reports concerned with the less-known rebel leadership and activities.

This kind of intelligence collection was a prime example of what has been called the "intelligence collection bias." The collector is biased toward obtaining information that can be collected the most easily. This he reports in quantity. Hard- to- get information which might be more important, tends to be overlooked. (Hilliard Roderick with Ulla Magnusson [eds.] Avoiding Inadvertent War: Crisis Management [Austin: University of Texas Press, 1983] p.75).

President Johnson's thirst for information spurred on the national intelligence effort during the intervention. His interest never waned throughout the crisis and he always wanted to know "right now" what was happening. This increased the crisis atmosphere in Washington, especially in the intelligence community, and was responsible in part for the setting up of a CIA permanent operations center which tied the agency into the NSC interagency network. Also, this sense of urgency caused the CIA to start issuing Dominican crisis situation reports every hour, twenty-four hours a day, during the initial days of the revolt (Phillips, The Night Watch, pp. 146, 147; Ray S. Cline, Secrets Spies and Scholars: Blueprint of the Essential CIA [Washington, D.C.: Acropolis Books Ltd., 1976], pp. 212, 213).

After the troop landings reporting improved as more channels of information became available. These included agents of the Federal Bureau of Investigation (FBI) and CIA, Special Force and military intelligence personnel, presidential envoys, members of peace delegations, and others. Also, television and press coverage increased.

3. Johnson, The Vantage Point, p. 200; Public Papers of the Presidents of the United States: Lyndon B. Johnson, v. 1, 1965, p. 465.

4. Tompkins, "Ubique," p. 35; Lowenthal, The Dominican Intervention, pp. 98-99.

5. Center for Strategic Studies, Dominican Action--1965, pp. 31, 32; Lowenthal, The Dominican Intervention, p. 99; Martin, Overtaken by Events, p. 655.

6. Center for Strategic Studies, Dominican Action--1965, p. 32; Atkins and Wilson, The United States and the Trujillo Regime, p.142.

7. Lowenthal, The Dominican Intervention, pp. 97, 100; Kelso, "The Dominican Crisis of 1965," pp. 84-87; Yates, Power Pack, pp. 47, 48.

8. Vice-Admiral Kleber S. Masterson, interview by John T. Mason, Jr., 9 April 1973, interview 7, transcript, U.S. Naval Institute Oral History Collection, U.S. Naval Institute, Annapolis, Md.

9. Lowenthal, The Dominican Intervention, 101; Johnson, The Vantage Point, 194; Kelso, "The Dominican Crisis of 1965," pp. 87-89.

10. Dare, "Dominican Diary," p. 42; Phiblant, Report of Participation, encl. 1, p. 2; Szulc, Dominican Diary, pp. 45, 56-57.

11. Lowenthal, The Dominican Intervention, pp. 101, 102; Martin, Overtaken by Events, p. 656; Kelso, "The Dominican Crisis of 1965," p.90; Yates, Power Pack, pp. 48-49. As Kelso points out, one hour prior to the decision to land the marines both McGeorge Bundy, President Johnson's national security adviser, and Thomas Mann, who was directing the State Department response to the crisis, were opposed to landing the marines. Apparently Washington, at this time, did not have an understanding of the real situation in the Dominican Republic. By then Wessin's forces had been routed, the Dominican navy was not sure of which side it would support, and the Dominican air force pilots were exhausted and discouraged. (Kelso, "The Dominican Crisis of 1965," pp. 88, 89). Mann believed that the embassy's pessimistic assessment of the loyalists' situation was exaggerated but he agreed with Bundy that the president should be briefed that afternoon on the situation in Santo Domingo.

CRITIC is a designation for urgent messages given the highest priority in transmittal and processing. A CRITIC cable is designed to reach Washington officials within a few minutes of being filed in the field.

12. Center for Strategic Studies, Dominican Action--1965, p. 36; Ringler and Shaw, U.S. Marine Corps Operations in the Dominican Republic, April--June 1965, pp. 24, 25; Phiblant, Report of Participation encl. 1, p. 2; Dare, "Dominican Diary," p. 42; Tompkins, "Ubique," p. 35.

13. Lowenthal, The Dominican Intervention, p. 102; Martin, Overtaken by Events, p. 656; Kelso, "The Dominican Crisis of 1965," pp. 90-92; Public Papers of the Presidents of the United States: Lyndon B. Johnson, v. 1, p. 461; Congress, Senate, Committee on Foreign Relations, Background Information Relating to the Dominican Republic, 89th cong., 1st sess., July 1965, pp. 57, 61 (hereafter cited as Committee on Foreign Relations, Background Information); Schoenbaum, Waging Peace and War, p. 448; Lyndon B. Johnson, The Vantage Point, p. 195; Yates, Power Pack, p. 49.

After Kennedy's assassination in 1963, President Johnson put first priority on preserving continuity within the administration. He therefore retained all of Kennedy's major military and foreign policy advisers including McNamara, Bundy, Rusk, Ball, and Taylor even after his own election to the presidency in the fall of 1964. Johnson apparently did not suffer from lack of advice during the early days of the revolt. He testified later that between 24 and 28 April, when the marines landed, he held 237 individual conversations and about thirty-five meetings with people in connection with the Dominican situation. See Richard W. Mansbach, Dominican Crisis 1965 (New York: Facts on File Inc., 1971), p. 73.

14. Mansbach, Dominican Crisis 1965, p. 73; Halper, Foreign Policy Crises, pp. 55, 215; Johnson, The Vantage Point, p. 195; Lowenthal, The Dominican Intervention, p. 103; Committee on Foreign Relations, Background Information, p. 61; Several sources have described Johnson's effort to get his principal advisers to agree with each other and his reluctance to take action unless they did (see William C. Westmoreland, A Soldier Reports (New York: Doubleday and Co. 1976), p. 120 and Morton H. Halperin, Bureaucratic Politics and Foreign Policy (Washington, D.C.: The Brookings Institution, 1974), p. 109.

15. Dare, "Dominican Diary," p. 42; Ringler and Shaw, U.S. Marine Corps Operations in the Dominican Republic, April--June 1965, pp. 25, 26; Tompkins, "Ubique," p. 35.

16. Mansbach, Dominican Crisis 1965, p. 75; Committee on Foreign Relations, Background Information, p. 56.

17. Public Papers of the Presidents of the United States: Lyndon B. Johnson, v. 1, 1965, p. 461; Department of State Bulletin (17 May 1965), pp. 738-739; Committee on Foreign Relations, Background Information, pp. 53, 56; Eric F. Goldman, The Tragedy of Lyndon Johnson (New York: Alfred A. Knopf, 1969), p. 397; Mansbach, Dominican Crisis 1965, p. 31.

Most U.S. political leaders supported the marine landings including ex-president Dwight D. Eisenhower, ex-vice- president Richard M. Nixon, and Senator Barry M. Goldwater. Congressional critics included Senators Robert F. Kennedy, Wayne L. Morse, and later J. William Fulbright, who in September 1965 in a Senate speech criticized the U.S. intervention and the administration's Latin American policies (Mansbach, Dominican Crisis 1965, pp. 39, 40, 77). Although a Gallup poll showed that 76 percent of Americans polled reacted favorably to sending troops to the Dominican Republic, most Latin American countries condemned the action. In general the French disapproved of the U.S. action while the British supported it (Mansbach, Dominican Crisis 1965, pp. 45-46; Halper, Foreign Policy Crises, p. 65).

For a discussion of the credibility of administration announcements referring to the Dominican crisis see Goldman, The Tragedy of Lyndon Johnson, pp. 394-397; also see Lowenthal, The Dominican Intervention, p. 105.

18. Lowenthal, The Dominican Intervention, p. 105; Center for Strategic Studies, Dominican Action--1965, p. 37; Johnson, The Vantage Point, p. 198; Lowenthal, The Dominican Intervention, p. 106.

19. ASI, The Air Force Role, p. 19; Ringler and Shaw, U.S Marine Corps Operations in the Dominican Republic April--June 1965, p. 25.

20. Lowenthal, The Dominican Intervention, pp. 106, 108; Martin, Overtaken by Events, p. 658. Johnson, The Vantage Point, p. 199.

21. Dare, "Dominican Diary," pp. 44-45; Phiblant, Report of Participation, encl. 1, p. 2.

22. Martin, Overtaken by Events, p. 658; Lowenthal, The Dominican Intervention, pp. 106, 107.

23. Johnson, The Vantage Point, p. 199; Public Papers of the Presidents of the United States: Lyndon B. Johnson, 1965, v. 1, p. 471; Center for Strategic Studies, Dominican Action -- 1965, pp. 38, 42. Yates, Power Pack, p. 66; Kelso, "The Dominican Crisis of 1965," p. 129.

24. Dare, "Dominican Diary," p. 45.

25. Ibid.; Lowenthal, The Dominican Intervention, p. 110; Yates, Power Pack, p. 67; Kelso, "The Dominican Crisis of 1965," pp. 125-129.

26. Dare, "Dominican Diary," p. 45; Tompkins, "Ubique," p. 35; Phiblant, Report of Participation, encl. 1, pp. 2, 3.

27. Johnson, The Vantage Point, pp. 199-201; Lowenthal, The Dominican Intervention, pp. 110, 111; Martin, Overtaken by Events, pp. 659, 660; Roberts, LBJ's Inner Circle, p. 208; Goldman, The Tragedy of Lyndon Johnson, pp. 378-381; Center for Strategic Studies, Dominican Action --1965, pp. 42-43; Kelso, "The Dominican Crisis of 1965," pp. 129-131.

28. Johnson, The Vantage Point, pp. 201-202; Public Papers of the Presidents of the United States: Lyndon B. Johnson, 1965, v. I, p. 466. U.S. Congress, Statement of Secretary of Defense Robert S. McNamara at the Hearings before a Subcommittee of the House Committee on Appropriations, pt.I, 89th Cong., 2d sess., 14 February 1966 (Washington, D.C.: GPO, 1966), pp. 12-38. Ringler and Shaw, U.S. Marine Corps Operations in the Dominican Republic April - June 1965, p. 121.
Use of overwhelming military force and rapid response in a similar preventive intervention in Lebanon in 1958 had proved successful in suppressing opposition before it became organized. Many military officers viewed the similarities between the two interventions as significant (see Martin Caidin, The Long Arm of America [New York: E. P. Dutton & Co., 1963], pp. 211-212). John N. Plank, "The Caribbean Intervention, When and How," Foreign Affairs (October 1965); Yates, Power Pack, p. 66.

29. Martin, Overtaken by Events, p. 661; Johnson, The Vantage Point, p. 200; U.S. Air Force, The Tactical Air Command in the Dominican Crisis, 1965 (Langley AFB, Va: Office of TAC History, May 1977), p. 12; U.S. Forces, Dominican Republic, "Report of

Stability Operations in the Dominican Republic," pt. 1, v. 2, sect. II, p. 4 (hereafter cited as U.S.F.D.R., "Stability Operations").

30. Roberts, LBJ's Inner Circle, pp. 208, 209; Public Papers of the Presidents of the United States: Lyndon B. Johnson, 1965, v. 1, p. 472; Lowenthal, The Dominican Intervention, pp. 114, 115; Center for Strategic Studies, Dominican Action --1965, pp. 38, 42; Halper, Foreign Policy Crises, pp. 70-77; Kelso, "The Dominican Crisis of 1965," pp. 133-134. For a discussion of the pros and cons of the American intervention see Congressional Digest (November 1965). The entire issue outlines U.S. policy toward communist activities in Latin America with emphasis on the Dominican action. The Selden Resolution passed by the House of Representatives in August 1965 is quoted. This resolution stated that any subversive intervention by international communism in the Western Hemisphere violated the principles of the Monroe Doctrine and of collective security and in such cases, in the exercise of individual or collective self-defense, nations could resort to armed force (see "Action Taken in the Current Congress," Congressional Digest (November 1965), pp. 267, 288; For a discussion of U.S. justification of the intervention see Edward J. Williams, The Political Themes of Inter-American Relations (Belmont, CA: Duxbury Press, 1971), pp. 79-101.

31. U.S.A.F., The Tactical Air Command in the Dominican Crisis, 1965, p. 19; U.S.F.D.R. "Stability Operations," pt. 1 v. 4, ch. 8, encl. 1, p. 1; Mansbach, Dominican Crisis 1965, pp. 31-34; Lawrence M. Greenberg, United States Army Unilateral and Coalition Operations in the 1965 Dominican Republic Intervention (Washington, D.C.: Analysis Branch, U.S. Army Center of Military History), p. 44 (hereafter cited as Dominican Republic Intervention).

4

Crisis Management

Although a familiar phenomenon during the European balance-of-power era, the term "crisis management," as it is known today, did not come into popular use until the late 1950s and early 1960s. A series of crises including Lebanon in 1958, the Congo in 1960, Berlin in 1961, and most important, the Cuban missile crisis in 1962, raised the possibility of nuclear conflict between the two superpowers. After the missile crisis, Secretary of Defense McNamara is said to have remarked, "Today there is no longer any such thing as military strategy; there is only crisis management." Although clearly an overstatement, this remark emphasized the critical role of the managerial aspect of the missile crisis. As a result, military and foreign policy matters and decisions, which formerly would have been settled in the field, were now increasingly referred to Washington.[1]

Although the Dominican intervention did not fit the pattern of a conflict between clearly defined opponents using bargaining to control the crisis, many of the same principles and processes of crisis management were involved. This has led to the use, in this study, of crisis management and its many elements as a framework for the analysis of management problems involved in conducting a military intervention. The term management, as used in this case study, refers to how governmental managers employed U.S. resources during the intervention to achieve their political and military goals. Managerial processes and actions previously considered include information collection and decision-making. Other actions and processes discussed below include goal definition, management techniques, organization, direction, control, communications, command relationships, military planning, and military doctrine and missions. Certain necessary elements of successful, governmental management such as the administration of a public information program are considered beyond the scope of this study and have been omitted.

POLITICAL GOALS AND OBJECTIVES

Goals and objectives give unity and purpose to the actions of individuals and organizations responsible for policy execution. Long- and middle-range goals set limits within which shorter range objectives can be developed. After the war with Spain in 1898 American policymakers fairly consistently followed three major long-range goals in Latin America: to exclude foreign influence and assure the independence of Latin American nations, to ensure U.S. leadership in the Western hemisphere and domination of the Caribbean area, and to maintain political stability throughout the region. Although the decision to intervene in the Dominican Republic fell within the bounds of all three of these policies, it most clearly reflected U.S. interests in maintaining stability in the Caribbean region.[2]

At the time of the Dominican revolt in 1965 the United States had been supplying military and economic assistance to established Latin American governments in order to grant them means of self-protection and to aid in their economic development. Critics interpreted this policy as reactionary for it supported maintenance of the political status quo. The policy of backing status quo governments had changed during the Kennedy and Johnson administrations. Beginning in 1960 in response to the Cuban revolution and based in part on the assumption that rightist dictatorships inadvertently fostered Castro-communist movements, the United States promoted democracy and economic and social reform in these countries. At the same time the United States dropped its ardent support of the doctrine of non-intervention and advocated strong action against the Right as well as the Left.[3]

Kennedy's attitude toward military takeovers can be illustrated by his response to a series of coups in 1962 and 1963. Consistent with the anti-dictator thrust of the Alliance for Progress, the United States censured military coups in Argentina, Peru, Guatemala, and Honduras followed by severance of diplomatic relations and the suspension of aid. This policy proved ineffective and after a 1963 coup in Ecuador the United States recognized the newly installed military junta. Kennedy took a pragmatic turn toward accommodating military governments. Government officials now recognized that the military formed an important part of the political and social structure of many Latin American countries and could play an important role in facilitating development and change.[4]

Policy during the Johnson administration continued to reflect this pragmatism. Some members of American military aid missions argued that for the sake of stability U.S. military assistance programs should aid existing military establishments even if corrupt and inefficient and try to reform them. This policy of pragmatism served as part of the rationale for the Johnson administration's renewal in December 1963 of diplomatic relations with the Dominican Republic and provided the framework within which Dominican policy developed in 1965.[5]

American policymakers also followed middle range political goals such as anti-fascism and anti-communism in Latin America. The disruption of international communism caused by splits within the Communist bloc affected American anti-communism by removing some of the restraints formerly imposed by the Soviet Union on overly ambitious revolutionary leaders. Also, Fidel Castro's conversion of a successful non-Communist revolution into a Communist government in Cuba made the United States more apprehensive of revolutionary movements in Latin America. The American goals of dominance and political stability in the Caribbean region and exclusion of foreign influence in the Western Hemisphere, combined with U.S. anti-communism, thus increased the chances of use by the United States of preventive intervention in response to the Dominican revolt of 1965.[6]

The long- and middle-range goals formed the framework within which U.S. government officials developed the short-range political objectives used during the intervention. President Johnson often mentioned these in speeches and at press conferences. Dominating all others was prevention of a communist takeover of the Dominican revolutionary movement. Allied to that was the goal of ensuring that the Dominican people could freely choose their own form of government. Another short-range objective was stabilizing the Dominican political situation, which meant first obtaining a cease-fire between the warring factions, then forming a temporary government with which the United States could deal, and finally arranging for a negotiated settlement under the auspices of the OAS. During the intervention governmental officials directed, controlled, and coordinated American actions to achieve these objectives.[7]

CIVIL-MILITARY MANAGEMENT

President Johnson used several significant management techniques in directing U.S. actions during the intervention including decision-making based on consensus, centralized civilian control, and the use of ad hoc task forces. Although Rusk, McNamara, and Bundy had served under Kennedy, Johnson's relationship with them differed from that of Kennedy. Kennedy deliberately drew upon the knowledge of outsiders and confronted his senior advisers with the views of younger aides who challenged existing assumptions. Johnson viewed dissent as a personal challenge, distrusted younger men as inexperienced, and relied on Rusk and McNamara to a greater degree than Kennedy. He believed military men too narrow in their appraisals of problems and prone to ignore the political implications of their actions. Instead he depended on McNamara for the military point of view and issued his orders to the armed services through him or General Earle Wheeler, chairman of the Joint Chiefs of Staff.[8]

In addition President Johnson used ad hoc task forces created by Kennedy as a reaction to Eisenhower's institutionalized approach to policy formation. Personnel from the State and Defense Departments, the CIA and other agencies made up the Dominican Task Force, which met in the State Department. This task force constituted a central point for the collection and processing of information related to the Dominican situation, for planning and making decisions not requiring presidential authority, and for directing the routine tasks necessary in organizing the government's response to the Dominican revolt.[9]

The management techniques of centralized civilian control and task forces formed to coordinate governmental actions bypassed bureaucratic control by large institutionalized governmental organizations and limited resource management to key personnel having the power and responsibility necessary to marshal and direct the government's resources quickly and efficiently. Since Kennedy and Johnson personally managed national security affairs using ad hoc techniques, critics complained of the seeming lack of permanent policy guidance during their administrations. Critics also pointed out the tendency to focus on the present rather than planning for the future. Such management techniques, however, suited situations such as the Dominican intervention where quick reaction and tight control were essential for success.[10]

ORGANIZATION, DIRECTION, AND CONTROL

The organization, direction, and control of governmental resources is an important part of management, especially during complex operations such as the Dominican intervention. Actions by the military to stabilize the political situation and prevent a communist takeover required coordination with diplomatic moves by State Department and embassy officials. Also military-civil affairs, disaster relief, and psychological warfare activities in the Dominican Republic required coordination with other American agencies such as the AID, the Peace Corps, and MAAG administering programs in the area. In addition, American military and diplomatic actions needed to be coordinated with representatives of the Inter-American Peace Force(IAPF), the United Nations, and the OAS in the Dominican Republic.

Command and Organizational Relationships

U.S. military commands during the crisis functioned at three major levels: the national level in Washington; the unified command level in Norfolk, Virginia, and Tampa, Florida; and the local command level in the Dominican Republic. During the alerting and staging phase of operations, orders from the national command authorities (the president, secretary of defense, and Joint Chiefs of Staff) passed to the commanders of the participating unified commands, the Atlantic Command in Norfolk and STRICOM in Tampa. STRICOM under General Paul D. Adams alerted and assembled the army and air forces designated for the operation in contingency plans and then turned them over to the Atlantic Command. This command in turn alerted and assembled the naval and marine forces committed to the operation and then assumed operational control of all the American military forces during the employment phase. Since the Atlantic Command normally included only naval and marine forces, continental-based army and air forces under STRICOM augmented these forces for joint operations in the Atlantic theatre. Change of operational control of the army and air forces from STRICOM to the Atlantic Command normally occurred when these forces arrived at their staging areas. This command relationship led to some confusion during the alerting and planning stages of the Dominican operations. Once control had been shifted, however, all forces came under one commander, CINCLANT.[11]

The CINCLANT Admiral Moorer, directly controlled three component commanders of the Atlantic Command. His component army and air force commanders each had three major areas of responsibility. General Paul L. Freeman, the Army component commander, was commanding general of the U.S. Continental Army Command based at Fort Monroe, Virginia, and commander in chief of both U.S. Army Forces, Strike Command (CINCARSTRIKE) and U.S. Army Forces, Atlantic Command. His counterpart, the air force component commander General Walter C. Sweeney, Jr., was commander of TAC based at Langley AFB, Virginia, and commander in chief of both U.S. Air Forces, Strike Command and U.S Air Forces, Atlantic Command. The navy and marine component commander, the commander in chief, Atlantic Fleet (CINCLANTFLT) based at Norfolk, Virginia also reported to CINCLANT.[12]

From CINCLANT orders passed directly to the joint task force commander in the Dominican area. The command structure at the Dominican level changed as American ground forces committed to the operation increased. Initially three co-equal task force commanders reported for operational control to the Joint Task Force 122 commander, Admiral Masterson. Major General Marvin L. McNickle, commander of the 9th Air Force, commanded Air Force Task Force 121 composed of air force forces; General Palmer, commanding general of the 18th Airborne Corps, commanded Task Force 120, which included army troops under General York and marine troops under Brigadier General John G. Bouker; and Vice-Admiral John S. McCain,Jr., commander of Amphibious Forces, Atlantic, commanded Task Force 124 composed of the naval forces.[13]

This command structure continued essentially unchanged until 7 May, by which time the large increase in troops ashore and the availability of air control and communications equipment in the objective area enabled the ground forces commander to assume total responsibility for all American troops located in the Dominican Republic. The Joint Chiefs of Staff designated this new command (headquartered in Santo Domingo) U.S. Forces, Dominican Republic. On 7 May the naval and air force task force commanders shifted from reporting to the joint task force commander to reporting to CINCLANT. Their task forces assumed supporting roles to the ground forces in the Dominican Republic and the ground and joint task forces 120 and 122 were dissolved. In September, 1965, the Joint Chiefs of Staff again reorganized the American forces in the Dominican Republic by dissolving air force and naval task forces 121 and 124 and establishing a permanent headquarters command in Santo Domingo for all U.S. forces in the Dominican Republic including air and naval forces.[14]

During the critical early phase of the Dominican intervention, the command relationship between the Joint Chiefs of Staff and the joint task force commander and his subordinate commanders at the Dominican level was closer than the military chain of command would indicate. Occasionally the Joint Chiefs of Staff directly contacted the Dominican task force commanders. Admiral Masterson, the joint task force commander, remarked that controlled response and centralized management required higher commanders to closely monitor his activities at the Dominican level, thereby increasing the difficulties of his exercise of command. He believed, however, that the president and Washington officials should make the decisions in situations such as the Dominican crisis and recognized that a political-military action called for more direct supervision at higher levels of command than would be necessary in a purely military operation.[15]

In addition to contacting the task force commanders directly the Joint Chiefs of Staff exercised control over operations through their use of the alerting system previously described and by ensuring that subordinate commanders obtained their final approval before implementing certain orders. The orders for airlifting the 82d Airborne, for example, included a special warning not to move these troops until directed by the Joint Chiefs. This prevented the 82d Airborne Division commander from calling his rear echelon headquarters in the United States for reinforcements without the approval of the Joint Chiefs.[16]

Organization of the American diplomatic response to the Dominican crisis followed a chain of command similar to that of the military extending from the president and secretary of state to the State Department and finally to the ambassador in Santo Domingo. Washington officials, however, communicated directly with the ambassador in the Dominican Republic rather than through an intermediate level of command comparable to the military unified commands. Thus, the president and secretary of state contacted Ambassador Bennett directly but the president and secretary of defense contacted Admiral Masterson, with exceptions as noted above, via his operational commander, CINCLANT. The effect of this organizational arrangement was to place Washington officials in closer contact with the ambassador than with the task force commander.[17]

Another factor affecting American military and diplomatic operations during the crisis was the diplomatic-military relationship at the Dominican level. Kennedy had clarified the relationship between American ambassadors and the military commanders of theater forces in a policy letter, written in 1961, that remained in effect in 1965. He placed the ambassador in charge of country teams formed of embassy foreign service officers and representatives of all U.S. government agencies having programs in the country such as MAAGs and Peace Corps personnel. The one exception to the rule of the ambassador as the senior in-country representative of the U.S. government who coordinated all governmental activities was his lack of control over the military forces of a theater command assigned to his area. During the Dominican intervention General Palmer continued to report to his operational commander instead of to the ambassador. Thus there was no single authority in the Dominican Republic responsible for both diplomatic and military operations and as a result coordination at this level suffered.[18]

Command, Control, and Communications

A command, control, and communication system refers to the personnel, equipment, procedures, and organizations used by a commander in planning, directing, and controlling operations. The system relies on timely, accurate, and complete information and its acquisition, processing, and dissemination. It requires centralized command and decentralized execution, responsive and reliable communications, and integration of system components. Often these requirements were not satisfied during the Dominican action.

Command posts were one of the most important elements of the command and control system. These centers, located at every command level, processed information necessary for decision making and supervision of operations and served as centers for alerting the forces committed to the operation. They also often served as the operating location of the component commander and tied together the commands, organizations, and agencies involved in the crisis. Staff personnel manned the facilities (known by various names as operations centers, war rooms, or command posts) on a twenty-four-hour basis and supplied the commander or agency chief with up-to-date summaries of crisis events.

One such facility, the White House situation room located in the basement of the White House, served as President Johnson's command post during the crisis period of the Dominican intervention. Under the direction of McGeorge Bundy, the president's national security assistant, staff personnel monitored the information flow and maintained a current situation display. Johnson surrounded himself with communications equipment including four telephones and two teletypewriters in his office, two telephones in his car, and three television sets near his office, each monitoring a major network. He kept in constant touch with the situation room. A program to improve communications capabilities had been initiated in connection with the emphasis on centralized civilian control and flexible response during the Kennedy administration. Johnson expanded the White House communications network and, although insufficient communications in Santo Domingo during the early phases of the intervention was a major problem, communications at the national level proved adequate during the crisis.[19]

An operations center set up shortly after the Bay of Pigs episode in 1961 served as the command post at the State Department. The Dominican Task Force formed during the crisis period operated from this facility, which maintained communications links with the White House, American embassies throughout the world, and other executive departments and agencies in Washington such as the CIA and the Department of Defense. A watch team composed of State and Defense Department representatives manned the Operations Center twenty-four hours a day and coordinated military and diplomatic actions at the national level during the crisis. To further unify military and diplomatic actions standard procedure called for the exchange of Operations Center officers with those of the National Military Command Center, the Pentagon's command post.[20]

The National Military Command Center (NMCC) acted as the nerve center of the national military command system by which the national control authorities directed American military forces throughout the world. The center operated various alerting and communications networks linking this facility with the unified commands. It also maintained communications with the White House situation room, the operation centers of the State Department and CIA, the command posts of every American major military command,

and with every major U.S. military base in the world. This center, manned on a twenty-four-hour basis by military and civilian watch officers from the State Department, CIA, and Department of Defense, furnished an up-to-date evaluation of the Dominican situation for review by the Joint Chiefs of Staff, the secretary of defense, and others.[21]

The unified commanders also maintained elaborate command and control systems. Watch officers manned the command post of CINCLANT located at the naval base in Norfolk, Virginia, on a twenty-four-hour basis, keeping records of the status of the developing crisis. The watch officer monitored the Joint Chiefs of Staff alerting communications network and could contact the commander in chief and his deputies in their cars or at other locations using a mobile telephone system. The watch officers also monitored a high-command communications net that linked all senior naval commanders with the chief of naval operations in Washington. Direct lines of communication connected the Atlantic command post with those of the army and air force component commanders in the Norfolk area. The geographic proximity of CINCLANT to his three component commanders--CINCLANTFLT, the commander of TAC, and the commanding general of the Continental Army Command--facilitated the command and control of the forces employed in the Dominican action. The Strike Command also maintained a command post comparable to that of the Atlantic Command.[22]

Satisfactory command and control of U.S. forces in the Dominican area required a rapid communications system secure from enemy communication analysis, compatible with other military communications systems in the objective area, and capable of linking up with a long-range communications system so that local commanders could contact their out-of-area superiors and officials in Washington. Communications during the first few days of Dominican operations met none of these requirements. Before the arrival of the Ready Group the only communications equipment available to the embassy capable of contacting the naval force consisted of an amateur radio set owned by one of the embassy staff.

Until 2 May, when reliable radio equipment reached the embassy, this radio set provided the only link between the embassy and the carrier <u>Boxer</u>. On 26 April embassy officials asked Fred Lann, an assistant information officer and owner of the radio equipment, to contact the Ready Group. At first Lann relayed all <u>Boxer</u> messages to the embassy from his house by telephone; later he used a walkie-talkie. On 28 April Lann moved his equipment to the embassy grounds and operated it from his car. Marines brought their own radio equipment to the embassy on the 28th but the <u>Boxer</u> could barely hear its transmissions and Lann's equipment continued to be used. During the early stages of the operation Lann and other amateur radio operators located in the Dominican Republic, Puerto Rico, and the United States conducted much of the miscellaneous radio traffic associated with the Dominican action.[23]

Admiral Masterson, the joint task force commander, noted the lack of secure communications during the early phases of the operation. He could not talk to Bennett over a secure radio net so the men or their deputies exchanged visits by helicopter. The naval forces supplied the army and air forces during this initial period with communications equipment from the amphibious force before their own equipment became available. Before the communications equipment of the other service components arrived, Masterson, using his own radio-telephone communications link with his commander in Norfolk and the Joint Chiefs in Washington, initially relayed all out-of-area embassy and military classified messages that required secure transmission. During this early phase of operations Bennett could only carry on telephone conversations through the rebel-controlled telephone exchange.[24]

The lack of voice security equipment seriously hampered direct coordination between the commanders afloat and diplomatic and military personnel ashore. In addition, the naval task force experienced a delay in establishing communication links to ashore commanders in the United States. Voice communications using high-frequency single-side band radio proved adequate in controlling the naval surface surveillance units, and a naval task force broadcast from the amphibious force flagship provided rapid dissemination of high-precedence classified traffic to the naval forces in the area. Ships and naval aircraft used ultra-high-frequency radio communications for local coordination with excellent results. This paralleled air force experience with this equipment in the ground control of its fighter aircraft.[25]

MILITARY PLANNING

Satisfactory management requires not only organization of resources and the means of directing them in pursuit of given objectives but necessary prior planning. The unified and subordinate commanders develop contingency plans for situations that might occur in their areas of responsibility. Such planning is important in increasing operational readiness, promoting efficiency, establishing force levels, and reducing reaction time by earmarking forces to be employed in the operation. Each plan requires months of detailed preparation so that by the time it is reviewed, approved, and published it may be out-of-date. This proved true of the Dominican contingency plans. By 1965 the Joint Chiefs had approved and the Atlantic Command had published Operation Plan 310/2-65, which applied to contingencies in the Dominican Republic. This plan served as a guide for detailed plans developed at lower echelons of command. It included provisions for several military actions such as a show of force, a blockade, air and ground landings, and the protection and evacuation of U.S. nationals.[26]

Task force organization, plans of maneuver, and many other details of the actual operation followed closely those items described in Operation Plan 310/2-65. Actual manning, however, differed widely from that planned. The Atlantic Command plan and those of subordinate commands required a much smaller troop commitment than that finally ordered by the Joint Chiefs during the Dominican intervention. Thus, additional planning became necessary in the limited time between alerting the first units designated for the operation on the evening of 26 April and the commitment of the air assault forces on 29 April. Additional planning was also necessary because the plans of some subordinate units had not been kept up-to-date and included personnel shortages. Other plans omitted important items such as provisions for airlift, critical communications frequencies, and even missions. These planning deficiencies caused confusion common to large joint operations.[27]

Preparations for the airborne assault began soon after the Joint Chiefs of Staff alerted the forces committed to Operation Plan 310/2-65. The Commander, Air Forces, Atlantic (CINCAFLANT) ordered an air force task force formed as a planning and control unit for all air operations in connection with the Dominican air assault and an airlift task force formed to plan and control the airlift operation. Staff personnel from these task forces, the 82d Airborne Division, and the 18th Airborne Corps in joint conferences worked out the details for the drop-zone axis, drop altitudes, order of flight, and other mission essentials for a paratroop drop adjacent to the San Isidro air base. The planners also arranged for fighter escort, weather and target reconnaissance, and communications support. Major General Robert H. Delashaw, commander of the air force task force, approved these plans.[28]

Although the 19th Air Force, an air force planning and control group, had developed a plan supporting the Atlantic Command Operation Plan 310/2-65, the airlift portion of it had not been published in time for use in the Dominican operation. While air force planning for the staging, enroute, and terminal phases of the airlift continued, the headquarters staffs of 18th Airborne Corps and its subordinate 82d Airborne Division refined their plans and briefed their personnel for a brigade parachute assault of two battalion combat teams in the vicinity of San Isidro. The 18th Airborne Corps contingency plan was also out-of-date. Troop lists including supporting elements had not been completed and the plan did not provide for the orderly escalation of the assault force from a two-battalion combat team to a brigade task force and finally to a divisional force.[29]

Dual assignment of units in contingency plans also caused problems. By the end of April the United States had committed American troops to Vietnam, including a number of Spanish-speaking individuals sorely needed in the Dominican operation. Air force reconnaissance aircraft were in short supply because of Vietnam and other commitments. Use of the 101st Airborne Division, which the Joint Chiefs alerted for the Dominican operation, would have depleted the U.S. forces of all active-duty airborne troops. The problem of insufficient manning, dual assignment, outdated contingency plans, and omission of vital planning elements highlighted the necessity for keeping contingency plans flexible and current in order to cope with varying force levels and the latest doctrine.[30]

MILITARY DOCTRINE AND MISSIONS

Beside contingency planning, satisfactory management requires additional means of conveying the goals and objectives of the policy-makers to those executing the policies. Doctrine and missions serve this function and since military commanders are the on-the-scene executors of the political use of force they must be familiar with both. Doctrine allows lower-echelon personnel and organizations to act independently in the absence of directives from higher authority. Commanders interpret the goals and objectives of the policymakers and transmit them to lower echelons of command often by means of doctrinal publications.

By 1965 the ideas of the armed forces regarding counterinsurgency had changed. In the early 1960s military men thought of insurgency in terms of relative firepower effectiveness with American army divisions pitted against the insurgents. By 1965, however, military doctrine recognized that the guerrilla depends for his combat effectiveness on support from within the population. Thus the new army manuals no longer used the term counterinsurgency but described broader concepts of nation-building and stability operations. These concepts affected the role of the American forces in the Dominican Republic so that in addition to engaging in military operations, the armed forces became involved in political, social, and economic activities such as civic action, humanitarian aid, and psychological warfare. In the Dominican action the political nature of the conflict required the military forces to maintain close liaison with the embassy, OAS peace negotiators, and other governmental officials attempting to arrange a political settlement. In order better to direct the military in coping with problems such as those which occurred during the Dominican action, each service issued manuals clarifying operational doctrine.[31]

The Marine Corps, for example, published a doctrinal manual that described the tactics and techniques to be employed by the marine landing force during counterinsurgency operations. The manual outlined the relationship of the landing force with other American agencies in the objective area and emphasized the necessity for coordination of marine operations with diplomatic actions. It emphasized participation of landing force representatives in the activities of the country team and on the civil affairs committee formed by the country team to coordinate civic action within the objective area. The doctrinal publication also described psychological warfare operations, including the use of leaflets, loudspeakers, and radio broadcasts to influence the local populace, and outlined a civic action program aimed at furnishing the local inhabitants with emergency food, medical supplies, and clothing. American military forces furnished disaster relief to both loyalists and rebels during the Dominican action under the guidance of such a program. The other American military services promulgated similar doctrinal publications outlining methods of coping with insurgency situations.[32]

Another series of publications described the interrelationship of the armed services during joint operations. The most important of this series was a Joint Chiefs of Staff publication concerned with unified action of the armed forces. This publication outlined the doctrine for joint use of the armed forces including the chain of command, the responsibilities of superiors and subordinates, the organization of commands, and the definition of terms such as "operational command." It served as a guide and management tool for commanders during the Dominican action and emphasized centralized direction, decentralized execution, and common doctrine.[33]

Ideally, doctrinal publications filled in gaps in directives from higher headquarters delineating missions. Several commanders complained that the Atlantic Command's Dominican contingency plan did not clarify command relationships nor assign specific missions and tasks. It became necessary, therefore, for subordinate commanders to derive their missions or goals from their knowledge of doctrine and the operational situation in the Dominican Republic.[34]

Although doctrine plays an important part in management, once a military commander makes a decision the product of the managerial process is the directive that converts policy into action and identifies the mission of subordinate commanders. The mission of the armed forces in the Dominican action originated in directives issued by higher commanders such as the president, secretary of defense, the Joint Chiefs of Staff, and the commanders of the Strike and Atlantic Commands. In addition, presidential speeches explained the purpose of the intervention and the specific missions of the troops. Announcements by the State Department and embassy officials sought to clarify the roles of the troops in the Dominican Republic.

A fact sheet distributed to individual soldiers summarized the overall missions of the U.S. forces as follows:

*To protect the lives of Americans and foreign nationals.
*To evacuate U.S. citizens and foreign nationals who desire to leave the Dominican Republic.
*To perform humanitarian missions as ordered including distribution of food and medical supplies without regard to nationality or faction.
*To assist in the establishment of stable conditions conducive to the development of an effective political settlement under the aegis of the OAS.
*To help prevent the establishment of another communist state in the Western Hemisphere in keeping with the principles of the Inter-American system.[35]

The fact sheet supplied the individual soldier with the rationale for the American intervention, but commanders issued directives and held briefings to further identify specific tasks necessary during the intervention. In order to satisfy the mission of stabilizing the political situation in Santo Domingo, for example, the army division commander issued orders to subordinate units to occupy positions, which ultimately resulted in separating the warring factions. Thus doctrinal publications, fact sheets, command directives, and briefings formed a chain from the commander to the individual soldier which transformed the command's mission into action.

NOTES

1. The reference to the McNamara remark is from Gordon A. Craig and Alexander L. George, Force and Statecraft (New York: Oxford University Press, 1983), p. 205. Also see Richard T. Loomis, "The

White House Telephone and Crisis Management," U.S. Naval Institute Proceedings (December 1969), pp. 67-73. There is a large volume of literature on crisis management, a sampling of which includes: Oran R. Young, The Politics of Force: Bargaining During International Crises (Princeton: Princeton University Press, 1968); Phil Williams, Crisis Management: Confrontation and Diplomacy in the Nuclear Age (London: Martin Robertson and Co., Ltd., 1976); Hilliard Roderick with Ulla Magnusson, ed., Avoiding Inadvertent War: Crisis Management (Austin: Lyndon B. Johnson School of Public Affairs, 1983); Gerald W. Hopple et al., eds., National Security Crisis Forecasting and Management (Boulder: Westview Press, 1984).

2. Atkins and Wilson, The United States and the Trujillo Regime, p. 5.

3. Robert S. McNamara, "Voluntary Service for all Youth," Vital Speeches of the Day, XXXII, no. 16, 1 June 1966, pp. 484-488; Herbert Dinerstein, Intervention Against Communism (Baltimore: The Johns Hopkins Press, 1967, pp. 36-37); John Gerassi, The Great Fear in Latin America (New York: The Macmillan Company, 1965); Slater, The OAS and United States Foreign Policy, pp. 184-185.

4. Atkins and Wilson, The United States and the Trujillo Regime, p. 22.

5. Ibid., pp. 23, 24; Mansbach, The Dominican Crisis 1965, p. 22.

6. Dinerstein, Intervention Against Communism, p. 45.

7. Mansbach, The Dominican Crisis 1965, p. 34. For further discussion of the goals and objectives of American policy in Latin America and the Dominican Republic see Gordon Connell-Smith, The Inter-American System (London: Oxford University Press, 1966), cited in Atkins and Wilson, The United States and the Trujillo Regime. Also see Slater, The OAS and United States Foreign Policy. For a discussion of armed intervention as a foreign policy tool in support of national interests see George, The Limits of Coercive Diplomacy, p. 17, and Donald E. Nuechterlein, United States National Interests in a changing World (Lexington, Ky.: The University Press of Kentucky, 1973), pp. 125-127; Bruce D. Larkin, ed., Vital Interests: The Soviet Issue in U.S. Central American Policy (Boulder: Lynne Rienner Publishers, Inc., 1988); Cole Blasier, The Hovering Giant: U.S. Responses to Revolutionary Change in Latin America (Pittsburgh: University of Pittsburgh Press, 1976).

8. Richard T. Johnson, Managing the White House (New York: Harper and Row, 1974), pp. 188-189. All the key personnel involved in the U.S. response to the crisis were strong personalities and excellent managers. Lyndon Johnson was his own desk officer and kept in personal touch with General Palmer, Ambassador Bennett, and his personal emissary in the Dominican Republic, former Ambassador Martin. He was cautious not only in his decision making, but in his

choice of a strategy to wear down the revolutionaries rather than crushing them with military force. For a discussion of this aspect of the U.S. response see: Michael J. Kryzanek, "The Dominican Intervention Revisited: An Attitudinal and Operational Analysis," in John D. Martz, ed., United States Policy in Latin America: A Quarter Century of Crisis and Challenge, 1961-1986 (Lincoln, Nebr.: University of Nebraska Press, 1988.)

Defense Secretary Robert McNamara was also an excellent experienced manager having come from his position as president of the Ford Motor Company. He had imposed centralized control in the office of the secretary and had introduced a system of program budgeting throughout the Department of Defense. He was widely known for his managerial talents in increasing efficiency. Johnson respected McNamara's intelligence and his administrative and managerial abilities. His role in the Dominican crisis was as the president's primary channel for military advice and for implementation of the chief executive's orders for the military. See Edward N. Luttwak, The Pentagon and the Art of War (New York: Simon and Schuster, 1984), p. 138.

Secretary of State Dean Rusk was also a strong manager, although during the Dominican crisis he delegated the routine handling of the State Department's role in the crisis to Undersecretary of State Thomas Mann. Rusk had become president of the Rockefeller Foundation at the age of 43. He adopted the management style of George Marshall. He believed in delegating authority to the assistant secretaries and desk officers and lectured them on not being afraid to make decisions. See Schoenbaum, Waging Peace and War, p. 269; Henry F. Graff, The Tuesday Cabinet: Deliberation and Decision on Peace and War under Lyndon B. Johnson (Englewood Cliffs, N.J.: Prentice-Hall Inc., 1970), pp. 16, 18, 185, 187. Richard L. Schott and Dagmar S. Hamilton, People, Positions and Power: The Political Appointments of Lyndon Johnson (Chicago: The University of Chicago Press, 1983).

9. Clark and Legere, The President and the Management of National Security, pp. 241-244.

10. Ibid.

11. U.S. Department of Defense Blue Ribbon Defense Panel, Report to the President and the Secretary of Defense on the Department of Defense (1 July 1970), p. 24.

The U.S. Southern Command and the Caribbean Sea Frontier also participated in the Dominican action. The Southern Command, a unified command based in the Panama Canal Zone, controlled the Military Assistance Program(MAP) in Latin America and thus administered MAAG in the Dominican Republic. This command also furnished logistical support for Dominican operations and supplied aircraft for transporting Latin American troops to Santo Domingo for participation in IAPF. The Caribbean Sea Frontier, a naval command headquartered in Puerto Rico, supplied logistical support to naval forces in the Dominican area and operational support including ships and aircraft (Dare, "Dominican Diary," pp. 44-45).

Philip A. Farris, "USARSTRIKE: Ready to Go," Army Information Digest (October 1965), pp. 12-16; "How Does STRICOM Get on the Move?," Armed Forces Management (July 1965), p. 62; Airborne Ready Forces, Airborne Quarterly (June - August, 1965), p. 10; Palmer, The 25-Year War, p. 137; Yates, Power Pack, p. 51.

This organization of the military forces reflected the principles of unified command which required the efforts of the separate military services to be closely integrated for effective utilization of joint military power. Unified commands, which by definition had broad continuing missions under a single commander and significant components from two or more services, were designed to ensure this unity of effort. In the Dominican crisis, however, the use of STRICOM in the manner described seemed to complicate matters. Because his army and air force component commanders originally controlled the units required by U.S.Atlantic Command(USLANTCOM), CINCLANT tended to talk directly to them thereby bypassing the commander in chief, U.S.Strike Command (CINCSTRIKE). This occurred at the same time that CINCSTRIKE exercised operational control over the augmentation forces prior to deployment. It had the effect of making Strike Command unessential to the operation (Yates, Power Pack, p. 57).

12. "To Moorer, the Dom Rep Action Proved -- CINCLANT has command and control," Armed Forces Management (July 1965), p. 68; Farris, "USARSTRIKE: Ready to Go," p. 26; "How Does STRICOM Get on the Move?," Armed Forces Management (July 1965), p. 62.

13. Tompkins, "Ubique," p. 39; Bruce Palmer, Jr., "The Army in the Dominican Republic," Army (November 1965), p. 44; Ringler and Shaw, U.S. Marine Corps Operations in the Dominican Republic, pp. 30-32; U.S.F.D.R., "Stability Operations," pt. 1, v. 1, chap. 2, p. 8.

14. Tompkins, "Ubique," p. 39; Yates, Power Pack, pp. 111, 112; ASI, Air Force Role, p. 33; Robert B. Mahoney, Jr., "U.S. Navy Responses to International Incidents and Crises, 1955-1975," (Washington, D.C.: Center for Naval Analyses, July 1977).

15. Masterson, Oral History. Bypassing the chain of command led to confusion, especially during the early days of the intervention, since subordinate commanders like Masterson sometimes received conflicting orders from both civilian and military authorities. General Palmer occasionally talked directly to the president and, because of delays in reaching Washington through CINCLANT in Norfolk, Virginia, sent information copies of his messages to his operational commander to Washington (Yates, Power Pack, p. 201).

Centralized management was a requirement for this type of stability operation. It was derived from the theories of flexible response and limited wars in which civilian-dominated, politically oriented use of military force was a requirement. There were many cases of tight military-civilian control from Washington during the intervention. These included permission from the Joint Chiefs of Staff to commit troops to action, continually changing rules of engagement, and instances of direct interference in military operations. The

Dominican crisis was a prime example of a political-military operation in which there were limits on the objectives, the means employed to attain the objectives, the resources committed to the operation, and even the geography of the objective area. These characteristics of the intervention clashed with traditional military thinking. More traditional views of army military operations saw military victory over the opposition as the chief objective. Applied to the Dominican case, this would mean an attack on the rebel stronghold by American troops. This led to frustrations on the part of the military, some of whom accepted political management as inevitable, for example Palmer and Masterson, but others of whom criticized overcontrol and micromanagement especially by civilians (Yates, Power Pack, p. 189).

16. ASI, Air Force Role, pp. 9-18; Palmer, "The Army in the Dominican Republic," p. 44; Another means of exercising control directly from Washington was the establishment of back channel communications. These are intraorganizational communication links that are not normally monitored by other agencies. They are sensitive and private and provide direct links between sender and receiver (Richard K. Betts, Soldiers, Statesmen and Cold War Crises (Cambridge, Mass.: Harvard University Press, 1977), pp. 151-153.) The chairman of the Joint Chiefs of Staff, General Wheeler, directed Palmer to ensure that all messages sent by him through the chain of command should also be sent directly to Wheeler through a back channel. This was done early in the operation because Wheeler considered communications from the area of operations via the Boxer and CINCLANT were too slow and unreliable (Yates, Power Pack, p. 86).

17. Department of Defense Blue Ribbon Defense Panel, Report to the President and the Secretary (July 1970), p. 24. Government officials did not follow the communications procedures described above during the early stages of the crisis when Admiral Masterson operated the only secure communications link to Washington and used it to pass information from embassy as well as military sources in the Dominican area.

18. Clark and Legere, The President and the Management of National Security, p. 145. For Martin's use of the country team and a discussion of the U.S. mission in the Dominican Republic including groups such as the Peace Corps, see Martin, Overtaken by Events, pp. 115, 145-147. Coordination at the local level improved after Palmer's arrival and he and Ambassador Bennett established a close working relationship and personal friendship (Yates, Power Pack, pp. 111, 112).

19. "Evaluation and Compatibility: 1965's Key Words in Tactical C and C," Armed Forces Management (July 1965), pp. 45-46; Lowenthal, The Dominican Intervention, pp. 91, 129, 149.

20. Burton M. Sapin, The Making of United States Foreign Policy (Washington, D.C.: The Brookings Institution, 1966), p. 111; William B. Connett, Jr., "Operations Center--Locus of Crisis Management," Department of State Newsletter (July 1964), pp. 16-18.

21. C. W. Borklund, The Department of Defense (New York: Frederick A. Praeger, 1968), p. 227; "The Management Team," Time (5 February 1965), p. 24; Hugh Ware, "New Tools for Crisis Management," U.S. Naval Institute Proceedings (August 1974), p. 21; Donald T. Poe," Command and Control--Changeless Yet Changing," U.S. Naval Institute Proceedings (October 1974), p. 27.

22. "To Moorer the Dom Rep Action Proved--CINCLANT has Command and Control," Armed Forces Management (July 1965), p. 69.

23. Ringler and Shaw, U.S. Marine Corps Operations in the Dominican Republic, April-June 1965, pp. 20-22.

24. Masterson, Oral History.

25. Phiblant, Report of Participation, encl. 3, p. 2. U.S. Air Force, 353d Tactical Fighter Squadron, TACOP Final Report, p. 4.

26. ASI, Air Force Role, pp. 9-10; U.S. Air Force, HQ, 9th Air Force, ALTF, TACOP Final Report, Power Pack, 24 May 1965, p. 2 (hereafter cited as ALTF, Final Report).

27. ASI, Air Force Role, pp. 9, 35; ALTF, Final Report, p. 2. The Atlantic Command's Dominican contingency plan included a warning to subordinate unit commanders that the plan was to be used as a guide to operations and that deviations from the plan would be inevitable.

28. ASI, Air Force Role, pp. 9-13, 21, 31; ALTF, Final Report, p. 12.

29. Phiblant, Report of Participation, p. 4; ALTF, Final Report, p. 11. The 18th Airborne Corps and the 82d Airborne Division had not received copies of the newly revised CINCLANT OPLAN 310/2-65. The 82d's OPLAN 310/2L-63 did not reflect the new major armywide reorganization called ROAD (Reorganization Objective Army Divisions), which had been completed in June 1964. The 1963 plan called for deployment of two or three battle groups. The battle group was the main combat element of the discarded pentomic division. TAC's plan was also geared to the deployment of two or three battle groups. Most important, none of the contingency plans from that of CINCLANT on down contemplated the possibility that an entire division might be needed for the deployment. (Yates, Power Pack, p. 59).

30. U.S.F.D.R., "Stability Operations," pt. 1, v. 2, pp. 16, 17; J.D. Yates, "The Dominican Crisis," p. 14. The importance of the planning function was emphasized in this operation. Fortunately there was time to revise outdated planning, but in situations in which troops meet determined opposition, time becomes more important. The planning process should allow doctrinal disputes and flaws in plans to be worked out ahead of time and tested in exercises based on the given plan.

31. H. Hayman, Jr., and W. W. Whitson, Can and Should the United States Preserve a Military Capability for Revolutionary Conflict, a report prepared by Rand-R-940-ARPA (Santa Monica, Calif.: Rand Corporation, 1972), p. 31; Harold K. Johnson, The Army's Role in Nation Building and Preserving Stability, Army Information Digest (November 1965), pp. 6-13.

32. U.S. Marine Corps, Operations Against Guerrilla Forces, FMFM-21, 14 August 1962, p. 39.

33. A Joint Chiefs of Staff publication (JCS Pub. 2) of November 1959 expressed the intent of Congress as set forth in the Department of Defense Reorganization Act of 1958. This act provided for the unified direction of the armed services by the secretary of defense and the establishment of unified commands such as the Atlantic Command. The chain of command for these unified elements ran from the president to the secretary of defense and through the Joint Chiefs of Staff to the commanders. The secretary of defense delegated to the Joint Chiefs of Staff the duty to serve as advisers and as military staff in the chain of operational command. The effect of this arrangement was to put operational control of the armed forces totally under civilian control. During the Dominican intervention the system worked out very well principally because Secretary McNamara had a close working relationship with General Wheeler, chairman of the Joint Chiefs of Staff. Wheeler had gained McNamara's favor for his cooperation in implementing the administration's changes in the Pentagon. Even Wheeler showed some concern over the influence of civilians in the Pentagon, however, when he complained, in a speech in late 1965, of overcontrol and overmanagement by Pentagon civilians (Betts, Soldiers, Statesmen and Cold War Crises, p. 11).

34. Phiblant, Report of Participation, p. 4. This applied in particular to the early days of the intervention before General Palmer's headquarters had been established.

35. U.S. Department of Defense, "The Dominican Crisis," Fact Sheet, DOD FS-16, 1965, p. 1; "Operation Dom Rep," Airborne Quarterly (June-August, 1965), p. 13; U.S. Department of Defense, Capsule Facts for the Armed Forces, Dominican Republic, AO-1, 5 May 1965.

5

Air Operations

Air operations focused on airlift of troops and supplies into the Dominican Republic, although the U.S. Air Force furnished fighters, reconnaissance aircraft, and many other services in support of Dominican ground operations. The size of the airlift and the complexity of air force involvement required the direct participation of ten major air force commands. Strategic Air Command supplied KC-135 jet tankers for fueling fighters during deployment, and a three hundred-man force at Ramey AFB, which helped in unloading transport aircraft committed to the airlift. Air Defense Command furnished a squadron of interceptor fighters to aid in air defense of the objective area. Aircraft from Military Air Transport Service, Continental Air Command, and Air National Guard assisted TAC in airlifting troops and cargo not only to Santo Domingo but in support missions to other areas. Air Force Logistics Command supplied logistics support for air force forces in the Dominican area and Air Forces, Southern Command(USSOUTHCOM), airlifted troops for the IAPF formed in Santo Domingo. USSOUTHCOM, with Air Force Headquarters Command, also jointly administered the Dominican military assistance program.[1]

AIRLIFT OPERATIONS

Transport aircraft delivered approximately 80 percent of the American ground troops to Santo Domingo in the largest airlift from a single loading base in U.S. history. By the morning of 7 May, airlift aircraft had flown 1,649 total sorties (round trips) carrying about 16,500 passengers including troops and evacuees, and 16,000 tons of equipment and supplies in support of the intervention. At one time over 300 aircraft participated in the airlift with 155 C-130s from TAC, 57 C-130s and 97 C-124s from the Military Air Transport Service, and 19 C-119s from Continental Air Command. These aircraft, in addition to transporting troops, evacuees, and cargo, relocated a one hundred-bed field hospital from Pope Air Force Base to San Isidro using twenty C-130 sorties and airlifted tons of beans, condensed milk, and flour into the Dominican Republic for civilian relief.[2]

The 1,200-nautical-mile airlift (codenamed Power Pack) of the 82d Airborne Division from Fort Bragg to the Dominican Republic began on Thursday 29 April. At 2030Z CINCLANT sent a verbal execution order to the Tactical Air and Continental Army Commands for the airlift of two 82d Airborne Division Battalion Combat Teams from Pope to Ramey AFB in Puerto Rico. This order did not affect fighter or reconnaissance aircraft that remained on alert, but TAC passed it to the airlift task force headquarters at Pope for action. The first aircraft of the assault force launched at about 2300Z with the last aircraft off two hours and forty-five minutes later. The 144-aircraft assault force consisted of 33 C-130 transport aircraft carrying troops followed by 111 C-130s carrying heavy equipment and supplies. The force flew at cruise altitude in serials of 36 aircraft trailing each other at two thousand-foot intervals slightly offset to avoid the wake turbulence of the aircraft ahead.[3]

Washington officials changed the destination of the assault force enroute to Ramey as a result of President Johnson's Thursday evening decision to rapidly increase American force levels in the Dominican area. The necessity for speed required diverting the airborne assault force from landing at Ramey AFB as originally planned to San Isidro airbase in the Dominican Republic. The Joint Chiefs notified Admiral Masterson of this change about two hours after the launch of the first assault aircraft from Pope and told him that the lead planes would arrive at San Isidro airbase about 0600Z on Friday morning. They left to the admiral's discretion the decision to redivert the aircraft to Ramey should conditions at San Isidro prevent landing the assault force there.[4]

The admiral could get little information on conditions at San Isidro from the American Embassy or military officials ashore who assumed that loyalists held the airbase. He sent a helicopter to Santo Domingo to bring back General Imbert to the <u>Boxer</u> for questioning. The general said the airbase was secure with the possible exception of a few wandering rebel bands, but that the control tower was unmanned and the field unlighted. About an hour before the expected landing, Masterson sent his aide and two marine officers to San Isidro to man the control tower, turn on the lights, and prepare for controlling the first aircraft landings.[5]

At 0150Z on 30 April CINCLANT directed the TAC to divert the assault force that was already airborne to the San Isidro airbase. The command post relayed this order to TAC's EC-135 airborne command post at Ramey and furnished it with frequencies for communications and navigational aids to be used with the <u>Boxer</u> and the San Isidro operations tower now manned by officers from Masterson's staff. The EC-135 proceeded to a designated orbit point, established contact with the assault force, and airborne air controllers directed the incoming aircraft to within range of the San Isidro tower. Colonel William L. Welch, the airlift task force advanced echelon commander aboard the lead aircraft, effected the diversion and landed at San Isidro at 0615Z on Friday with thirty-three troop transport aircraft and forty-six aircraft transporting heavy equipment. He assumed command of the airfield and directed the first group of aircraft to land. All transports carrying the two battalion combat teams had landed within an hour. Most of the C-130 troop transports carried sixty-four paratroopers each, thus, by 0715Z more than two thousand troops of one brigade of the 82d Airborne Division had landed.[6]

The change in plans to airland the paratroopers and equipment at San Isidro instead of staging them through Ramey for an air drop in the vicinity of San Isidro made unloading and rerigging the aircraft difficult since equipment such as jeeps had been rigged on pallets for airdrop. The small size of the San Isidro field also complicated unloading. Neither special equipment nor manpower was available to unload items rigged for airdrop. Aware of such limitations General Delashaw, aboard the airborne command post, requested authority to airdrop all support equipment. Washington officials denied the request forcing sixty-five heavy-equipment aircraft, which lacked sufficient fuel to orbit while waiting to land at San Isidro, to proceed to Ramey. Both at San Isidro and Ramey inaccessibility of the loads inside the aircraft and lack of unloading equipment necessitated unloading much of the heavy equipment manually. Personnel used axes to cut nylon webbing and lines tying down vehicles on wooden platforms rigged for airdrop. They then drove the vehicles off the platforms and aircraft ramps. Unavailability of equipment to remove loads from the taxiways at San Isidro slowed aircraft arrivals and departures. At Ramey three hundred Strategic Air Command personnel, who had neither the equipment nor the expertise for such work, unloaded the sixty-five Power Pack aircraft manually. Reloaded and rigged for airlanding, these aircraft returned to San Isidro.[7]

After unloading at San Isidro, transport aircraft returned to Pope or Ramey to pick up additional cargo. Poor lighting at the San Isidro base caused many delays and did not improve until the arrival of a portable lighting system on 1 May. Two and one-half hours after the first assault aircraft landed at San Isidro the airfield became overcrowded, necessitating a three-hour delay in air activity. After elimination of this condition, groups of nine planes each began arriving at fifteen-minute intervals from Ramey, again overcrowding the field.[8]

Limited traffic handling capacity was not confined to the San Isidro airbase. Over 125 transport aircraft returning from the assault landing at intervals of one to two minutes at Pope also exceeded the ability of handling crews to park, refuel, and prepare the aircraft for the next mission. Pope's combat airlift support unit could not control the assembly and dispatch of loads to aircraft in such congestion. As a result ground crews loaded some aircraft that had not been properly serviced and were out of commission at the time of the next scheduled flight. It then became necessary for the loading crews to transfer loads from these aircraft to others ready for flight, thereby delaying departure times.[9]

One personal account of the assault airlift details aircrew operating conditions during the flight to San Isidro. A C-130E copilot described how he and his crew went without sleep for thirty-six hours during the assault mission. His aircraft, placed on fifteen-minute alert before dawn on Thursday at Charleston AFB, later that morning flew to Pope. After a briefing on the Dominican situation, the crew then joined the assault force. The copilot stated that more than one hundred planes flew all the way to San Isidro in trail formation with a continuous stream of red beacons visible for miles. Using this formation the airlift pilots experienced difficulty in maintaining separation between aircraft, particularly at night while flying at a planned 190-knot indicated airspeed. Pilots had to vary airspeed between one hundred knots with full flaps to 250 knots in order to maintain position.[10]

As each aircraft returned to its home base, a fresh crew took over to fly the plane on the next sortie. During the initial days of the airlift each plane carried extra pilots and the crew took turns sleeping as they shuttled back and forth. Each aircraft had a crew of five and averaged from five to six hours to cover the 1200-nautical-mile distance between Pope and Santo Domingo, although the initial assault aircraft remained airborne about seven hours before landing at San Isidro.[11]

Large scale operations bringing in more troops, equipment, and supplies continued with increasing frequency through 4 May and then declined. By the end of the first week in May all nine battalions and support troops of the 82d Airborne Division, totaling about 12,000 men, and four battalions and support troops of marines, totaling about eight thousand men, had arrived in the Dominican Republic. On 7 May transport aircraft performed forty sorties, but later resupply and air evacuation missions decreased to an average of nine per day. After 7 May ships provided the principal means of logistic support for the Dominican operation.[12]

FIGHTER AND RECONNAISSANCE OPERATIONS

Although the air force supplied three hundred transport aircraft for the Dominican airlift, only two squadrons of air force fighters and elements of another squadron of air force reconnaissance aircraft deployed to the objective area. This limited deployment occurred because of the small likelihood of counterair operations by hostile forces, the lack of requirements for air strike support for American troops, and the availability of U.S. marine, naval, and Puerto Rican National Guard fighter aircraft in the objective area. The Dominican air force, controlled by loyalist personnel friendly to the United States, had only about seventy fighters of World War II vintage. Any real threat would come from the Cuban air force of more than 120 fighters including fifty-five jets. Although the authorities did not expect Cuba to interfere with American air operations in the Dominican area, the airlift transports provided such inviting targets for unfriendly fighters that fighter support was considered necessary.[13]

The priorities set by the Joint Chiefs on airlift of troop combat elements caused fighter support for the Dominican operation to arrive at Ramey 43 hours after the assault landing at San Isidro. This did not accord with doctrine that required fighter support to be available at the time of the assault landing. The Joint Chiefs of Staff chanced this breach of doctrine because of the low probability of air opposition. The TAC alerted the 354th Tactical Fighter Wing based at Myrtle

Beach AFB on 27 April, and on 2 May 18 F-100 fighter aircraft from the wing's 353d Tactical Fighter Squadron deployed to Ramey AFB in Puerto Rico. A total of about four hundred personnel from the 354th organizational, field, munitions, armament, and electronics maintenance squadrons and supply and hospital personnel deployed in support of fighter operations.[14]

Ground crews at Ramey configured the F-100s to fly combat air patrol missions with a full internal load of twenty-millimeter ammunition, two 335-gallon external fuel tanks, and missiles. On 4 May four aircraft from the 353d assumed a thirty-minute alert and another four a sixty-minute alert from thirty minutes prior to sunrise until thirty minutes after sunset. Later the air force task force commander cancelled this alert requirement and substituted a one-hour launch cycle keeping two aircraft airborne at all times during daylight hours.[15]

Twelve Air Defense Command F-104 aircraft from the 331st Fighter-Interceptor Squadron deployed from Webb Air Force Base, Texas, to Ramey on 6 May to augment the F-100s. Although the fighter forces returned to their home bases in the United States on 1 June, TAC developed contingency plans for quick reaction should tactical air support be required later in the Dominican Republic. Eight F-100 aircraft at Homestead AFB and eight F-4Cs at MacDill AFB in Florida remained on twelve-hour alert to render this support if necessary.[16]

By 2 May the 363d Composite Reconnaissance Unit composed of six RF-101s and three RB-66s had arrived at Ramey AFB to provide reconnaissance support for Dominican operations. This unit furnished visual and photographic reconnaissance and photographic processing and interpretation, and disseminated intelligence products to requesting organizations. Reconnaissance aircraft initially concentrated on coverage of airfields throughout the Dominican area then provided aerial photographs of selected targets and fifteen- to eighty-mile long strip coverage. Both inclement weather and restrictions on flight below 1,500 feet over Santo Domingo hampered operations. In addition to processing routine requests for photographic coverage from the ground forces, the unit photographed the entire objective area stressing main lines of supply, rivers, and approach valleys.[17]

Although requests for reconnaissance never exceeded the squadron's ability to provide photographic coverage, excessive demands for prints and duplications increased delivery times. Airlift aircraft from Ramey provided delivery of photography to the requesting unit since flight restrictions prevented the use of fighter aircraft for aerial drops of photography. This arrangement further increased delivery times. Even after 7 May photograph delivery times averaged well over five hours, an excessive delay for ground force support in a fluctuating operational situation such as American forces faced in Santo Domingo.

For the first two weeks reconnaissance missions ranged from two to nine sorties per day. While in the Dominican Republic the RB-66s flew thirty-one and the RF-101s ninety-six reconnaissance missions. Air force reconnaissance activity ceased when three RB-66s redeployed from Ramey on 21 May. These were followed by three RF-101s on 25 May, and the remaining three RF-101s on 4 June.[18]

HELICOPTER OPERATIONS

During the Dominican operation the marines, army troops, and naval forces employed helicopters extensively in command and control and to increase the mobility of troops. The versatility of rotary wing aircraft made them ideal for rapid transport, liaison, observation and reconnaissance, medical evacuation, supply, and communications. Such use of helicopters in the Dominican Republic served as a prelude to their employment in South Vietnam.

Helicopter pilots from marine Helicopter Squadron 264 aboard the Boxer worked twelve to fourteen-hour days from 28 April to 4 May averaging ten hours of flying time a day. Squadron pilots flew 1,605 sorties and airlifted 386 tons of supplies and approximately 5,500 personnel. In addition to evacuating personnel, they performed liaison duties between the embassy, the San Isidro air base, and the ships of the task force. These duties were particularly important during the initial phase of the Dominican action when rebels controlled the central telephone switchboard in Santo Domingo and there was a shortage of American radio equipment ashore.[19]

The buildup in American helicopter strength in the Dominican Republic was considerable. On 30 April army helicopters from a reconnaissance troop of the 17th Cavalry arrived at San Isidro and by 4 May, twenty-eight officers and 222 enlisted personnel equipped with twelve UH-1B and fourteen OH-13 helicopters had arrived to support the 82d Airborne Division. UH-ID helicopters from the 11th Air Assault Division, an army unit organized to test the concept of an air assault division employing air-transportable weapons and aircraft-mounted rockets, also arrived. The army thus had an opportunity to try out its air mobility concept in a limited counterinsurgency situation prior to its full use in Vietnam.[20]

Although use by the armed services of so many helicopters caused air traffic control problems over Santo Domingo, the helicopters proved their worth in many ways. Even individual ships such as the Raleigh carried helicopters. The surveillance area assigned the Raleigh was a shallow bay and numerous caves that two Raleigh helicopters, operating together, surveyed each day during daylight operations. These helicopter operations included detailed close-in investigation of the numerous caves along the shoreline. Operations such as these proved that helicopters could cover more than twice the surveillance area assigned to one ship in the same time and with greater efficiency. Helicopters from the Roosevelt Roads Naval Station in Puerto Rico and marine and army helicopters together with those organic to the amphibious force also performed utility services such as staff liaison, mail transfer, quick transfer of critical spare parts, and liaison with surveillance units. The wide use of helicopters by all the armed services during the Dominican action proved the flexibility, versatility, and military usefulness of this form of air power.[21]

COMMAND, CONTROL, AND COMMUNICATIONS

General Delashaw, the initial air force task force commander, exercised command and control of the assault phase of the airlift from

TAC's EC-135 airborne command post. This aircraft controlled air traffic and acted as a primary communications link during the airlandings. On 1 May Major General Marvin L. McNickle assumed command of Air Force Task Force 121 and General Delashaw continued as his deputy. The headquarters of the air force task force remained at Ramey AFB until 5 May when it moved to San Isidro. At the new location the command post, a tactical air control center with air operations planning, coordinating, and control functions, and a control and reporting center providing radar control and surveillance of aircraft combined into a joint air control coordination center that controlled air operations in Dominican air space for the remainder of the operation.[22]

Coordination of air operations in the Dominican Republic was excellent despite the high density of air traffic over Santo Domingo, the large number of organizations operating aircraft in the area, poor weather conditions, and restrictions imposed by Washington authorities on flight operations. The fact that there was no anti-aircraft or air opposition of course helped. Difficulties developed during the early phases of the airlift in coordinating airlift requests. Coordination between the airlift task force at Pope AFB and 18th Airborne Corps and 82d Airborne Division headquarters at nearby Fort Bragg was adequate during the planning and execution stages of the assault mission. The coordination conferences between these organizations primarily concerned employment concepts and tactics rather than detailed items such as how to process requests for additional airlift. When the two army headquarters moved to the Dominican Republic coordination of airlift requests broke down.

The ground force commander determined the requirements for airlift within limits set by the Joint Chiefs and common doctrine. Initially the 18th Airborne Corps rear echelon at Fort Bragg forwarded airlift requests from the ground force commander in the Dominican Republic through the headquarters of Army Forces, Atlantic, at Fort Monroe and Air Forces, Atlantic, at Langley AFB to the airlift task force command post at Pope. This cumbersome procedure resulted in the airlift task force commander receiving his requirements piecemeal. Later an airlift task force liaison officer was assigned to army headquarters at Fort Monroe. He relayed packaged airlift requirements directly to the airlift task force commander, eventually solving this problem.[23]

Another problem affecting air operations involved air traffic control. Before army and air force communications equipment had arrived in the objective area, the air force's airborne command post and similarly equipped aircraft relayed out-of-area message traffic. In addition, the air force deployed a C-130 "Talking Bird" with a communications package that operated on the ground at the San Isidro base using portable antennas. Air force communications personnel employed this installation in air traffic control. Also, General Palmer used it in communicating with the president on 2 May. Air force communications associated with air traffic control, air support, and the relay of message traffic to higher headquarters in the United States relied heavily on airborne command and control during the critical time prior to the establishment of air force permanent communications systems in the Dominican Republic.[24]

The priority placed on Power Pack combat elements by the Joint Chiefs delayed movement of required point-to-point communications equipment, thereby extending the operational periods of the airborne command post. Once communications personnel and equipment arrived the primary workload for command and control communications shifted to ground installations. The Air Force Communications Service sent personnel and equipment from three of its mobile communications groups to the Dominican Republic. These groups furnished mobile navigational aids, air traffic control service, and local and long-range communications. Communications Service technicians working with Bendix Corporation representatives installed an MRC-98 tropospheric-scatter communication link between the Dominican Republic and Ramey AFB. This two hundred-mile communications link with multi-channel voice and teletype capabilities became operational early in May, connecting the Dominican objective area with Defense Communications System terminals in Puerto Rico. This system linked communications in the area of operations with a major worldwide long-range communications system.[25]

Analysis of Dominican air operations indicates limitations in basic planning, procedural instructions, logistical support, and personnel resources. Nevertheless, the participating forces performed remarkably well in moving a complete army division in one week from the United States 1,200 miles to an airfield having very limited facilities in spite of poor weather conditions, large formations, minimum navigational aids, and grueling flight conditions. Once an airhead had been established, air support provided the ground forces with logistic and fighter and reconnaissance support, which, although limited by flight restrictions, adequately met ground force requirements.

NOTES

1. U.S. Air Force, The Tactical Air Command in the Dominican Crisis, 1965 (Langley AFB, Va.: Office of TAC History, May 1977), p. 9.

2. U.S. Air Force, TAC/OI, TAC-Its Story, 1971; "The Military Air Transport Service," Air Force and Space Digest (September 1965), pp. 126-127; U.S. Air Force, OSAF, "Speaking of U.S. Air Force Operations in the Dominican Republic," Air Force Policy Letter for Commanders, No. 10-65, 15 May 1965; U.S. Air Force, TAC/OI, Press Release, OIO-P-65-242, 7 May 1965.

3. ASI, "Air Force Role," pp. 9, 21; Airborne Ready Forces, Airborne Quarterly (June-August 1965), p. 11; Ault, Dominican Republic Crisis p. 31; Robert F. Barry, ed., Power Pack (Portsmouth,- N.H.: Messinger Printing Co., 1965), pp. 11, 24. The military designated the operation "Power Pack" because of the package concept inherent in army organization in 1965. The Reorganization Objective Army Divisions was the name given to the army's tactical reorganization designed to meet the requirements of flexible response. Under this reorganization each division had a fixed base including a

Air Operations   75

headquarters company, reconnaissance squadron, engineer, signal, medical and supply battalion. Using a building block principle the numbers and types of attached battalions were then varied depending on the situation (see John K. Mahon and Romana Danysh, Infantry Part I: Regular Army (Washington, D.C.: U.S.GPO, 1969). All times used in this study are local except as noted. Use of Zulu time (Greenwich local time) in this chapter eliminates the confusion caused by time differences between the United States and the Dominican Republic.

4. Kleber S. Masterson, vice-admiral, U.S. Navy, Oral History, U.S. Naval Institute, Annapolis, Md., 1973; Tompkins, "Ubique," p. 36. The Joint Chiefs consulted the Air Forces, Atlantic command post concerning the feasibility of an enroute diversion. Brigadier General Robert F. Worley, as battlestaff director of the command post, consulted with the Atlantic Command operations officer; the commander, 9th Air Force; the Air Force Task Force commander; and the commander, TAC before passing approval of the diversion to the Joint Chiefs. (Memorandum, Colonel Thomas W. Morris, DCS Operations, TAC to Schoonmaker, CSH, subj: Enroute Diversion, 11 August 1976).

5. Tompkins, "Ubique," p. 36.

6. ASI, "Air Force Role," p. 22; "Airborne Ready Forces," Airborne Quarterly (June-August 1965), p. 11; Bruce Palmer, "The Army in the Dominican Republic," Army (November 1965), p. 43.

7. ASI, "Air Force Role," pp. 22-25; Greenberg, Dominican Republic Intervention pp. 38-39; Yates, Power Pack, p. 69.

8. ASI, "Air Force Role," pp. 22-25, 40-41; "Airborne Ready Forces," pp. 11, 36; Ault, "Dominican Republic Crisis," p. 32.

9. ASI, "Air Force Role," p. 41; ALTF, Final Report, pp. 29-30, 41-42.

10. Rudolph A. Pyatt, "Dominican Republic Airlift Just Routine for MATS," News and Courier, Charleston, S.C., 4 May 1965, p. 2-A.

11. Ibid.

12. ALTF, Final Report, pp. 2, 3, 15, 17. ASI, "Air Force Role," pp. 25-26, 42; Maurice Matloff, ed., American Military History (Washington, D.C., U.S. GPO 1969), p. 599; Tompkins, "Ubique," p. 39.

13. U.S. Air Force, 363d Tactical Reconnaissance Wing, History, 17 June 1965, p. 3; U.S. Air Force, Press Release, TAC/OI, 5 May 1965.

14. ASI, "Air Force Role," pp. 28-29; U.S. Air Force, 353d Tactical Fighter Squadron, TACOP Final Report for Power Pack, 3 June 1965, pp. 1-3; U.S. Air Force, 354th Tactical Fighter Wing, History, 1 January-30 June 1965, p. 19.

15. U.S. Air Force, 353d Tactical Fighter Squadron, TACOP Final Report for Power Pack, 3 June 1965, pp. 3, 1. This configuration caused excessive drag on the F-100 aircraft, which needed to accelerate to supersonic speeds several times during Dominican operations in order to intercept unidentified targets. ASI, "Air Force Role," pp. 27-28.

16. ASI, "Air Force Role," pp. 28-29.

17. ASI, "Air Force Role," pp. 29-31; U.S. Air Force, 363d Tactical Reconnaissance Wing, TACOP Final Report, 17 June 1965, pp. 1-7.

18. Ibid.

19. Tompkins, "Ubique," pp. 34-35.

20. U.S. Navy, Atlantic Fleet, Amphibious Group Four, Report of Participation in Dominican Republic Operations, 29 June 1965, encl. 2, p. H-1.

21. Phiblant, Report of Participation, tab C, encl. 7.

22. ASI, "Air Force Role," p. 32.

23. Ibid., pp. 32-34.

24. Robert Worley, "Striking a Balance in Advanced Command and Control Gear," International (December 1965), p. 41; U.S. Air Force ATC/DM "Summary of Airborne Communications Packages Associated with TAC," Items of Interest (13 September 1965), p. 2; "The Air Force Communications Service," Air Force and Space Digest (September 1965), p. 156.

25. "The Air Force Communications Service," Air Force and Space Digest (September 1965), p. 156. "A Systematic Approach to Command/Control," DATA (January 1966), p. 13; "International Defense Report," Armed Forces Management (July 1969), p. 35.

6

Military and Diplomatic Coordination (30 April-5 May)

American military and diplomatic activity continued simultaneously during the Dominican action. Use of both military and diplomatic means to further American foreign policy goals in the Dominican Republic placed heavy demands on coordination of the activities of military and embassy personnel. Lack of this coordination showed in John Bartlow Martin's cease-fire arrangements with the rebels on 1 May, which had not been properly coordinated with the military. American military and diplomatic officials, however, cooperated on the establishment of the corridor between the separated enclaves of U.S. troops. The complexity of the Dominican situation highlighted the necessity for tight command and control of military and diplomatic actions, an awareness of their interrelationship, and an understanding by the military of the importance of restrictions on military action in a political situation.

Late Thursday evening, 29 April, after the president had decided to increase the size of American forces in the Dominican Republic, the council of the OAS met to discuss the Dominican situation. The meeting carried over to early Friday morning when the council passed a resolution asking for a cease-fire and the immediate establishment of an international security zone. The United States had called for the meeting and fully supported the resolution. Washington officials now turned their attention to the deployment of American troops in Santo Domingo and the establishment of contact with the rebel faction.[1]

The White House also established an informal channel of communications with Juan Bosch through Chancellor Jaime Benitez of the University of Puerto Rico, a friend of Bosch, and Abe Fortas, an adviser of President Johnson. In addition, Washington officials began consultations with former President Romulo Betancourt of Venezuela, former Governor Luis Muñoz Marin of Puerto Rico, both of whom were in the United States when the Dominican revolt began, and former President José Figueres of Costa Rica. They also contacted

Martin, who agreed to act as President Johnson's personal emissary to Santo Domingo.[2]

INTERNATIONAL SECURITY ZONE

On Friday morning 30 April, the State Department sent Bennett a resume of policy. He should now ask San Isidro's cooperation with the OAS request for a cease-fire. San Isidro officials should ensure, however, that honoring the cease-fire would not result in the ascendancy of Communist groups to political power. Bennett should also warn the San Isidro officials that the U.S. government would not join the junta in actions against rebel forces. U.S. objectives were to establish the security zone and to secure the San Isidro air base and the bridge over the Ozama River. The Department also instructed Bennett to cooperate with the papal nuncio in achieving a cease-fire. Establishment of an International Security Zone would reduce the junta perimeter and allow loyalist troops to concentrate on reasserting control of the downtown area. Because the Benoit junta commanded the only existing organized Dominican force friendly to the United States, it must be preserved as the basis for an eventual government. The embassy should impress upon the junta the need to avoid rash military actions that might either jeopardize its existence or force direct American participation in rescue operations. Junta forces could be used to patrol the area between the Security Zone and the Duarte Bridge, thereby forming a defensive line around the main rebel-held portion of the city. With the help of the American troops junta forces would be able to rest, regroup, and then establish their authority over the rest of the city and the countryside.[3]

Washington told the embassy that Admiral Masterson had been instructed to send an officer from his staff to Benoit's headquarters to improve the morale of the junta forces, to act as an adviser on military tactics, and to arrange for whatever supplies and equipment the junta might require, including the establishment of adequate communications facilities between junta headquarters and the American joint task force. Undersecretary Ball also stressed by telephone to Bennett, that Washington did not plan to attack the rebel stronghold using American troops.[4]

Two important conferences occurred Friday morning, one at the White House and the other at the embassy in Santo Domingo, further clarifying the American military role in the Dominican Republic. When the administration's principal foreign policy advisers met at the White House it appeared that military opposition to the rebels had collapsed. The embassy reported that the rebels had captured the strategic Ozama Fortress at the eastern edge of the downtown area. This fortress, the last junta enclave in rebel territory, was a major prize in the conflict. Five to six hundred riot police had defended it, but by mid-morning the rebels had overpowered the fortress and captured large quantities of light and heavy machine guns and bazookas and a large store of ammunition. Fighting in the waterfront area was heavy and embassy officials thought that the San Isidro forces might collapse during the day. Martin, who attended the White House conference Friday morning in preparation for his departure to Santo Domingo, wrote that a major issue of the discussion involved whether or not American troops should be sent into the city to shoot Dominicans.[5]

At this conference the president instructed Rusk and Ball to seek OAS help in resolving the crisis. Johnson emphasized his intention to work through the OAS and reaffirmed his interest in securing Latin American understanding and support. Venezuela's President Raúl Leoni condemned the intervention, and public opposition had developed throughout the hemisphere. Washington officials decided to send former Alliance for Progress coordinator and Venezuela ambassador, Teodoro Moscoso, to Caracas to reassure Leoni regarding American intentions and to seek his support for establishing an OAS committee to resolve the crisis. Averell Harriman would visit key Latin American capitals to explain American intentions and Undersecretary Mann would follow up his contacts with Betancourt. In addition Washington enlisted the aid of the OAS in finding an interim government acceptable to both sides of the Dominican conflict and in arranging free elections. This process began on Friday when Secretary General José A. Mora left for Santo Domingo to establish an initial OAS presence.[6]

At this same White House conference, the president asked Secretary McNamara and General Wheeler what they would need in military forces to occupy the Dominican Republic. They answered one or two divisions. The president authorized the use of that much force and whatever additional might be necessary to prevent a communist takeover and ordered the "best general in the Pentagon" sent to command the American forces in Santo Domingo. He told Martin to help Bennett in contacting the rebels, the OAS, and the papal nuncio to arrange a cease-fire. Martin's task would be to study the complex political situation in the Dominican Republic and report back directly to the president. Martin's reports from Santo Domingo would significantly influence Johnson's assessments of an active communist role in the revolt.[7]

As a result of the White House conference on Friday, General Wheeler sent Lieutenant General Bruce Palmer, Jr., to assume command of American ground forces in Santo Domingo. Wheeler assigned Palmer an announced mission of saving American lives but an unstated mission of preventing the Dominican Republic from going communist. He told Palmer that he could count on as many troops as necessary, and that the entire 18th Airborne Corps, consisting of the 82d and 101st Airborne Divisions, could be used.[8]

At noon Friday the Joint Chiefs alerted the 4th Marine Expeditionary Brigade and two additional battalion combat teams plus supporting elements from the 82d Airborne Division. Shortly after 1400 the Joint Chiefs alerted three more battalion combat teams from the Third Brigade of the 82d Airborne and the entire 101st Airborne Division of about 12,900 men. The troops alerted at this time totaled about 11,000 men less those of the 101st. This sizeable addition to the Dominican commitment represented President Johnson's emphasis on preventing a communist takeover and avoiding a second Cuba.[9]

Embassy officials and American military officers attended a conference also on Friday to plan for the day's military operations in Santo Domingo. General York participated as commander of U.S. ground forces in the Dominican Republic. After landing with the first elements of the 82d Airborne Division at San Isidro early Friday morning he had gone to the base operations tower where he received Admiral Masterson's orders.[10] While his division readied itself for action, York helicoptered to the Boxer to meet Masterson and to verify his orders, which directed him to secure the San Isidro base and the Duarte Bridge across the Ozama River, the only bridge leading into the city from the east. Masterson directed York to take command of all ground forces ashore and designated him Commander, Task Force 120.

York then went with Masterson's marine deputy commander to the embassy to obtain Bennett's concurrence with the planned day's operations. They met with the ambassador and outlined the proposed plan. The 3d Battalion of the 6th Marines, leaving a detachment to secure the polo grounds and man certain roadblocks, would move out east and north to establish the International Security Zone using tanks and armored personnel carriers followed by marines on foot and by truck. Roving patrols would sweep the area from the polo grounds to the forward positions on the perimeter.[11]

The perimeter later established by the marines formed an approximate rectangle running along the seafront from the polo grounds to a point about three miles to the east then north for less than two miles. It included the embassy compound in the northeastern corner of the security zone and most of the foreign embassies that had been under fire. From a point designated Checkpoint Charlie, about a block and a half north of the embassy, the perimeter ran west to Checkpoint Alpha two on Abraham Lincoln Avenue then swung south again to take in the Embajador Hotel area. While the marines established the Security Zone the 3d Brigade of the 82d, leaving a detachment to secure the San Isidro base, would occupy the Ozama River bridgehead, relieving the junta troops who would patrol along a route between the marine and 82d Airborne positions. Bennett, acting for the United States, and Benoit, acting for the junta, approved this plan.[12]

In mid-morning on Friday 30 April, the 3d Brigade of the 82d Airborne moved down the highway linking San Isidro to Santo Domingo. The troops advanced without opposition until they neared the eastern approaches of the Duarte Bridge. Here the rebels, equipped with small arms and sheltered in houses, opened fire on the column. The flank elements of the paratroopers swung south and cleaned out these rebel positions, suffering four wounded, the first American casualties of the Power Pack operation. During the afternoon the 82d took over the bridgehead on the western side of the Ozama River. Within three hours the American troops had cleared a semicircle with a six-block radius on the west bank and taken over the electric power plant. The loyalist forces, relieved at the Duarte Bridge, retired to the training center at San Isidro, taking with them ten half-tracks, thirteen tanks, eight armored cars, and artillery including six towed 105mm guns.

The paratroopers also established positions on the eastern bank of the Ozama River, occupying eight-story flour silos from which their fire could cover the western bank of the river, including the Ozama Fortress and the entire downtown rebel stronghold. They moved on to the narrow tongue of land jutting into the sea from the eastern side of the river. This peninsula, known as Sans Souci, controlled the Santo Domingo harbor entrance. It faced a section of George Washington Avenue that ran along the seacoast, forming the southern flank of the downtown rebel stronghold. Thus the paratroopers entrenched on the east bank of the river and at the entrance of the harbor faced the rebel positions on two sides.[13]

On the other side of the city the marines came under sniper fire in securing the International Security Zone. Rebels fired at them with small arms and .50-caliber machine guns from the shelter of buildings occupied by civilian families. The marines could not use their 106mm recoilless rifles in clearing out these positions but relied on infantry sweeps through the area. Two marines were killed and eight wounded in this action. The marine commander decided to halt operations for the day, believing that more troops would be needed to effect a linkup between the two separated U.S. forces.

The identity of the snipers in and around the zone remained a question. Although the rebel military command spokesmen reported that sniping at foreign embassies and at the marines in the zone was contrary to the interests of the revolution, it continued even beyond the cease-fire, arranged by the papal nuncio. Apparently the rebel commanders could not control the snipers. Although it might be assumed that communists and their allies directed some of the sniper fire because of their interest in increasing friction between the United States and rebel forces, many of the snipers were "tigres," young thrill-seeking hoodlums who enjoyed carrying out their own private guerrilla warfare in the city.[14]

CEASE-FIRE AND GROUND FORCE OPERATIONS

The possibility that American forces might soon engage in bloody fighting with the rebels caused Johnson to assign urgent priority to an immediate cease-fire. When he learned that the papal nuncio had secured preliminary agreement on a cease-fire from rebel and junta representatives and from Bosch in San Juan, the president ordered his subordinates to assist in getting the cease-fire adopted. The State Department instructed the embassy to reassure the junta leaders that the United States would maintain its determination to prevent a communist takeover and to assist the nuncio in securing a formal cease-fire agreement.

The department noted the embassy's skepticism about the nuncio's efforts and the usefulness of a cease-fire while the rebels controlled most of downtown Santo Domingo but reported that Washington now considered a cease-fire essential. Washington officials rejected complaints from General York that compliance with a cease-fire would hinder the capacity of the American forces to prevent a second Cuba and instructed York to cooperate in establishing the proposed accord. Bennett telephoned Mann to express doubt that a cease-fire would control the rebels, but Washington, convinced that the nuncio's efforts should be supported, told both Bennett and Admiral Masterson to secure junta cooperation in working for a cease-fire.

The embassy provided the nuncio with a helicopter that flew him to San Isidro for cease-fire talks with Wessin y Wessin, Benoit, and the junta. Martin and Harry Shlaudeman, the Dominican desk officer at the State Department who had accompanied him to Santo Domingo, reached San Isidro late Friday afternoon and joined the cease-fire negotiations in progress at the junta headquarters. Present were Bennett, York, the papal nuncio, Wessin y Wessin, Benoit, other junta members, and rebel representatives Héctor Conde and Fausto Caamaño, Jr., the rebel commander's brother.[15]

Martin saw four dangers in the situation in the Dominican Republic: a communist takeover, a full-scale American military occupation, an entrenched Dominican dictator supported by the United States, or "another Hungary." The last would mean a frontal assault on the rebel stronghold in Ciudad Nueva, with American troops killing thousands of Dominicans. Determined to avoid these dangers Martin began his activities by assisting with the cease-fire negotiations. The talks had continued for sometime and seemed to him about to break up. He persuaded General Wessin y Wessin to sign an agreement ratifying the nuncio's earlier cease-fire accord. Wessin y Wessin signed first, then De Los Santos, Benoit, and the members of the junta and the two rebel representatives initialed for Caamaño. Bennett and the head of the Dominican Red Cross also signed. Both sides acceded to the internationally supported call for a cease-fire, although a bitter hatred had developed between the opposing camps. After the signing, Radio San Isidro transmitted the cease-fire text, which consisted of a guarantee of the personal safety of individuals on both sides of the conflict and called for a commission from the OAS to arbitrate the differences between the groups. This cease-fire, although broken by both sides, served as a first step toward a peaceful settlement of the conflict.[16]

On Friday evening Johnson announced in a televised speech that a cease-fire plan had been accepted. Neither side took the truce seriously and firing continued as before. The president renewed his appeals for an end to hostilities and urged the OAS to move rapidly to establish a permanent peace. In this address Johnson gave the first public indication that "people trained outside" the Dominican Republic had sought to gain control of the revolution. A new peace attempt began when OAS Secretary General José A. Mora departed for Santo Domingo. The failure of the cease-fire became evident on Friday night. That night the marine platoon at the embassy, now joined by a platoon from the 82d Airborne Division, encountered sniper fire. Military authorities decided to remove the embassy from the front lines by moving the line two blocks to the east. During the same night 82d Airborne troops killed a scuba diver in the Duarte Bridge area, probably one of the elite navy frogmen who had defected to the rebels and now guarded the rebel leaders.[17]

By Friday the Dominican armed forces had disintegrated. The San Isidro generals now commanded no more than fifteen hundred army, nine hundred air and 150 tank personnel, plus several thousand troops scattered in garrisons throughout the country and about one thousand police. The demoralized generals would not fight. Since Wessin y Wessin's troops had not patrolled the area between the American forces as originally planned, it appeared that U.S. troops might be required to enter the city and secure a corridor between the separated troops. This would lead to combat with the rebels. American military

Military and Diplomatic Coordination

officers in Santo Domingo and staff members of the Joint Chiefs of Staff in Washington began planning for this operation, which many feared might turn the intervention into another Hungary. Such planning led to further requests from Santo Domingo for troop increases to accomplish the linkup operation and to man the resulting corridor. Troop disposition became a major problem in the next few days, demanding the closest coordination between American diplomatic officials and military commanders.[18]

Martin decided to learn more about the origins of the revolt and the current situation in the Dominican Republic. He assigned a high priority to getting the facts and transmitting them directly to the president. Since he could not enter the rebel zone at night, Martin decided to visit Imbert on a fact-finding mission. During the crisis Imbert had kept apart from the San Isidro generals. They had never accepted Imbert and, while they stayed at San Isidro, Imbert remained in the city in a section now part of the security zone. Since Martin did not know Caamaño, who had served under Imbert in the police, he assumed Imbert would be able to report on the rebel leader and the Dominican political scene. Thus began a series of conferences between Martin and Imbert leading to formation of an interim government under Imbert lasting from 7 May through August.[19]

Imbert told Martin that communists and Caamaño led the revolt. This information reinforced Bennett's personal opinions and embassy reports and led to Martin's belief that the revolt was communist-led, which he reported to the president and to Bosch whom he visited later in San Juan. While talking with Imbert, Martin received an urgent message from the embassy that Bosch had called him from Puerto Rico. He hurried to the embassy and telephoned Bosch who told him the American troops had attacked rebel positions and that Wessin y Wessin's troops had advanced behind them. Martin replied he would investigate and told Bosch that the San Isidro generals had signed a cease-fire that afternoon (Friday) and that he intended to see it honored. Bosch said that he would see that Caamaño also signed and adhered to the agreement. Martin met with Caamaño Saturday morning to establish links with the rebel leadership. Martin's efforts, however, led to a breakdown in American military-diplomatic coordination.[20]

By Saturday morning differences about deployment of troops had developed between Washington, the embassy, and American military officers in the Dominican Republic. The military officers, concerned by attacks on their troops and their separated positions on either side of the city, asked for more troops and helicopters, for permission to link their forces, and even for authorization to enter the city and put down the rebel movement. General Palmer arrived at San Isidro about midnight Friday and, after reporting to Admiral Masterson, relieved General York as commander of ground forces in the Dominican Republic. When York told him of the cease-fire that American officials had signed, Palmer pointed out the dangerous military situation of the separated U.S. forces and indicated that he did not recognize any cease-fire. Some American military officers now wanted to do exactly what Martin wanted to avoid. In order to prevent further use of military force, Martin opposed sending American forces into the city to crush the revolt. Both in the Dominican Republic and in his calls to the White House he tried to ensure that the cease-fire agreement would remain firm and that United States troops would honor it, as he had promised Bosch on Friday night.[21]

Bennett opposed U.S. support for the cease-fire, however, claiming that only the junta had honored it. Snipers had been active all Friday night, especially in the vicinity of the American Embassy. The Ambassador backed American troop commanders' requests for more troops and helicopters and urged Washington to grant the U.S. forces permission to linkup and contain or cordon off the rebels. Concerned primarily with preventing a Communist takeover in Santo Domingo, Bennett supported his pleas to Washington with reports of rumored rebel acts and intentions and repeatedly stressed the Castro-like flavor of the rebel radio broadcasts. He complained that the cease-fire protected the rebels by giving them an unwarranted political advantage, allowing them to consolidate their strength and improve their bargaining position. Washington approved the request for more troops but limited their use and continued to press for observance of the cease-fire. Air force aircraft airlifted two additional battalion combat teams from the 2d Brigade of the 82d Airborne Division to Santo Domingo at noon on Saturday. That evening the main elements of the 1st Battalion of the 6th Marine Regiment and General Bouker with part of his 4th Marine Expeditionary Brigade staff arrived.[22]

Washington officials worried not only about the risk of a second Cuba but about American diplomatic prestige throughout the world. Although the United States had won a measure of support in the OAS with the cease-fire appeals and creation of the International Security Zone, many Latin American governments disapproved of the American intervention. American officials were careful about taking any action that might further alienate these governments and the OAS. The Soviet Union brought up the Dominican issue in the United Nations, charging that U.S. actions constituted intervention and formally requested a meeting of the United Nations Security Council for 3 May. Because of these diplomatic considerations Washington wanted the embassy and American military in Santo Domingo to adopt a neutral stance, fearing that any rash military move in the Dominican Republic might affect American relations in other parts of the world.[23]

Washington officials rebuked Bennett for making encouraging comments to junta leaders over non-secure radio links. They instructed the embassy to resist any attempts by the junta to transfer its headquarters from San Isidro to the American-controlled security zone. Washington also instructed the military command in Santo Domingo to avoid identification with the junta forces and to ensure that actions by the United States conformed to the objectives of the intervention. Coordination between the military commanders and diplomatic officials in Santo Domingo broke down over cease-fire arrangements.[24]

At noon on Saturday Martin, Shlaudeman, and the papal nuncio met with Colonel Caamaño and other rebel leaders to discuss the cease-fire, which Caamaño had already signed. Caamaño insisted that American troops adhere to the cease-fire and not cross the agreed lines. He complained that embassy marines had supplied advance cover beyond these lines for Dominican police, who fired over their heads at the rebels from the National Police Headquarters near the embassy. Martin told Caamaño that he was unaware of this, but later he learned that two marines had been killed near the embassy outside the zone. No one had told them the limits of the zone.

Both embassy officials and American military commanders lacked information on the actual positions of U.S. troops. The inherent chaos of any battle situation partly caused this confusion but also the military commanders lacked sufficient control of the troops early in the crisis. Martin studied the troop positions with Caamaño using an ESSO city map supplied by the embassy that sketched the approximate marine positions as of the previous evening. This map showed the northern boundary of the zone as different from the one American forces intended to patrol and inadvertently left outside the zone the fair grounds where the congress and other Dominican government buildings were located.[25]

Caamaño agreed to the zone lines as shown on Martin's map and to an extension of the line two blocks eastward. This extension was made so that the American Embassy would be secure from sniper fire. Also, Martin discussed the area occupied by the 82d Airborne paratroopers. Caamaño claimed that he had sent civilians to repair the electric power plant in that area in the morning and they had been fired upon. He further claimed that junta troops had broken the cease-fire and that two 106mm recoilless rifles had been fired into the rebel zone from across the river, destroying a house. Martin answered that he knew nothing of the incidents but that during the first hours of a cease-fire such incidents were inevitable. Caamaño wanted to ensure that the American troops remained in their positions, but Martin and Shlaudeman insisted they did not know the exact location of the troops. Martin and Caamaño, however, agreed to the cease-fire and Caamaño said he would welcome OAS observers.[26]

Martin had not coordinated these arrangements with the joint task force and ground force commanders. While the conference between Martin and the rebel leaders continued, the positions of the American troops had changed. Shortly after dawn on Saturday the marines again started moving eastward in an attempt to linkup with the 82d Airborne troops moving west from the Duarte Bridge. The rebels again fired on the marines from the housing area, killing one marine and wounding three. The marines worked their way north and then swung east. At the same time an 82d Airborne motorized reconnaissance patrol moved west. This paratrooper force, consisting of a reconnaissance and a weapons platoon, lost two killed and five wounded during the day. At 1245 hours the marine and paratrooper patrols met on Avenida San Martin and began joint patrols. This meeting, one block south of Radio Santo Domingo's studios, occurred about the time Martin left the Caamaño conference.[27]

Learning of this movement of U.S. forces Caamaño called Martin to protest and Martin promised to check with the military. Caamaño also called Bosch in San Juan, who told him not to resist the American advance. Martin then called officials at the White House who had already asked for more information through military channels. State Department officials seemed confused about the positions of both the American and rebel forces. Because of the confusion Washington halted the advance of American forces and ordered the army and marine patrols to return to their original positions pending a decision on how the troops would be used.[28]

As a result of this action the left flank of the marine position extended from a point south of the northern boundary, which the American ground forces had decided to defend. Also, the corridor or line of communications between the American ground forces established later passed south of the radio station, an installation critical to rebel psychological warfare operations. American military officers could do nothing about the worsened military situation since it would be too difficult to renegotiate troop dispositions with the rebels.[29]

RULES OF ENGAGEMENT

The political nature of the conflict demanding close coordination between military and diplomatic officials and the character of the urban guerrilla warfare made the command and control of the ground forces difficult. During the Dominican operations the enemy consisted primarily of individual snipers or small groups using hit-and-run guerrilla tactics. Shortages of intelligence and operations personnel and inadequate information processing delayed the dissemination of information. By the time the appropriate personnel had debriefed the American troops, located and plotted observed sniper positions, evaluated the probable enemy concentrations, and determined what troops to use and what routes to employ in the attack, the enemy had moved. The problem was analogous to employing tactical air to strike small guerrilla forces. The solution in both cases required rapid intelligence processing and instant response, neither of which was available to the ground forces at least during the early days of the Dominican action.

Because of the confusion generated by the 1 May example of poor coordination between the American military and diplomatic authorities, Washington officials tightened the rules of engagement of American troops. The troops could still fire and maneuver in self-defense, but now they had to return to their original positions after each such operation, and Washington restricted the arms they could use. After the marine and army troops established a line of communications, Washington authorities ordered stringent rules of engagement placed on American troops on the perimeter. These rules prohibited the troops from firing unless in danger of attack. The individual soldier, therefore, took cover when fired upon and requested permission from his commander to return the fire. This permission was rarely granted. During the Dominican action these rules and restrictions on movement led many American military officers to believe that political leaders made decisions without taking into account important military considerations.

An incident that took place in May illustrated the problems the military faced when engaged in limited urban warfare. In this incident snipers in the rebel zone fired on paratroopers in the corridor causing the paratroopers to react violently. Standing orders of the unit commanders authorized them to enter the rebel zone in pursuit of snipers whenever necessary for the protection of American soldiers.

Military and Diplomatic Coordination

After the paratroopers penetrated a few hundred yards into the rebel area, heavy rooftop machine gun fire pinned them down. The gunfire killed one paratrooper and wounded several. To enable the medical personnel to reach the wounded men the paratroopers fired at the rebel machine gun positions with 106mm recoilless rifles, since unit commanders possessed discretionary power to use these powerful weapons in an emergency. The 106mm rounds blew the penthouses off the rebel-occupied roofs of the buildings, presumably killing the machine gunners. The rebels complained that a number of civilians also died in this action. Martin feared incidents such as these might lead to "another Hungary." He even doubted that it could be avoided and cited the example of overhearing a young marine say, "I almost got one today," and his friend's answer, "I got my first one yesterday." The necessary restrictions in this type of warfare frustrated the military but could be understood in terms of the political objectives involved.[30]

In addition to specific restrictions placed on the type of weapons fired and their use, other rules of engagement restricted military operations. In counterinsurgency warfare restraints on military actions often ran counter to the principles of traditional warfare such as concentration of firepower, pursuit, concentration of force, and offense, which demanded an attack on the downtown rebel strongholds. Because American military commanders believed strongly in these principles, they understandably opposed the rules of combat dictated to them by political necessities and politicians. One of the restrictions already mentioned was the limit on flight operations below 1,500 feet over Santo Domingo, which limited overhead reconnaissance. Other restrictions included prohibiting troops from firing into the National Palace grounds and the use of 106mm recoilless rifles in the city. These restrictions continually changed during the early days of the crisis.[31]

PARATROOPER-MARINE LINKUP

On Saturday, 1 May, Martin met with OAS Secretary General Mora. In this meeting, attended by Bennett and the San Isidro generals, Mora emphasized the need to observe the cease-fire and save lives. Junta officials assured him the cease-fire would be honored, but Benoit talked about beheadings and Commodore Rivera complained bitterly about Radio Havana. The rebel representative, Héctor Conde, angrily argued that the people wanted Bosch back but the San Isidro generals replied they were the people. This meeting accomplished nothing, and it was with the impasse in mind that Martin took stock of the situation for his report to the president on the next day, Sunday. As a result of his participation in conferences and personal interviews with Dominicans of all political persuasions, and after weighing all the evidence of the intelligence agencies, Martin concluded that the revolt had fallen under the domination of Castro-communists in the last few days, that Caamaño might become a Dominican Castro, and that Caamaño used communists as political advisers in Santo Domingo. He also believed that it had made little difference when Castro became a communist and would make little difference when Caamaño became one. He concluded that after all the violence and hate there was no chance for a political settlement, and that sending American forces against the rebels would be unacceptable.[32]

Martin detected a rising determination on the part of the military to attack the rebels directly. Several Dominican generals wanted the American forces to do this and U.S. military men including General Palmer considered the U.S. troop positions tactically untenable. Martin believed the generals right from a purely military viewpoint, but wrong from a political one. He thought that the gravest danger lay in provoking the American troops into a massacre, and that after the troops landed and the Communists knew they could not win, the Communists might attempt such provocation. He concluded that the United States should seek to gain time, maintain the cease-fire, and hope that openings for conciliation and new leaders or political constellations might arise. After telephoning these conclusions to the president, Martin held a press conference in which he suggested that the American troops should be used to prevent a Castro-Communist takeover. He mentioned specifically that "what began as a PRD revolt had in the last few days fallen under the domination of Castro-communists and other violent extremists." The president relied heavily on Martin's opinions, and that night expressed the same idea in a radio-television speech to the American public. General Palmer agreed with Martin over the communist threat but opposed him on the use and disposition of American ground forces.[33]

Officials in Santo Domingo and Washington argued over the disposition of American troops in Santo Domingo on Saturday and Sunday. General Palmer reported to the Joint Chiefs on Saturday afternoon that the United States could not exploit its military power to stabilize the situation in Santo Domingo unless the Joint Chiefs permitted a ground linkup of American forces regardless of the politically motivated commitment not to move U.S. troops. Honoring the cease-fire of 30 April and restricting the movement of American forces, Palmer warned, would risk letting the rebels take over the Dominican Republic. He suggested establishment of a cordon through the heart of downtown Santo Domingo. This cordon would confine the rebels to downtown Santo Domingo and give American troops control of the city's telecommunication facilities, its main post office, the major banks, and other key downtown installations identified in the Dominican Republic contingency plan.

This action would lead to a direct confrontation between American and rebel troops, and Palmer suggested, as an alternative, establishing a cordon along the route patrolled earlier Saturday by the army and marine reconnaissance patrols. Using this route meant leaving the rebels in control of key facilities and enlarging their territory, but it would also contain the rebels in the city and facilitate the protection and supply of the security zone. Without such a move, Palmer pointed out, the security zone including the embassy could be reached and supplied only by helicopter or by sea over the beach, for the docks were in rebel-held territory. Palmer requested authorization to establish a cordon using one route or the other.[34]

Bennett and Martin opposed Palmer's direct confrontation plan, which would establish a corridor through the heart of downtown Santo

Domingo. Bennett agreed that his major concern of a communist takeover could now be discarded with the arrival of the large American force and that the best course would be to buy time. Eventual disarmament of the rebels might still require direct American military action, but emphasis for the present should be to establish the junta's authority outside the rebel stronghold. After Palmer requested Washington's permission to establish a corridor, General Wheeler sent a message to Admiral Masterson asking him to estimate the forces and time required to establish a corridor along each of three different routes. Admiral Masterson advised the Joint Chiefs that to cut through the city might require twelve to fifteen battalions and would take twenty-four hours. Since only six battalions were on hand in the Dominican Republic (two marine and four army), Masterson's estimate appeared to rule out a frontal attack.[35]

Early Sunday afternoon the Joint Chiefs directed Palmer and York to linkup with the marines as they had requested. Palmer, York, and Masterson's marine Chief of Staff worked out a plan for linking the two separated U.S. forces. They chose the shortest route for the corridor between the 82d's bridgehead and the nearest point in the security zone held by the marines. This route avoided known rebel strongholds and passed south of the route patrolled by the army-marine troops earlier. The officers discussed the plan in detail with Martin and Bennett and the Joint Chiefs and CINCLANT approved it. Washington insisted that an attempt be made to obtain prior approval of the linkup operation from members of the OAS Peace Commission who arrived in Santo Domingo Sunday afternoon.

This five-man special committee or peace commission headed by Argentina's OAS delegate, Ricardo M. Colombo, included representatives from Guatemala, Brazil, Columbia, and Panama. Its principal purpose was to aid in mediation efforts in the Dominican Republic. Embassy officials met with the commission soon after its arrival and obtained approval of the plan for establishing the corridor. Washington then granted the embassy permission to proceed with the operation and the Joint Chiefs agreed to its execution any time after midnight on 2 May.[36]

General Palmer set H-hour for one minute after midnight in order to take advantage of the principle of surprise and to limit Dominican civilian and American casualties, as well as damage to the city. The operation began when troops from the 82d Airborne Division advanced west from the Duarte bridgehead, leap-frogging by battalion through deserted streets. The troopers received only light fire from rebels and snipers on rooftops and behind open windows. They fired back and advanced from house to house. At the same time the marines moved east and linked up with the paratroopers. The entire operation ended after about an hour and a half. Paratroopers then secured the three-mile corridor moving into some of the houses along the corridor and climbing to the roofs in the search for snipers. They also cleared houses for a block or two on either side of the corridor to prevent sniper access to the traffic. Two battalions of paratroopers secured the corridor or line of communications, keeping it open to traffic.[37]

The corridor sealed off the principal rebel forces in downtown Santo Domingo (Ciudad Nueva) from the rest of the country. North of the corridor in the industrial area of Santo Domingo and adjoining neighborhoods, the rebels maintained a measure of control. These forces, however, consisted mainly of irregulars whom the junta forces eventually cleared out (see map 3). Establishment of the corridor linked together the two separated enclaves of American troops, improving communications, and made the military positions mutually supportable. More important, after establishment of the corridor much of the fighting between the rebels and junta troops ended, although the sniper attacks continued unabated and snipers killed or wounded American troops almost every day. Some of the decrease in fighting could be attributed to the arrival of the OAS commission, which offered the chance of a political solution to the Dominican crisis.[38]

The corridor not only improved communications between American military positions but proved useful to civilians. When the peace commission members arrived Sunday afternoon, before establishment of the corridor, they could not use surface transportation from San Isidro through the city to the security zone because of rebel sniper fire. Instead they used helicopters to travel to their headquarters in the Embajador Hotel. By Monday afternoon, however, traffic moved freely between the security zone and the Duarte Bridge. The linkup also allowed the 82d Airborne Division to resupply its troops from the Port of Haina, thereby decreasing its dependence on air freight. Despite the advantages of the corridor and the fact that American troops now surrounded the principal rebel stronghold, the rebels still controlled the economic heart of the city including several major banks, the telephone exchange, the two largest newspapers, and the city's largest stores. They also controlled Radio Santo Domingo, located only two blocks north of the newly established corridor.[39]

The operation establishing the corridor exemplified close military-political coordination at the local level. In the weeks that followed, this coordination and cooperation between General Palmer and Ambassador Bennett, and later between these two and Ambassador Ellsworth Bunker, representing the OAS, remained excellent. Establishment of the corridor by sealing off the main rebel forces in downtown Santo Domingo also permitted the American forces to adopt a more neutral stance in the days that followed. The immediate dangers perceived by President Johnson, Martin, and others of American confrontation with the rebels and possible diplomatic isolation almost disappeared. Attention in Washington could now be turned toward finding a political solution to the crisis that would permit the eventual withdrawal of American forces.[40]

The mission of the American forces in the Dominican Republic was publicized in a speech by President Johnson on Sunday, by Martin's news conference the same day, and through official Washington statements. A State Department spokesman at a Embajador Hotel news conference Monday, 3 May, described the mission of the troops as not only to protect Americans and other foreign nationals, but to help Dominicans find a democratic solution to their problems. As later explained, this meant that U.S. forces would remain in the Dominican Republic until the establishment of a viable non-Communist government.[41]

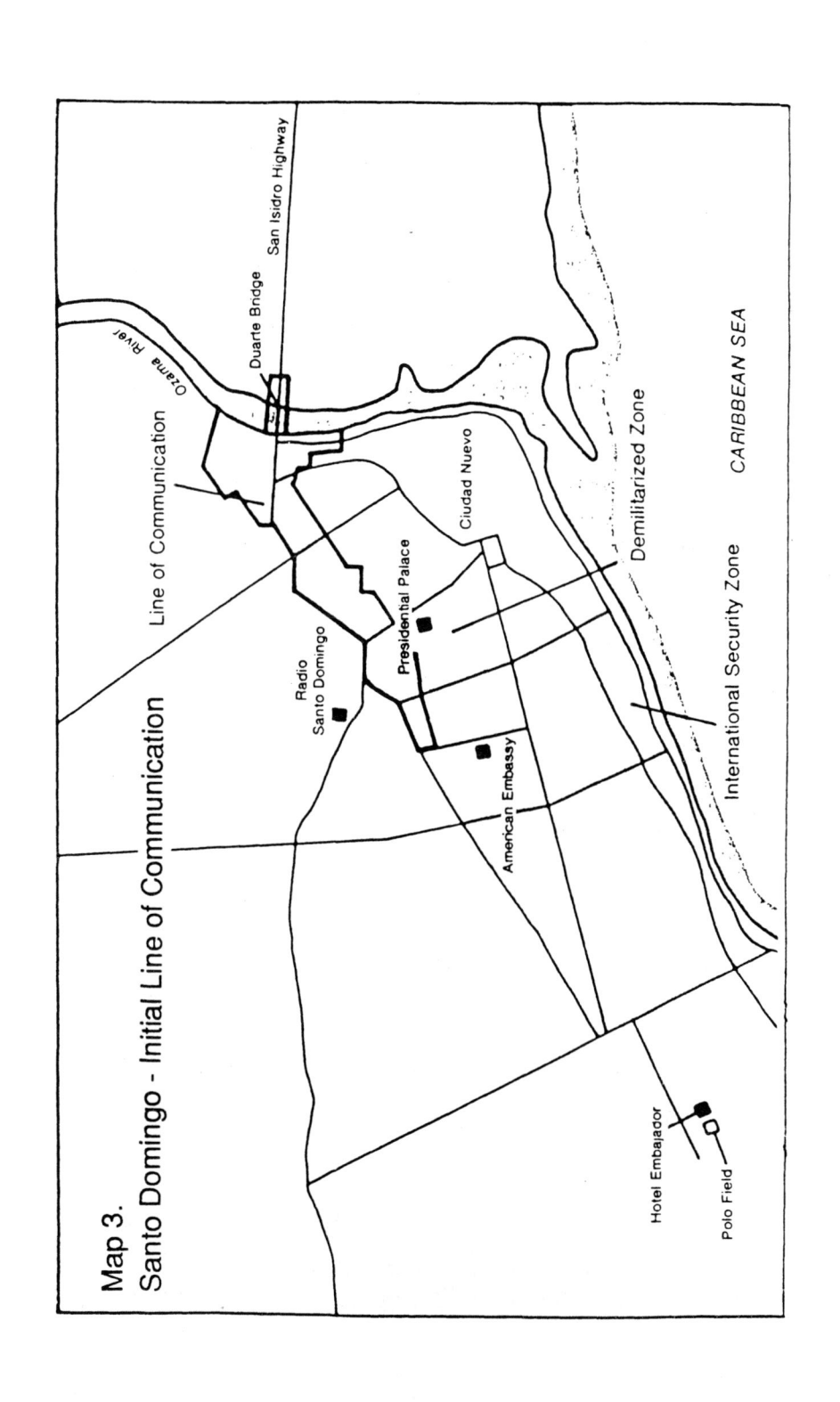

Map 3.
Santo Domingo - Initial Line of Communication

NOTES

1. Center for Strategic Studies, Dominican Action--1965, p. 45; Martin, Overtaken by Events, pp. 658, 660.

2. Lowenthal, The Dominican Intervention, p. 114; Martin, Overtaken by Events, p. 660.

3. Lowenthal, The Dominican Intervention, p. 118; Martin, Overtaken by Events, p. 660.

4. Center for Strategic Studies, Dominican Action--1965, p. 48; Lowenthal, The Dominican Intervention, p. 118.

5. Lowenthal, The Dominican Intervention, p. 115; Center for Strategic Studies, Dominican Action--1965, p. 48; Martin, Overtaken by Events, p. 661;

6. Lowenthal, The Dominican Intervention, pp. 116-117; Martin, Overtaken by Events, p. 661, Johnson, The Vantage Point, p. 202; Center for Strategic Studies, Dominican Action-- 1965, pp. 44-46.

7. Martin, Overtaken by Events, p. 661; Charles C. Moskos, "Grace Under Pressure," Army (September 1966), p. 42; Slater, Intervention and Negotiation, p. 63. At its maximum strength, the U.S. command included about 14,000 army troops, 8,000 marines, 1,000 air force, and 11,500 navy personnel. (U.S.F.D.R., "Stability Operations," pt. 1, v. 4, ch. 8, encl. 1, p. 1).

8. Lowenthal, The Dominican Intervention, p. 116; Roberts, LBJ's Inner Circle, p. 209; Greenberg, Dominican Republic Intervention, p. 43.

9. Lowenthal, The Dominican Intervention, pp. 116-117. The 101st Airborne Division did not participate in the Dominican action, fortunately for Strike Command, which otherwise would have been without any airborne troops to use in case of another contingency operation; Greenberg, Dominican Republic Intervention, p. 43.

10. U.S.F.D.R. "Stability Operations," pt. 1, v. 2, ch. 6, sec. II, p. 5.

11. Tompkins, "Ubique," p. 37; Phiblant, Report of Participation, encl. 1, p. 3; Greenberg, Dominican Republic Intervention, p. 39.

12. Center for Strategic Studies, Dominican Action--1965, p. 47; Greenberg, Dominican Republic Intervention, p. 39; Yates, Power Pack, p. 78.

13. Tompkins, "Ubique," p. 37; Lowenthal, The Dominican Intervention, p. 120. During this period both the marines on the west side of the city and the 82d Airborne paratroopers on the east continued to evacuate civilians. Yates, Power Pack, pp. 79-82.

14. Lowenthal, The Dominican Intervention, p. 120; Ringler and Shaw, U.S. Marine Corps Operations in the Dominican Republic, April-June 1965, pp. 33-35; Tompkins, "Ubique," p. 37; Yates, Power Pack, p. 82.

15. Phiblant, Report of Participation, p. 3; Martin, Overtaken by Events, pp. 150, 662; Center for Strategic Studies, Dominican Action--1965, p. 47.

16. Martin, Overtaken by Events, p. 663; Lowenthal, The Dominican Intervention, p. 122; Center for Strategic Studies, Dominican Action--1965, p. 47.

17. Public Papers of the Presidents of the United States: Lyndon B. Johnson, 1965, v. 1, p. 465; Center for Strategic Studies, Dominican Action--1965, p. 49; Tompkins, "Ubique," p. 38.

18. Martin, Overtaken by Events, p. 664; Lowenthal, The Dominican Intervention, pp. 115-120; Tompkins, "Ubique," p. 37; Yates, Power Pack, p. 90.

19. Martin, Overtaken by Events, pp. 661, 662, 665, 666; Mansbach, Dominican Crisis 1965, p. 101.

20. Martin, Overtaken by Events, pp. 666-668; Lowenthal, The Dominican Intervention, p. 123.

21. Phiblant, Report of Participation, encl. 1, p. 4; Tompkins, "Ubique," p. 38; Lowenthal, The Dominican Intervention, pp. 123-124; Yates, Power Pack, pp. 86-91; Martin, Overtaken by Events, p. 666.

22. Lowenthal, The Dominican Intervention, p. 124; Slater, Intervention and Negotiation, p. 73; Tompkins, "Ubique," p. 38; Phiblant, Report of Participation, encl. 1, pp. 3-4.

23. Lowenthal, The Dominican Intervention, pp. 124-125; Center for Strategic Studies, Dominican Action--1965, p. 46.

24. Lowenthal, The Dominican Intervention, p. 125.

25. Tompkins, "Ubique," p. 38; Lowenthal, The Dominican Intervention, p. 126; Yates, Power Pack, p. 85; Martin, Overtaken by Events, pp. 668-671.

26. Martin, Overtaken by Events, pp. 669-670.

27. Tompkins, "Ubique," p. 38; Lowenthal, The Dominican Intervention, p. 127; Yates, Power Pack, p. 88.

28. Tompkins, "Ubique," p. 38; Martin, Overtaken by Events, p. 671; Lowenthal, The Dominican Intervention, p. 127; Yates, Power Pack, p. 88.

29. Tompkins, "Ubique," p. 38.

30. Lowenthal, The Dominican Intervention, p. 127; Yates, Power Pack, pp. 119-123; Martin, Overtaken by Events, p. 672.

31. Bernard Brodie, Strategy in the Missile Age (Princeton: Princeton University Press, 1959), p. 24; Martin, Overtaken by Events, p. 676; Yates, Power Pack, p. 122; U.S.F.D.R. "Stability Operations," pt. 1, v. 2, p. 8.

32. On 3 May the constitutionalists elected Caamaño president, solidifying his leadership of the revolutionary movement (see Mansbach, Dominican Crisis 1965, p. 49).

33. Martin, Overtaken by Events, p. 676; The army Chief of Staff, General Harold Johnson, wanted American troops to enter the city. At a later conference the president asked the general if he would have done anything differently during the Dominican crisis. The general answered, "I would have cleaned out part of the city and gone in with the same numbers." See Jack Valenti, A Very Human President (New York: W.W. Norton, 1975).

34. Lowenthal, The Dominican Intervention, pp. 127-129; Yates, Power Pack, p. 92; Greenberg, Dominican Republic Intervention, pp. 44-47.

35. Lowenthal, The Dominican Intervention, p. 129; Yates, Power Pack, p. 92.

36. Tompkins, "Ubique," p. 39; Mansbach, Dominican Crisis 1965, p. 51; Yates, Power Pack, p. 93; Greenberg, Dominican Republic Intervention, pp. 46-47. By now about six thousand American paratroopers had landed at San Isidro and an air force fighter squadron and reconnaissance element supported ground operations from Ramey AFB in Puerto Rico. The navy had fourteen ships on station off Santo Domingo and naval aircraft operated from Roosevelt Roads, Puerto Rico. About three thousand marines manned the international security zone perimeter.

37. Tompkins, "Ubique," p. 39; Phiblant, Report of Participation, encl. 1, p. 4; Greenberg, Dominican Republic Intervention pp. 46-47; Yates, Power Pack, p. 94.

38. Tompkins, "Ubique," p. 39; Greenberg, Dominican Republic Intervention, p. 47.

Military and Diplomatic Coordination

39. Tompkins, "Ubique," pp. 38-39.

40. Lowenthal, The Dominican Intervention, p. 131; Greenberg, Dominican Republic Intervention, p. 47.

41. Szulc, Dominican Diary, p. 111; Yates, Power Pack, p. 96.

7

Support Operations

In addition to combat, marines and paratroopers took part in a host of other activities requiring their active participation in a variety of roles. Some of these activities, such as special operations, and the collection and processing of military intelligence information, directly supported combat operations. Other activities, such as civil affairs and psychological warfare, were related more to the political dimension of the stability operation. The navy took part in many of these activities in addition to carrying a heavy load in the early evacuation of U.S. and foreign nationals from the Dominican Republic.

NAVAL OPERATIONS

One unusual naval activity took place early on Monday morning, 3 May. A marine detachment from the Newport News, a cruiser which had replaced the Boxer as Admiral Masterson's flagship, landed at Haina and moved by truck to the University of Santo Domingo in the security zone in search of a reported cache of arms. This small-scale operation, although unsuccessful, was unique in that combat landings from a cruiser using ship's boats instead of landing craft had become rare.[1]

On 4 May the American troop buildup continued with the arrival aboard the Okinawa of another battalion of marines from the 2d Marine Division. In supporting this battalion the navy experienced the same problems faced by the air force in supplying and transporting the 82d Airborne troops. Insufficient time to load supplies for this battalion and another airlifted to San Isidro early on 2 May caused inefficient utilization of amphibious lift. Ships ordered to furnish the sea lift arrived at the Morehead City, North Carolina, embarkation point without regard to logistical requirements, and personnel loaded these ships upon arrival as troops and equipment became available. This resulted in some ships departing for the objective area not fully loaded with as much as 55 percent of their cargo space not utilized. By

4 May almost eight thousand marines had landed in the Dominican Republic and Vice-Admiral John McCain, Jr., aboard the LaSalle assumed duty as commander, Task Force 124, relieving Captain Dare as commander of all naval forces in the Dominican area. Dare now assumed the post of commander of the Amphibious Task Group aboard the Boxer.[2]

The activities of the American naval forces in the Dominican operation, like those of the ground and air forces, varied widely. In addition to evacuating personnel, naval ships stoodby ready to furnish gunfire support. Also, until early June, air and surface naval forces blockaded the island of Hispaniola to prevent Cuban or other forces from interfering with U.S. operations in the area. Naval surveillance of the sea approaches to the island to detect any infiltration of arms or personnel began on 8 May. Destroyers, minesweepers, and amphibious-type vessels were used on patrol stations. The destroyers employed their high-speed capability, the minesweepers their shallow draft, and the amphibious ships their landing craft in performing the patrol tasks. The task force commander designated forty-mile patrol areas and set up a surveillance reporting center aboard the naval task force flagship to coordinate the patrol effort.[3]

The patrol force varied in size from a maximum of twelve ships during the first weeks of May to three ships in June. All patrols ended on 3 June. Surface contacts, mostly detected by naval aircraft, totaled about two thousand during the twenty-five days of the patrol. Naval patrol aircraft operated from Guantanamo Bay, Cuba, and Roosevelt Roads, Puerto Rico, surveying the sea approaches to Hispaniola continuously from 10-25 May. By 2 June this coverage had been reduced to one circuit of the island during daylight hours. The blockade included constant surveillance of the Dominican ships in Haina harbor as part of the political requirement to prevent junta military operations against the rebel stronghold in downtown Santo Domingo. Causeway sections placed at the entrance of Haina harbor aided in preventing the uncontrolled movements of Dominican naval ships. This ensured control without the necessity for use of naval gunfire. Also, American naval ships established special patrols to warn of any commando raids or shore bombardments by the Dominican navy directed against the rebel stronghold.[4]

Another naval task involved the dispatch of warships to the mouth of the Ozama River to locate, photograph, and possibly retrieve bodies of Dominicans rumored to have been executed. In this connection the Luce, one of several ships that picked up Dominican dead floating out to sea, on 5 May recovered six bodies and turned them over to the Dominican navy. American naval units visited Dominican ports to deliver medical supplies and food and performed towing and salvage tasks. When several Dominican ships parted their lines and drifted out to sea in Haina harbor, ships of the task group took them under tow and aided those that ran aground. Thus naval operations exhibited the same diversity that characterized U.S. army and air force activities during the Dominican crisis.[5]

HUMANITARIAN OPERATIONS AND CIVIL AFFAIRS

Humanitarian operations included the evacuation of American and foreign nations from the Dominican Republic and the provision of food and medical aid to needy Dominicans. On 27 April naval ships evacuated about 1,200 Americans from Santo Domingo to San Juan, Puerto Rico. By 30 April, three thousand refugees had been evacuated, but as late as 2 May others, mostly Dominicans, still filled the lobby of the Embajador Hotel. The State Department reported that U.S. forces had evacuated 2,700 Americans and 1,400 foreign nationals by 5 May, and on 28 May the president stated that a total of more than 6,500 refugees from forty-six different countries had been evacuated and more than eight million pounds of food distributed.[6]

As they moved into the city American soldiers began a civil affairs program in Santo Domingo and the surrounding countryside. Street fighting, bombing by Dominican aircraft, and rioting for ten days had caused extensive damage. The city lacked electric power and water in most areas, garbage and debris filled the streets, and people were starving and needed medical attention. The 82d Airborne Division troopers immediately began helping to alleviate these conditions. Eighty-second Airborne civil affairs officers arranged for immediate medical aid as required and supervised distribution of rice and dry milk brought by airlift from the United States to both warring factions and the Dominican people. They also helped restore power to the city.[7]

The army issued rules for controlling personnel in the corridor. These rules permitted unarmed individuals free access to the corridor at designated checkpoints controlled by American forces. Thus any unarmed person in the rebel zone could enter the corridor to obtain food, water, or medical assistance. As soon as the marines landed they began to give food to the Dominican needy and even before the first American government surplus food had been distributed, airborne troopers began sharing their C-rations with the impoverished Dominicans. The Division Civil Affairs section established a program of food and medical supply, which supplied over 15,000 tons of food and 15,000 pounds of clothing to needy Dominicans. In addition, 82d Airborne wives sent more than two thousand pounds of used clothing to the troopers for distribution.[8]

Distribution of food to needy Dominicans was a difficult job. At first relief agencies distributed food stored in Santo Domingo by AID and CARE but in mid-May naval ships began bringing in food from the United States. Relief agencies established distribution points throughout the cleared areas of the city, each point often caring for as many as four thousand people daily. Hungry crowds sometimes threatened to get out of control but generally distribution continued at a steady pace.[9]

Although the 82d Airborne established an organization for issuing food and clothes, the best source of aid proved to be the individual trooper who shared his ration with the Dominicans. The troopers acted as ambassadors of goodwill and in general their behavior was friendly, generous, and peaceful; they created a favorable impression on the Dominicans. Lack of proper cultural training accounted for some Dominican resentment. American soldiers directing traffic, for example, did not know that Dominican police controlled traffic with their bodies more than with their arms. The troopers confused the Dominicans by unconsciously signalling one traffic direction by their body positions and another with their hands.

Also, Dominicans disliked the immorality of some American soldiers who did not distinguish between professional prostitutes and ordinary Dominican women. Part of the Dominican resentment resulted from the nature of the duties of the American soldiers, which included breaking up demonstrations, forcing teenagers to collect garbage, and in some cases shooting Dominican troublemakers. Another source of resentment was the Dominican belief that the U.S. troops were in the Dominican Republic as an occupying power. On balance American troops behaved satisfactorily in a difficult situation and the Dominican people returned their friendship.[10]

Although the 82d Airborne accomplished most of its humanitarian work in Santo Domingo, division doctors and chaplains made many trips to outlying towns and villages. A team from Company B of the 307th Medical Battalion set up mobile medical centers and in the first four days of operations treated about 350 people in remote villages. Eighty-second Airborne Division doctors treated more than 58,000 Dominican civilians for everything from head colds to appendectomies. Division chaplains held religious services and baptized children in remote areas in the absence of Dominican priests. Also, the soldiers of the 307th Engineer Battalion, initially employed in mine-clearing operations and position fortifications, later established water supply points in outlying towns and trucked water into Santo Domingo to alleviate the serious water shortage. Eighty-second soldiers also made daily trash runs, assisting in restoring sanitation to the city.[11]

SPECIAL OPERATIONS AND PSYCHOLOGICAL WARFARE

Special forces troops performed many useful activities during the Dominican action. The most important of these was intelligence information collection. Early in the intervention President Johnson wanted information concerning the extent of the insurgency in the countryside and if the rebellion in Santo Domingo was spreading. In addition to sending into the interior nine CIA agents, who reported the countryside was quiet, army troops, the embassy, the CIA, and AID joined in a program called Green Chopper. This program was made up of assessment teams that visited over thirty towns in the interior between 3 and 5 May in order to determine the political feelings of the people and the political, military, and economic conditions in the countryside. The results from this program confirmed the CIA estimate that the only serious trouble was in Santo Domingo. On 5 May this mission was taken over by Special Forces.[12]

Special Forces from the 7th Special Forces Group established six detachment sites in the countryside from which they surveyed economic needs, reported on local political conditions, developed working relations with local police and military units, gathered information on rebel resistance, and looked for signs of Cuban involvement. Beside covering many towns in the interior, the Green Berets established residency in their assigned towns and were resupplied by military helicopters and C-123 aircraft provided by an air force commando squadron. Their reports also confirmed the relative peace and quiet in the countryside. As the CIA chief of station reported after touring the interior, the "firebrands and young activists" had left to join the rebels early in the revolt. No one else seemed very concerned or politically involved.[13]

The approximately twenty officers and seventy enlisted men in the Army Special Forces in the Dominican Republic were involved in a number of other activities such as locating, seizing, and detaining rebels who published an underground newspaper. They reinforced Juan Bosch's personal bodyguard and kept him under surveillance. They also covertly moved the family of a prominent rebel leader to Santo Domingo from a town in the north. One of the more exotic activities of the Special Forces was to help the 82d paratroopers in a sewer war. When they had difficulty in crossing the corridor manned by the paratroopers, the rebels used the sewer system to go under the line of communications. A Special Forces team obtained a plan of the sewer system, which they gave to corps and division headquarters. This facilitated countermeasures to stop the infiltration across the line. Special Forces also assisted the paratroopers in reconnaissance missions in the sewers.

In a joint operation, Army Special Forces personnel teamed up with a Navy sea-air-land (SEAL) team to investigate a reported cache of Cuban arms located near Samana Bay. This reconnaissance indicated that there was no arms cache and confirmed intelligence reports of no Cuban involvement in the revolt other than propaganda radio broadcasts from Havana. A Special Forces team also investigated a sunken boat suspected of carrying Cuban ammunition and weapons and found nothing of importance. One of the most important contributions of the Special Forces teams was the successful air assault against the rebel Radio Santo Domingo transmitter sites. This radio station, which changed hands several times during the revolt, was the mainstay of the rebel propaganda effort. The day after the Special Forces seized one of the transmitters, a combined team of paratroopers and Green Berets severed the telecommunications lines serving the radio station. Although this operation did not shut down the radio station it disrupted the rebel telephone system, which, along with walkie-talkies, was the principal method of rebel tactical communications.[14]

In spite of all these, what might be called, ad hoc activities, probably the greatest contribution of the Special Forces operations was the network of detachments set up in the countryside to collect intelligence and engage in civic activities. A typical detachment generally consisted of an officer, one intelligence sergeant who was cross-trained as a medical specialist, and two radio operators. All or a major proportion of the team personnel were Spanish linguists. Some of the detachments operated undercover and wore civilian clothes; others were openly military. The Green Berets kept files on key local officials, leftists, and pro-American Dominicans who might be utilized as agents, collaborators, or supporters of civic action projects. Some of the detachments were able to change the attitudes of the Dominicans from apathy and open hostility to enthusiasm and approval by helping the people in civic actions such as school construction and especially by providing them with medical care.

Probably the detachments' most significant achievement was in providing higher headquarters with timely and accurate information concerning Dominican political personalities and in predicting political trends. Another important contribution was the army and air force use of Special Forces personnel in U.S. psychological warfare operations in the Dominican Republic.[15] The loyalists, rebels, and U.S. personnel used radio broadcasts and written materials to influence the attitudes and behavior of groups opposed to them. In its program the United States employed the Voice of America, locally generated radio broadcasts, truck and ground-emplaced loudspeakers, and air-dropped and truck-distributed leaflets to carry its message to the Dominican people.[16]

The goal of the American psychological warfare campaign was to explain the U.S. intervention not as a mission of conquest but rather as necessary to safeguard the lives of Americans and other nationals and to restore order to the country without taking sides in the dispute. President Johnson made these goals clear in a television speech on 2 May, which is often quoted for its reference to "what began as a popular democratic revolution . . . was taken over and really seized and placed into the hands of a band of Communist conspirators."[17] In the same speech he declared that many who had joined the revolt did not seek a communist tyranny and he joined with the OAS in appealing to them to lay down their arms. He added that the United States had not interfered in the affairs of the Dominican Republic, that revolution in any country should be a matter for that country to deal with, and that it became a matter for hemispheric action only when the object was the establishment of a communistic dictatorship. U.S. Information Agency personnel incorporated this explanation of the intervention into the material prepared for dissemination by American psychological warfare teams in the Dominican Republic.[18]

The U.S. Information Agency, under the policy guidance of the State Department, had overall responsibility for psychological warfare operations during the Dominican action. Units from the CIA and the Department of Defense also participated in the program. At the request of the Information Agency, army psychological warfare teams from the 1st Psychological Warfare Battalion based at the Special Warfare Center at Fort Bragg, North Carolina, deployed to the Dominican Republic early in the airlift. Units from this battalion conducted leaflet, loudspeaker, and radio psychological operations. Psychological warfare teams, for example, employed helicopters equipped with specially adapted loudspeakers over Santo Domingo on the afternoon of 2 May. These aircraft hovered low over the city broadcasting President Johnson's explanation of U.S. policy. Thus began a broad-based program of psychological warfare initiated by the United States early in the crisis.[19]

Army personnel from the 1st Psychological Warfare Company (loudspeakers and leaflets) included experts in radio station and mobile broadcasting, printing, and the Spanish language. Radio teams from this unit and Voice of America personnel rehabilitated a one thousand-watt transmitter for relay of Voice of America broadcasts from Greenville, North Carolina, to the Dominican Republic. These broadcasts continued for thirty-five days. On 5 May an American mobile five thousand-watt broadcasting station became operational and later two mobile army transmitters and a fixed broadcasting station augmented this unit in the Dominican Republic. Psychological warfare teams mounted loudspeakers along the east bank of the Ozama River and used loudspeaker trucks, which attracted large Dominican crowds eager for information. The possibilities that the information program offered Dominicans for passing family news to distant relatives helped to stimulate this interest. While active in the Dominican Republic psychological warfare teams completed six hundred hours of loudspeaker operation and nine hundred hours of locally produced radio broadcast.

Production of propaganda leaflets by copying machines began in the Dominican Republic even before the arrival of portable presses. After the mobile printing equipment arrived, trucks distributed printed material to the Dominican people. Information pamphlets became highly sought items and eventually sold for five cents a copy. Psychological warfare teams distributed over twenty-five million propaganda items in the Dominican Republic.[20]

On 30 April the Special Air Warfare Center of TAC sent two C-47 aircraft for Dominican psychological warfare operations. Within two weeks four C-123 and two U-10 aircraft and a small photographic laboratory had deployed to aid in the program. On 3 May the two C-47 aircraft, manned by personnel from the 1st Air Commando Wing, began operations over Santo Domingo dropping leaflets and broadcasting messages using four hundred-watt aircraft-mounted speakers. This speaker system required the aircraft to fly no higher than 1,500 feet in order to maintain the intelligibility of the broadcasts, thereby subjecting the aircraft to ground fire. The 1st Air Commando Wing operated the C-47s on two-hour missions, three times a day, in order to cover the city.

A major problem during these operations was how to overcome the dangers involved in low-level flight. Although the wing did not lose a single aircraft, groundfire hit several planes and wounded one crew member throwing leaflets from a plane. The Special Air Warfare Center sent the wing a leaflet dispensing system that partially solved this problem. Lack of navigational and identification equipment aboard the air commando aircraft operating in the high-density traffic of the objective area also led to difficulties. Air commando personnel delivered psychological warfare material unaware of its contents. It became apparent that an air force representative should review this material after the air commandos learned that leaflets had been dropped confirming to snipers that their groundfire was effective against leaflet-dropping aircraft. Also, U.S. Information Agency personnel insisted that entire speeches be broadcast, which increased the length of aircraft exposure to ground fire. This problem was solved by broadcasting only vital extracts of the speeches, limiting aircraft exposure time, and increasing broadcast intelligibility.[21]

Allied to the U.S. psychological warfare program was a communication jamming effort to counter the rebel propaganda campaign. Early in the revolt the rebels seized the government radio station and began broadcasting propaganda on a wide range of transmitter frequencies. Their broadcasts reached large numbers of Dominicans eager for information of the revolt, damaged the U.S. military effort, and increased tensions among the Dominican people. Rebel broadcasts emphasized anti-U.S., anti-Bennett, and anti-loyalist themes directed at the Dominican people. The rebels used propaganda effectively especially when compared to the loyalists who directed their program at the American military forces. During the first few days of the revolt the Wessin y Wessin air and ground forces attacked the rebel-held radio station and the station changed hands several times. On 13 May junta forces attacked the station but it returned to the air on 15 May. On 19 May junta troops captured the station and retained it for the remainder of the civil strife.[22]

American armed forces teams attempted to jam the rebel broadcasts using electronic interference equipment located on ships, aircraft, and at ground installations. Although the United States did not interfere with junta broadcasts, American communications personnel did monitor loyalist broadcasts and communications nets. The jamming program was largely unsuccessful because of lack of suitable interference equipment, the high power of the rebel radio transmitters, and the rebel capability of varying broadcast frequencies over a wide band. American government authorities, therefore, cancelled the program late in May.[23] Although the jamming program was discontinued, an active intelligence collection effort was maintained throughout the Dominican operation.

OPERATIONAL INTELLIGENCE

Intelligence requirements vary with the tactical situation, the mission, and the command level. The essential elements of information at the national level consisted of such questions as what was the strength of the communist movement in the Dominican Republic and to what degree did the communists control the rebellion. Also, Washington needed to know the strengths and weaknesses of the loyalists and their capabilities and intentions. At the army corps level more detailed information was needed regarding the insurgents' strengths, locations, weapons, likely courses of action, arms caches, communications facilities, radio stations, and many other similar types of information important to the conduct of operations in an urban area. At the individual combat soldier's level the most crucial problem was how to identify the enemy especially, since the rebels often wore jungle fatigues similar to those worn by the U.S. armed forces.[24]

There were many sources for the kind of intelligence needed during the intervention but many of these did not become available until after the U.S. troops had arrived in the Dominican Republic. Up to that time operational intelligence was scarce. For example, during the period 27-29 April, the 82d Airborne Division received only ten intelligence information messages. These appeared to be summaries of newspaper reports that were not current. It was not until 29 April that up-to-date, evaluated information began to be received. The marines experienced the same difficulties in obtaining evaluated intelligence in the early days of the Dominican action. They reported that in many cases, although the information was available within the Defense Intelligence Agency, it was not immediately available to the forces in the Dominican Republic because the marines were not on the standard distribution list.[25]

The situation changed, however, once the troops were ashore. The most pressing need at that time was order of battle data on rebel forces. Intelligence personnel from the 82d Airborne Division intelligence section, augmented by the 519th Military Intelligence Battalion, initially contacted CIA, embassy, MAAG, JTF 122, Marine Corps, and Dominican intelligence personnel who had already collected information needed by the intelligence section. Military Intelligence (MI) established liaison with these groups and after about a week had its own program set up. One of the best sources of information was combat troops. After the army-marine linkup on 1 May, the participating troops were able to report on rebel roadblocks, sniper and machine-gun positions, the kinds of small arms the rebels were using, and even the fact that the rebels had some tanks captured from Wessin's forces. With the establishment of the LOC and the increased flow of information from the combatant forces, a major intelligence problem developed in that intelligence collection began to outstrip the production of intelligence. Army, air force and navy forces all experienced this difficulty, especially during the early phases of the intervention.[26]

Another major source of intelligence information became available to the army through "detainees"--rebels who surrendered or were captured. Army commanders set up a corps detainee center on the Sans Souci peninsula at the southernmost point of the Ozama's east bank. Once these facilities became operational after receiving initial interrogations at brigade holding areas, detainees would be sent to Sans Souci. The Sans Souci center detainees not only provided their interrogators with MI information but with political information concerning the motives, background, organizations, and personalities of the rebels. At corps level, political intelligence was essential, given the political-military nature of the intervention. Another source of information was from agents recruited by MI personnel from defecting rebels and sent back into the constitutionalist zone for espionage purposes. Also, MI and Special Forces personnel infiltrated the rebel perimeter and returned with valuable information.[27]

Although air reconnaissance was useful, especially in map making, and communication intercepts were vital in city street fighting, the most important source of intelligence information was derived from human sources. This is true in most, if not all, cases of low-intensity urban conflict, especially in Third World countries. In these situations there is a requirement for cultural information, political information important because of the large number of factions involved, and information on public services, street numbering systems, radio and newspaper facilities, power plants, and many other essential elements of information. This information is best and sometimes only provided by human sources.

In spite of problems in intelligence production such as the processing of the large volume of unevaluated information during the initial phases of the operation, by mid-May the U.S. forces had produced a fairly accurate order of battle and other essential information about opposing forces in Santo Domingo. It was estimated that the number of rebels at this time was between two and four thousand operating in fifteen- to twenty-man commando units, each responsible for a certain portion of the city. Although the commando units were ostensibly under Caamaño's control, the degree of control was doubtful. These commando units often operated behind the facade of an organization such as a student body or political party, but the intelligence services were able to identify the commanders of most units.[28]

In addition to the intelligence collection program, U.S. specialists developed a program for counterintelligence. Military counterintelligence operations were closely coordinated with the CIA and later with the FBI. Counterintelligence personnel compiled personality files and lists that categorized rebel activists according to their political affiliation, ideological commitments, and degrees of involvement in the revolt. Initially these files and lists had to be built from raw information because the CIA and embassy staffs had burned many of their records early in the revolt when they thought the embassy might be overrun. Of particular value in this effort were the detainee interrogation reports from the Detainee Center. The counterintelligence information was particularly useful for U.S. soldiers manning checkpoints on the corridor. They were able to stop and detain individuals whose names appeared on the counterintelligence list.[29]

NOTES

1. Tompkins, "Ubique," p. 39; Phiblant, Report of Participation, encl. 2, p. 2.

2. Phiblant, Report of Participation, encl. 2, p. 5; Tompkins, Ubique, p. 39.

3. Phiblant, Report of Participation, encl. 3, pp. 1-3.

4. Phiblant, Report of Participation, encl. 4, p. 1.

5. Phiblant, Report of Participation, encl. 3, p. 3 and tab B and encl. 4, p. 2.

6. Mansbach, Dominican Crisis 1965, p. 31; Dare, Dominican Diary, p. 45.

7. U.S.F.D.R., "Stability Operations," pt. 1, v. 2, p. 48; Szulc, Dominican Diary, p. 110.

8. Szulc, Dominican Diary, p. 110; Yates, Power Pack, pp. 133-135; "All American Teamwork," Army Digest (January 1967), p. 21.

9. "All American Teamwork," Army Digest (January 1967), p. 21.

10. Moskos, "Grace under Pressure."

11. "All American Teamwork," p. 21; Szulc, Dominican Diary, p. 110.

12. Phillips, The Night Watch, p. 149; Yates, Power Pack, p. 107, 108.

13. Phillips, The Night Watch, p. 158; Yates Power Pack, p. 108; Greenberg, Dominican Republic Intervention, p. 51.

14. Greenberg, Dominican Republic Intervention, pp. 51, 53; Yates, Power Pack, pp. 128, 130, 131.

15. U.S.F.D.R., "Stability Operations," pt. 4, v. 2, ch. xx-3.

16. Yates, Power Pack, pp. 136-140; U.S.F.D.R., "Stability Operations," pt. 2, ch. 1, p. 45.

17. Mansbach, Dominican Crisis 1965, p. 33; Yates, Power Pack, pp. 136-139; U.S.F.D.R., "Stability Operations," pt. 1, v. 4, ch. 11.

18. Robert F. Delaney, "The Psychological Dimension in National Security Planning," Naval War College Review (January-February 1973), p. 57; Wallis J. Moulis and Richard M. Brown, "Key to a Crisis," Military Review (February 1966), pp. 9-14.

19. Moulis and Brown, "Key to a Crisis," pp. 9-14; Szulc, Dominican Diary, pp. 102-103; Ron D. McLaurin, ed., Military Propaganda Psychological Warfare and Operations (Boulder: Frederick A. Praeger, 1982), pp. 282-285.

20. Moulis and Brown, "Key to a Crisis," pp. 9-14.

21. Ibid.; Munro MacCloskey, Alert the Fifth Force (New York: Richard Rosen Press, 1969), pp. 149, 150, 154; U.S.A.F. The Tactical Air Command in the Dominican Crisis, pp. 30-33.

22. Yates, Power Pack, pp. 131, 132; U.S.F.D.R., "Stability Operations," pt.1, v. 1, ch. 2, 11, and v. 2, p. ii-24; Phillips, The Night Watch, pp. 152, 153.

23. Lowenthal, The Dominican Intervention, pp. 205, 206; Yates, Power Pack, pp. 131, 132.

24. Yates, Power Pack, pp. 102, 103; James B. Motley, "Intelligence Requirements," Journal of Defense and Diplomacy 1988 v. 6, no. 4, pp. 50-52.

25. U.S.F.D.R. "Stability Operations," pt. 1, v. 2, sect. III, pt. C, p. 21; Ringler and Shaw, U.S. Marine Corps Operations in the Dominican Republic, April-June 1965, p. 69.

26. Yates, Power Pack, pp. 103, 104.

27. Ibid., pp. 104-106.

28. Yates, Power Pack, pp. 106-107; Motley "Intelligence Requirements," p. 52.

29. Yates, Power Pack, p. 104; U.S.F.D.R., "Stability Operations" pt. 1, v. 1, ch. 3, p. 3.

8

Peace Force and Political Settlement (May 1965-Sept. 1966)

One of the most important duties of the American forces was to support diplomatic efforts to achieve a political settlement and provide troops for the IAPF. After the OAS peace commission arrived and American troops cleared the corridor joining the marine and paratrooper positions, the duties of the troops consisted of maintaining order in Santo Domingo, ensuring that rebel forces were contained in their stronghold in downtown Santo Domingo, and restraining the loyalist forces from attacking the rebel stronghold.

During the first few days of the crisis, when American officials thought the rebel faction might win, U.S. policy favored the junta and American military forces supplied the loyalists with communications equipment and other support. After the U.S. military buildup American policy shifted toward a more neutral stance and Washington used military force to restrain the junta from attacking the rebel stronghold. Finally, U.S. policy shifted toward backing a Dominican provisional government and, as part of the peace force, U.S. units participated in actions in support of the new government.[1]

IMBERT GOVERNMENT

President Johnson sent Ambassador Martin to the Dominican Republic to obtain information, to arrange a cease-fire, to contact the rebels, and to investigate the possibilities of a political settlement. In order to accomplish the last, Martin investigated General Imbert as a possible candidate to form a new government. American officials wanted to broaden the base of the rightist San Isidro government, for it seemed Caamaño and the rebels would never reach an understanding with Wessin y Wessin and the San Isidro generals. Washington did not want to associate the United States too closely with the Wessin y Wessin-backed Benoit junta, which represented a symbol of oppression to the Dominican people. Martin decided to back Imbert, for a rapprochement between Caamaño and Imbert appeared possible.

Largely because of Martin's arrangements with Imbert the loyalists formed a new five-man, civilian-military government under Imbert and Benoit. The new regime, called the "Government of National Reconstruction," was sworn in on 7 May. This interim government, which was never recognized by the United States, served as a step in cutting Washington's ties with the Wessin y Wessin group. On 4 May the pro-Bosch rebels had installed Caamaño as constitutional president of a provisional regime. Creation of the Imbert government served as an alternative to the Caamaño regime. On 5 May the Caamaño and Wessin y Wessin forces signed a formal truce, negotiated by the OAS peace commission and embassy officials.[2]

Sniper incidents continued on a daily basis even during the truce. Some of the incidents occurred because of mistakes made by American troops in leaving their assigned lines. On the morning of 6 May seven marines in a jeep and a three-quarter-ton truck drove out of the security zone along the corridor on their way to San Isidro, made a wrong turn, and entered rebel territory. The rebels fired, killing two marines and fatally wounding a third. The incident occurred one day after the signing of the 5 May cease-fire. As a result of this truce the fighting between the rebels and junta forces had died down, but now the rebels were fighting with U.S. forces. Incidents such as these continued throughout the period of American involvement in spite of measures taken to ensure safe traffic flow along the corridor such as posting police at intersections to direct traffic and setting wooden and barbed-wire barricades to aid in traffic control.[3]

American officers, their troops under persistent sniper attack, believed they faced communist forces and wanted to attack the rebel strongholds in Santo Domingo. Bennett agreed but Washington restrained both him and the officers. By the middle of May the possibility of American military action had lessened because of OAS involvement, domestic and international criticism of the American intervention, and evidence that the communist threat had subsided. Intelligence reports indicated that communist leaders had decided after the American troop buildup that, while rank-and-file members of the three communist parties would fight on, the top leaders would withdraw. By mid-May Washington had decided to play a less prominent role in the crisis hoping that the OAS would assume the primary responsibility for negotiating a political settlement.[4]

After establishment of the Imbert government Martin attempted to bring the Imbert and Caamaño forces together for talks. On 11 May Caamaño told Martin that it would be impossible for the rebels to negotiate with Imbert as long as the San Isidro generals led by Wessin y Wessin remained in the country and backed Imbert. American officials now took on the task of ridding the Imbert junta of the appearance of an improved version of the San Isidro junta. Caamaño and Imbert made lists of the rightist generals who must leave and Imbert exiled eight of these generals by placing them aboard a Dominican warship which put out to sea.[5]

On 9 May Ambassador Bennett and General Palmer visited General Wessin y Wessin, the most unpopular and dictatorial of all the San Isidro generals, and asked him to leave the country. After considerable argument he agreed to resign on condition that the other loyalist generals leave also. Later he refused to leave but in September, after pressure from Washington, the Dominican provisional government, and General Palmer he was forced into exile. Wessin y Wessin's forced departure illustrated the deep involvement of American political and military officers in Santo Domingo in setting up an interim government that would provide a basis for a negotiated settlement to the conflict and future free elections.[6]

Imbert became a problem in arranging a negotiated settlement. Although Bennett and Martin had created the Imbert government only to counterbalance that of the Caamaño regime, Imbert believed he would become the savior of the Dominican Republic. He also believed that a quick military victory over the Caamaño forces was essential and began planning to attack the rebels. Caamaño, convinced that the Imbert forces would attack his forces, stepped up his defensive preparations. These political animosities led to renewed fighting between the loyalists and rebels on 13 May. U.S. marines had extended the security zone eastward on 12 May, occupying seven blocks of rebel territory. This extension, concurred in by the rebels, protected the French Embassy, which had been receiving sniper fire. Rebel leaders claimed that the United States had violated the cease-fire by this action but Palmer pointed out that the U.S. representative had not signed the 5 May cease-fire document.[7]

On 13 May five P-51 planes from Imbert's air force equipped with rockets attacked the rebel radio station, located about a mile north of the American Embassy. The rockets damaged the station but ground fire from U.S. and rebel positions destroyed one of the planes. The United States protested to the OAS peace commission, charging that a junta aircraft attack on the corridor, occurring at the same time as the rocket assault on the radio station, was a violation of the 5 May cease-fire. The rebels also protested the attack to the peace commission. At a briefing at the Embajador Hotel a State Department spokesman confirmed the details of the air attack and stated that U.S. policy prohibited such attacks. He stated that the incident proved the absence of coordination between the American and Dominican commands. The spokesman added that the United States had taken immediate steps to prevent the recurrence of such attacks.[8]

U.S. policy now became neutral. On 16 May Washington directed General Palmer to neutralize the loyalist-backed navy and air force. American naval ships began a blockade of the Port of Haina using ships steaming in column four miles off Santo Domingo which were prepared to move in and prevent any Dominican ships from shelling or blockading the city. The commander of the naval task force ordered helicopters to standby in the event rapid reaction forces might be required. American army trucks, supported by 82d Airborne troops armed with bazookas, took positions across the runways of the San Isidro air base preventing junta aircraft from launching. Imbert's army troops were more difficult to contain. Imbert had assembled about one thousand troops in the northwest sector of the capital, brought in six hundred fresh troops from San Christobal, ferried tanks by sea from San Isidro to Haina, and on 15 May launched a drive eastward to clear the area north of the corridor of rebel forces.[9]

At the same time U.S., United Nations, and OAS representatives attempted to arrange a cease-fire and negotiate a political settlement. On 14 May the United Nations Security Council approved a resolution calling on Secretary U Thant to send a representative to the Dominican Republic to report on the situation. U Thant appointed José Antonio Mayobre as his representative and a United Nations advance party headed by Indian Army Major General Indar Jit Rikhye, U Thant's military adviser and organizer of the United Nations peacekeeping forces in the Congo and Cyprus, arrived in Santo Domingo on 15 May. The five-man OAS peace commission returned to Washington on 18 May, asserting in its report to the OAS council of foreign ministers that United Nations intervention in the Dominican strife had interfered with the commission's work at the critical stage. The peace commission resigned on 20 May and the OAS Secretary General Mora took over its assignment in Santo Domingo.[10]

BUNDY MISSION

On 16 May McGeorge Bundy, special assistant to the president for national security affairs; Undersecretary of State Thomas C. Mann; Undersecretary of Defense Cyrus R. Vance; and Assistant Secretary of State Jack H. Vaughn arrived in Santo Domingo. Their mission was to establish a broad-based government in the Dominican Republic. The Americans talked to Imbert, the San Isidro generals, rebel leaders, and to Antonio Guzmán, Bosch's former minister of agriculture. The Bundy mission planned to create an acceptable government with Guzmán in charge. Washington told Martin to halt his efforts to bring Caamaño and Imbert together. Martin believed administration policy had swung to a Boschist formula probably in reaction to harsh press criticism. Caamaño agreed to step aside in Guzmán's favor, but Imbert, winning in the north, and Caamaño's advisers balked.[11]

The degree of Imbert's resistance became evident on 17 May, when he summoned the American military attachés and his military leaders to his house. On his return to the American Embassy the naval attaché stated that he feared for his life while at the meeting with Imbert. The day before Imbert, informed of Bundy's mission, had told Martin that he would denounce the United States and continue alone. Bundy, Mann, Vance, Vaughn, and Martin were talking by phone to President Johnson when the attachés returned to the embassy after seeing Imbert. The president asked each if he preferred Guzmán to Imbert. Martin told the president that he preferred Guzmán's political coloration to that of Imbert but doubted that he represented anybody, or that anything would come of the effort to establish his government. After Martin's conversation with the president he decided to visit Imbert, but the others at the embassy meeting, fearing for Martin's life, dissuaded him. Imbert now believed that the United States, after helping him to form a government only nine days earlier, had forsaken him in attempting to form a new government around Guzmán.[12]

The Bundy mission failed in setting up a new government, mostly because of Imbert's successful offensive in the north. Imbert was convinced he might be able to win a complete military victory over the rebels and he therefore resisted any attempts to compromise. Also, Washington had apparently decided not to back Guzmán after all. Although the Bundy group did not accomplish its political mission, it did gather valuable information that helped in formulating future American policy. Mission members acted to ensure that the Imbert forces would be held in check and prevented from attacking the rebel stronghold in downtown Santo Domingo. On 20 May Vance announced in Santo Domingo that U.S. forces would not permit junta troops to cross the American-held security corridor to attack the rebels in Ciudad Nueva. Martin had proposed this solution to stop Imbert's military drive. He estimated that when Imbert's troops reached the Ozama River, they would turn south and could be met at the corridor by U.S. troops interposed between the Imbert and Caamaño forces.[13]

The fighting which had begun on 13 May continued for a week until the rebels and loyalists signed a twelve-hour humanitarian truce permitting the removal of the dead and wounded from the streets. This truce was extended to twenty-four hours and on 21 May continued indefinitely. During the fighting in the north about four hundred persons had been killed and one hundred wounded. After the suspension of hostilities on 21 May, although the usual sniper activity continued, no serious fighting broke out until 15 June when American troops clashed with the rebels.

Officials of OAS, the United Nations and the International Red Cross negotiated the 21 May truce between the loyalists and rebels. Just before the cease-fire went into effect Imbert announced that his forces had completed their drive against the rebels in the northern sector of the city and had assumed full control of that area. The 21 May truce was an informal arrangement by which both sides agreed not to fire at each other unless provoked. During the negotiations Imbert informed Mora and the United Nations representative, Mayobre, that he sought peace and did not plan to initiate any warlike action. Caamaño told Mora that his forces would not be the first to resume the fighting and announced at a news conference that he considered U.S. current policy to be effectively neutral. He offered to relinquish his position and negotiate with the United States but not with Imbert. There had been an overnight switch in positions by the loyalists and rebels, probably caused by the Bundy-Guzmán formula. Imbert now violently opposed U.S. policy and Caamaño now considered the United States a friendly neutral.[14]

INTER-AMERICAN PEACE FORCE

Although there had been an emphasis on nonintervention by the United States in the Caribbean region since the 1933 Good Neighbor Policy of Franklin D. Roosevelt, a complex inter-American security system had been developed. The OAS, chartered in 1948 at Bogota, consolidated in a single organization what had been an informal union of nations. This organization became the core of the new inter-American system. Before 1965 the organization had never established a combined military force to quell internal unrest in a neighbor state, but in 1965, as a one-time experiment, the OAS did just that.

Difficulties in the establishment of such a force stemmed from several factors. For one thing, Latin American nations were now challenging the traditional twentieth-century role of the United States as the Western Hemisphere's political leader. Also, there were differences in the way the United States and Latin American nations viewed instability, Communist influence, and unilateral U.S. intervention. In spite of these differences and because of the gravity of the situation in the Dominican Republic, OAS missions sent to investigate the civil strife reported on 3 May that the introduction of Latin American troops was necessary so that U.S. involvement could be reduced. President Johnson heartily concurred.

On 6 May the OAS foreign ministers meeting in Washington approved by a 14-5 vote a U.S. resolution to establish a peace force. This force would operate under OAS direction to "cooperate in the restoration of peace in the Dominican Republic, maintain the security of its inhabitants, . . . , and establish an atmosphere of peace and conciliation to permit the functioning of democratic institutions." Peace force contingents included troops from the United States, Brazil, Honduras, Nicaragua, and Paraguay and a platoon of police from Costa Rica. The resolution establishing the force stipulated that the OAS ministerial council would remain in session to continue to review the Dominican situation and would determine when the peace force should be withdrawn.

On 22 May the ministerial council named General Hugo Panasco Alvim of Brazil to serve as commander in chief of the force with an American general to act as his deputy. Prior to General Alvim's arrival, General Palmer assumed command of the force. The IAPF command was formally established at a ceremony at the Embajador Hotel on 23 May with the OAS Secretary General Mora presiding. By 23 May all the Latin American contingents except that of Paraguay had arrived and the force began operations immediately. Three-man peace force observer teams began patrolling junta territory on 26 May. The teams, each composed of an American, a Honduran, and a Costa Rican, enforced the terms of the truce agreement. The rebels agreed to permit the patrols to enter their sectors but only on condition that no U.S. troops be used.[15]

The IAPF at its maximum strength contained fewer than two thousand Latin American troops, the majority of whom were Brazilian. The United States had pressed for a more genuinely international force and had agreed to the progressive equalization of national contingents. During the last week in May, airlift activity increased again as U.S. Air Force units took part in Operation Press Ahead, the airlift of Latin American forces to the Dominican Republic. In cooperation with the U.S. Southern Command, the commander in chief, U.S. Air Forces, Atlantic(CINCAFLANT) furnished thirty-five C-130 aircraft for the movement of peace force personnel from Latin and South American countries to San Isidro. Honduras made the first formal offer of troops for the peace force and the United States airlifted the first contingent of these to San Isidro on 14 May. By 15-16 May, 250 troops from Honduras, 164 infantrymen from Nicaragua, and twenty-five police from Costa Rica had joined the force. Eight C-130s from the 463d Troop Carrier Wing of TAC airlifted 695 Brazilian army troops from Santa Cruz Air Base, Brazil, to the San Isidro base during the period of 24-26 May, with additional missions flying out of Ramey AFB through 30 May. With the arrival of 183 Paraguayan troops in Santo Domingo on 26 June, the total peace force strength reached approximately 14,000 men. Of these about 12,000 consisted of U.S. troops.[16]

MILITARY OPERATIONS AND THE PROVISIONAL GOVERNMENT

With the buildup of Latin American forces for the peace force the number of U.S. troops in the Dominican Republic declined. After the arrival of the first contingent of Brazilian troops, the president directed the withdrawal of six hundred marines. At maximum strength in late May, 1965, U.S. forces in Santo Domingo had numbered about 14,000 army troops, eight thousand marines, and one thousand air force personnel. The gradual reduction of marines committed to Dominican action begun on 26 May continued until 6 June when the final marine units departed.[17]

With the buildup of the peace force and the gradual withdrawal of U.S. forces, the final stages of the search for a peace formula and political settlement began. On 2 June the OAS foreign ministers in Washington approved a U.S.-Brazilian resolution to send a three-man Peace Committee to Santo Domingo to mediate the dispute between the Imbert junta and the Caamaño rebel regime. This ad hoc committee, composed of ambassadors to the OAS, Ilmar Penna Marinho of Brazil, Ellsworth Bunker of the United States, and Ramon de Clairmont Duenes of El Salvador, accomplished what diplomatic representatives of the United States, United Nations, and the former OAS commission had been unable to accomplish--the establishment of a Dominican coalition government to be followed by free elections. Ambassador Bunker stated on 4 June that the committee was to assist the Dominican people in establishing a provisional government of national unity that could eventually lead to a permanent representative regime through the democratic process.[18]

The resolution creating the committee also empowered it to give political guidance to the inter-American force. The United States in effect turned over its mediation role to this new committee, which conducted negotiations in the Dominican Republic 4-16 June in an effort to settle the political impasse. Committee members met with leaders representing Imbert and Caamaño, the United States and the United Nations, and with Dominican businessmen and professional leaders outside of Santo Domingo aligned with neither side of the political dispute. Rebel-junta differences centered on which constitution should guide the proposed government. The rebels called for restoration of the 1963 constitution and the junta wanted the 1962 constitution. While these negotiations continued the IAPF, now organized into a Latin American brigade and a U.S. command, relieved the withdrawing marines in the security zone. The Brazilians took over responsibility for security of the National Palace after three hundred junta troops evacuated the building. A token force of twenty-five junta troops remained in the palace, but the area became a demilitarized zone.[19]

Incidents between troops of the peace force and the rebels occurred daily, and on 15 June serious fighting broke out between 82d Airborne troops in the corridor and the rebels. U.S. peace force troops in this action secured control of over thirty additional city blocks. The fighting spread to the Latin American brigade which held its positions on the security zone perimeter. U.S. forces arrested about five hundred men, releasing some and holding others for questioning. Fighting between rebel and U.S. troops broke out again on 16 June at the same location. In the 15-16 June fighting the paratroopers heavily shelled rebel positions using mortars, and at least two hundred persons, many of them civilians, were killed or wounded. Three paratroopers were killed and twenty-eight wounded and five Brazilian soldiers were wounded. U.S. peace force troops now held positions dominating the rebel-held area in Santo Domingo. OAS representatives in Santo Domingo stated that the inter-American force would continue to occupy the rebel area it had seized until the insurgents pledged not to open fire again. President Johnson accused rebel elements of totally unjustified firing on the inter-American force. In the 16 June incident, the president stated peace force troops did not shoot back until twenty-three minutes after rebels had fired on them.[20]

By the end of June, agreement was near on the composition of a provisional Dominican government. The OAS ad hoc committee proposed Héctor García-Godoy, who briefly had been Bosch's foreign minister, for provisional president. The committee also proposed an institutional act in lieu of a constitution, under which García-Godoy would govern until the Dominicans held free elections in June. Prior negotiations helped in making García-Godoy's selection as provisional president acceptable to both the rebels and the loyalists. The rebel negotiating committee split with a pro-Bosch faction overriding a Caamaño faction in accepting the García-Godoy selection. Bundy's earlier Guzmán formula may have begun this split and Vance's negotiations with Imbert's generals probably helped that side in accepting a settlement.[21]

Imbert and Caamaño resigned and accepted García-Godoy who took office as president of the provisional government on 3 September. This government ruled the country for eleven months. U.S. authorities had pressured the junta to accept a provisional government by stopping funds allotted to pay the salaries of junta public servants and members of the armed forces. The United States had contributed about $21 million for the May-June junta payrolls through the OAS. U.S. withdrawal of payroll support forced Imbert to use immediate revenues to meet junta public salaries so that his regime faced bankruptcy. The United States recognized the provisional Dominican government on 4 September 1965. During his term of almost a year in office, García-Godoy acted independently of the United States. With Ambassador Bunker's misgivings but acquiescence he brought numerous former rebels or constitutionalists into his government, failed to crack down on leftist tendencies in the universities, and deported the conservative minister of the armed forces and the army and navy chiefs.[22]

On 5 September García-Godoy abolished CEFA and called for its integration into the Dominican army. He told Wessin that the general would have to leave the country. Wessin agreed to leave but on the next day began to mobilize his unit for a march on the city. The CEFA forces were quickly intercepted by IAPF troops and escorted back to their compound where they were kept confined. IAPF troops also surrounded Wessin's headquarters and occupied a landing zone near the general's house. With this amount of military force arrayed against him, Wessin capitulated and agreed to leave the country. The departure of the general was a blow to the forces of the Right. Since the rebels refused to surrender their weapons for fear of attack by the Dominican military led by Wessin, his departure was the first step toward demilitarization of the rebel zone.

In another step, on 13 and 14 October, military police and 82d troops escorted the rebels desiring to be reintegrated into the Dominican military from Ciudad Nueva to the 27th of July barracks. On 15 October, IAPF troops removed the corridor barriers and check points separating the rebel and loyalist territories. One task remained and that was to reintegrate the rebel zone with the remainder of the city. Since García-Godoy distrusted his own military, peace force troops were called again. They moved into the rebel zone and, without bloodshed, secured the area on 25 October. The clearing operation uncovered few arms caches but did uncover some incriminating Communist documents. The operation was one more example of how García-Godoy's distrust of his military led him to call on peace force troops without using his own resources. This policy also encouraged leftists to enter the government at all levels on the mistaken belief that the IAPF would be used "indefinitely to prevent the Dominican military forces and police from taking effective counter-action." Although the IAPF forces were used to separate the rebels and loyalists, General Palmer was determined that they would not be used to further the drift of the García-Godoy government to the left.[23]

Violence broke out sporadically for the remainder of the winter. On the night of 21-22 November, riots broke out in two outlying cities, Santiago and Barahona, when former constitutionalists seized local radio stations and announced the establishment of a new Dominican government. This time Dominican troops put down the attempted coup, but they were backed up by a company from the 82d Ready Reaction Force. On 19 December, a more serious incident occurred outside Santiago. About three hundred former loyalist troops surrounded the Hotel Matum, where Caamaño and about one hundred of his followers had fled, and opened fire. A battle lasting several hours began. García-Godoy authorized the IAPF command to dispatch troops to quell the disturbance. A company of the 82d responded and the paratroopers were able to interpose themselves between the opposing forces and evacuate Caamaño and his men by helicopter back to Santo Domingo.[24]

Strained relations between the former junta forces and ex-rebels had caused the 19 December clash. The rebels had pressured the provisional government for ouster of the rightist leaders since the end of the conflict, and the rightists had demanded similar action against Caamaño's group. Bunker proposed a solution whereby military leaders from each side would leave the country. Although García-Godoy agreed to this proposal when he issued a decree on 6 January 1966 announcing the overseas posting of his military chiefs and certain constitutionalist officers including Caamaño, some of his military chiefs rebelled and seized the main radio station. The IAPF once more was called upon to put down an attempted coup, this time from the

Right. Backed by their troops, Alvim and Palmer met with the leaders of the uprising and arranged an end to the crisis.

In January Caamaño left the country for London and a Dominican military attaché's post and in February the service chiefs resigned. In all García-Godoy ordered thirty-four military officers exiled with twelve assigned abroad as military attachés and twenty-two assigned to a training and study mission in Israel. The effect of this readjustment within the military was to cancel U.S. plans to reorganize and reform the Dominican armed forces for fear of further demoralization of the officer corps.[25]

CONSTITUTIONAL GOVERNMENT AND TROOP WITHDRAWAL

By the time of the June 1966 elections Dominican political parties had fragmented. The National Civic Union, the second largest party in the 1962 elections, and Bosch's Dominican Revolutionary Party had split into warring factions. Of the major parties only Balaguer's Reformist party had escaped fragmentation. By 1966 polarization had narrowed Dominican political choice to two major candidates--Balaguer, representing order and the traditional status quo, and Bosch, symbolizing revolution. The OAS and García-Godoy government took pains to ensure that the elections were covered by outside observers. The paratroopers monitored the election process augmenting three sets of international observers. Even persons likely to be biased against the election were invited to attend. There were OAS observers from eighteen countries and over sixty foreign correspondents. All but a few of the correspondents and even members of the embassy staff predicted a Bosch victory. One exception to this almost universal prediction was the CIA station chief, who having made a fairly recent trip into the interior of the country, predicted a Balaguer victory. He was correct, as on 1 June 1966 the Dominicans elected Balaguer as president with 57 percent of 1.3 million votes. The decisive factor in his victory was his following in the rural areas. Although Bosch carried Santo Domingo, Balaguer carried all but four of the twenty-six Dominican election districts or provinces.[26]

On 1 July, in his inaugural address, Balaguer announced an austerity program, the need for continued U.S. economic assistance, and the necessity of eliminating corruption and graft in the bureaucracy and military services. In the weeks that followed he formed his cabinet and reached an agreement with Bosch and the opposition Dominican Revolutionary Party on a policy of military reforms and party cooperation. Balaguer confirmed ex-provisional government president García-Godoy as ambassador to the United States. In his last act as provisional president García-Godoy on 29 June signed a law reintegrating the former constitutionalist rebels into the armed forces, thereby officially recognizing the end of the civil strife begun in April 1965.[27]

One of the important aspects of use of the IAPF, as far as the U.S. was concerned, was the ease with which it was possible to integrate the staffs and Latin American and U.S. troop contingents into an effective military organization utilizing common military terminology, doctrines, and procedures. General Palmer believed that this had been made possible by the U.S. Army's foreign student program in service schools, the establishment of military advisory groups and missions throughout Latin America, the attaché system, and the U.S. Army School of the Americas in the Panama Canal Zone. These agencies, although not completely succeeding in turning the Latin American military into professional apolitical elements on the U.S. model, had, however, contributed to creating forces that, as in the Dominican crisis, remained, General Palmer believed, "the only effective indigenous force capable of preventing a return to the chaos and mob rule of April 1965 or of countering a seizure of power by Leftist extremists following the withdrawal of the IAPF."[28]

As the IAPF arrived in the Dominican Republic the U.S. forces departed so that by October 1965 American troops numbered only about 8,500. By mid-January 1966 the IAPF consisted of two brigades with about one-third of the troops from Latin American countries, and in June, after the elections, the OAS ministerial council passed a resolution calling for the withdrawal from the Dominican Republic of the 8,200-man peace force within three months. The troops began leaving on 1 July and the last of the 6,800 U.S. troops of the force left the Dominican Republic on 19 September. Operations of the IAPF formally ended one day later.[29]

On 14 September as the U.S. troops were leaving, Dominican terrorists killed two U.S. soldiers, bringing the total of U.S. killed in action to twenty-seven. There were 172 U.S. troops wounded in action, twenty non-combat U.S. dead, seventeen Latin American troops wounded in action, and one Latin American non-combat dead. This brought the total IAPF casualties to 237. The financial cost to the United States for both humanitarian and military-related costs was about $311 million. For the Dominicans the costs of the civil war in terms of lives lost has been estimated at a minimum of three thousand killed. Even critics of the intervention agree, however, that had not the United States stepped in to end the hostilities, the Dominican loss of life would have been much higher. The government that emerged after the intervention has been relatively stable and the country relatively prosperous. This has resulted in part from the achievements of the negotiated settlement ending the civil war, in part from the continued interest of the United States in this neighboring country, and mostly from the Dominican people themselves who have been able to solve many of their political, economic, and social problems in an environment free from political chaos.[30]

NOTES

1. Slater, Intervention and Negotiation, p. 56.

2. Martin, Overtaken by Events, pp. 681-684, Mansbach, Dominican Crisis 1965, pp. 49, 51, 56; Slater, Intervention and Negotiation, p. 63; Yale H. Ferguson, "The Dominican Intervention of 1965; Recent Interpretations," International Organization (Autumn 1973), p. 531.

3. Szulc, Dominican Diary, p. 147; Ringler and Shaw, U.S. Marine Corps Operations in the Dominican Republic, April- June 1965, p. 54.

4. Slater, Intervention and Negotiation, pp. 73-75; Martin, Overtaken by Events, p. 686. Still worried about the extent of the Communist threat President Johnson announced on 24 May that a team of FBI agents would be sent to the Dominican Republic to investigate the nature and extent of the Communist influence (see Congressional Digest [November 1965], p. 266). An article in the World Marxist Review (December 1965) stated that the Communist leaders went underground after arrival of the U.S. troops (see Martin, Overtaken by Events, pp. 770-790).

5. Martin, Overtaken by Events, p. 688.

6. Yates, Power Pack, pp. 162-163; Mansbach, Dominican Crisis 1965, p. 104; Martin, Overtaken by Events, pp. 700-701.

7. Mansbach, Dominican Crisis 1965, p. 61.

8. Ibid., pp. 62, 63; Martin, Overtaken by Events, p. 694.

9. Yates, Power Pack, pp. 116, 117; U.S.F.D.R. "Stability Operations" pt.1, v. 1, ch. 2, pp. 13, 14; Phiblant, Report of Participation, encl. 2, p. 21.

10. Mansbach, Dominican Crisis 1965, pp. 67, 68, 70.

11. Martin, Overtaken by Events, pp. 695, 696; Ferguson, "The Dominican Intervention of 1965; Recent Interpretations," p. 532; Atkins and Wilson, The United States and the Trujillo Regime, p. 145; Joseph Kraft, Profiles in Power, pp. 164, 165.

12. Martin, Overtaken by Events, pp. 695, 696.

13. Ibid., p. 694; Mansbach, Dominican Crisis 1965, pp. 61, 81, 82.

14. Mansbach, Dominican Crisis 1965, pp. 81, 82; Kelso, "The Dominican Crisis of 1965: A New Appraisal," p. 180.

15. OAS, Report of the Secretary General Regarding the Dominican Situation, Washington, D.C. and Pan American Union, 1 November 1965, pp. 11-13; Committee on Foreign Relations, Background Information, pp. 64-68; Greenberg, Dominican Republic Intervention, pp. 60-68.

16. Mansbach, Dominican Crisis 1965, pp. 54, 84; Greenberg, Dominican Republic Intervention, pp. 69-74; U.S. Air Force, MATS, 772d Troops Carrier Squadron, Final Report Operation Press Ahead, 11 June 1965.

17. Phiblant, Report of Participation, encl. 2, pp. 25, 29. Withdrawal of American forces began on 26 May when the 6th Marine Expeditionary Unit began reembarking aboard ship and naval authorities reconstituted the Caribbean Ready Group. This force with

its embarked marines reverted to the control of CINCLANT, but remained within four hours steaming distance from Santo Domingo for the duration of the crisis. Ringler and Shaw, U.S. Marine Corps Operations in the Dominican Republic, April-June 1965, pp. 60-63; Tompkins, "Ubique," p. 39.

18. "Dominican Crisis," Department of State Bulletin, no. 7971 (October 1965), p. 3; Ferguson, "The Dominican Intervention of 1965: Recent Interpretations," p. 532; Mansbach, Dominican Crisis 1965, p. 87; Yates, Power Pack, pp. 145, 146.

19. Mansbach, Dominican Crisis 1965, p. 84; OAS, "Report of the Secretary General Regarding the Dominican Situation," pp. 18-19.

20. Mansbach, Dominican Crisis 1965, pp. 91-93; Yates, Power Pack, pp. 158-159; U.S.F.D.R. "Stability Operations," pt. 1, v. 1, ch. 2, p. 17 and pt. 2 ch. 2, 3, 5, 8, 16; James H. Clingham, "All American Teamwork," Army Digest (January 1967, p. 22.

21. Mansbach, Dominican Crisis 1965, pp. 97, 98, 101; Martin, Overtaken by Events, pp. 700-701.

22. Yates, Power Pack, pp. 159-163; Ferguson, "The Dominican Intervention of 1965: Recent Interpretations," p. 533; U.S.F.D.R., "Stability Operations," pt. 2, ch. 1, pp. 8-10; Phillips, Night Watch, pp. 166, 167; Henry Wells, "The Dominican Search for Stability," Current History (December 1966).

23. Mansbach, Dominican Crisis 1965, pp. 104, 108; Yates, Power Pack, pp. 164, 165; Bracey, Resolution of the Dominican Crisis, p. 32; U.S.F.D.R. "Stability Operations," pt. 2, ch. 1, pp. 19-24, 26-29, 31.

24. Mansbach, Dominican Crisis 1965, pp. 112, 113; Yates, Power Pack, pp. 165, 166; U.S.F.D.R., "Stability Operations" pt. 3, ch. 1, p. i-3.

25. Mansbach, Dominican Crisis 1965, pp. 114-116; Yates, Power Pack, p. 168; Phillips, The Night Watch, p. 176.

26. Phillips, The Night Watch, pp. 179-181; Bracey, Resolution of the Dominican Crisis, p. 41; Eldredge R. Long, Jr., "The Dominican Crisis 1965: An Experiment in International Peace Keeping," Student thesis, Newport, R.I.: U.S. Naval War College, 1967; Johnson, The Vantage Point, pp. 203, 204; Mansbach, Dominican Crisis 1965, pp. 121, 122.

27. Mansbach, Dominican Crisis 1965, pp. 124, 124; Atkins and Wilson, The United States and the Trujillo Regime, p. 147.

28. U.S.F.D.R., "Stability Operations," pt. 2, ch. 16, pp. 8, 11.

30. Mansbach, Dominican Crisis 1965, pp. 125, 126; Greenberg, United States Army Unilateral and Coalition Operations in the 1965 Dominican Republic Intervention, pp. 84, 85; Yates, Power Pack, p. 169.

9

Conclusions

One must study the entire eighteen months of American participation in the Dominican intervention to answer such controversial questions as whether U.S. policy was truly neutral. American policy changed during the period from favoring a rightist junta, to a neutral policy, to finally favoring a very liberal, provisional government. An important factor in this shift was the changing military situation. Early in the crisis, when it appeared the rebels might win and there were few American troops in Santo Domingo, U.S. policy favored the Wessin y Wessin junta. American military officials supplied the junta with communications equipment, military assistance officers and attachés conducted joint planning with the San Isidro generals, and the joint task force furnished the junta with liaison officers. With the American troop buildup and the resulting decreased communist threat U.S. policy became increasingly neutral. After completion of the buildup and containment of the rebels in downtown Santo Domingo, American policy shifted to restraining the Imbert forces from attacking the insurgents and persuading the Imbert junta to accept a left-leaning provisional government. Not only had American foreign policy requirements limited U.S. military operations, but military operations had allowed foreign policy to shift as the military situation improved.

Complexity also characterized the Dominican factional dispute, American military operations in the Dominican Republic, and the activities of groups associated with the search for a cease-fire and negotiated peace. The crisis began with a coup that overthrew the existing government, then became a limited war between two factions, both claiming to be the legitimate Dominican government. Then the provisional government formed in September 1965, exiled the leaders of the contending factions and served as an interim government until the formation of a constitutional government in July of 1966. American military operations likewise changed from a relatively simple rescue of endangered Americans by five hundred marines into a preventive intervention of over 23,000 U.S. troops and airmen. This force then rapidly decreased to one-third its original size as U.S. forces became part of an inter-American peace force in the Dominican Republic. Also, the United Nations, OAS, and the United States sent representatives to the Dominican Republic to aid the papal nuncio and the United States ambassador in seeking a peace formula, thus adding to the complexity of the political negotiations.

Varying interpretations of communist influence in the rebellion also confused observers. At the time of the coup, the threat of communism was limited. Later when the situation became truly chaotic, when the government and police were powerless, and when the rebels began supplying arms freely to whoever wanted them, the threat from organized communist elements increased. After American troops had landed, some of the communist leaders decided to go underground and the danger of a communist takeover disappeared, although continued communist agitation apparently played a part in causing fighting between the rebels and troops of the inter-American force. The Communist issue illustrated some of the weaknesses of American intelligence. Intelligence organizations overestimated the amount of control over the revolt by communists, a miscalculation that proved crucial in the president's decision to intervene in force in the Dominican Republic.

One major shortcoming of the intelligence collection effort was its emphasis on reporting the activities of communists. The volume of this reporting by the military attachés and CIA personnel magnified the Communist role in the revolt and detracted from reporting concerned with the insurgent leadership. The tendency of intelligence collection agencies and the embassy to focus on communists identified with Castro's Cuba caused this distortion. Another shortcoming was the close association between collection personnel and members of the existing regime. Because of attempts to improve the internal security of the Dominican Republic as part of the counterinsurgency program, U.S. military attachés and military advisory officers maintained close ties only with their loyalist military counterparts. The ambassador and political attachés maintained close liaison with the existing regime but lacked contacts or knowledge of competing political elements within the Dominican government and military forces. Thus governmental procedures and processes helped to prevent a true picture of events in the Dominican Republic from reaching the Washington decision-makers.

Faulty analysis and screening procedures compounded the errors of the intelligence collection program. Lists of communists supplied embassy briefers by CIA personnel, for example, reported as active in the revolt communists who were either in jail or out of the country. Embassy staff, intelligence personnel, and observers also attached credibility to rumors of rebel atrocities current in the early days of the revolt. These rumors, reported at embassy briefings, appeared in Johnson's speeches. The high volume of reports used by the military forces in the Dominican Republic prevented the proper processing and evaluation of information. By the time reports on rebel concentrations had been processed and forwarded to the ground forces in the operational situation, the rebels had shifted positions. Reconnaissance photography often reached the requesting agency too late to be useful because of long processing times, overemphasis on print duplication, and slow delivery procedures.

The quality of intelligence was important to Washington decision-makers because information concerned with communists and disorder in Santo Domingo heavily influenced the president and his advisers in

Conclusions

deciding to intervene and in what form. The president did not rely completely on established intelligence channels but sent Martin and the Bundy mission to the Dominican Republic, not only to help in finding a solution to the crisis but to report on the situation. Johnson also used other channels of information, including agents of the FBI and the Abe Fortas-Bosch link in San Juan. Martin's assessment of the communist threat reinforced the president's decision to increase the American troop commitment, although he had already decided to prevent a communist takeover of the revolt with whatever troops were necessary even before Martin's departure from Washington. Thus the president's reliance on independent sources of information partially compensated for the inadequacies of intelligence available to Washington decision-makers through regular channels.

Another factor important to Johnson's decisionmaking was the number and quality of his advisers. Although the president consulted with Latin American experts such as Mann at the State Department and with members of Congress such as Senator Richard Russell of Georgia before making his decisions, he relied mostly on the advice of a small group of key, highly qualified personnel, especially Bundy, Rusk, and McNamara. Johnson had selected his principal advisers because of the similarity of their outlook to his and to retain continuity of leadership with the preceding Kennedy administration. Rusk, McNamara, and Bundy favored a large troop commitment which corresponded with the president's views. His reliance on the advice of a small number of advisers and his insistence on consensus gave the impression that his analysis of the Dominican situation lacked thoroughness. This was not the case. Based on the information received the president and his advisers believed that other actions such as a show of force would be inadequate.

In making the decision to land the marines the president and his advisers believed they had no choice but to grant Bennett's request for military support. No one questioned the necessity for this initial action, which, according to the president, was based "99 percent" on the desire to protect American lives in Santo Domingo. The President, however, exercised some caution in increasing the troop commitment and waited until Thursday evening before deciding on a rapid intervention in strength to prevent a communist takeover. His decision on the size of the intervening force was based not only on overwhelming strength but on the missions of the troops. Although analysts usually have focused on the initial decision to land the marines, successive decisions by Johnson on committing army troops were more important and turned the intervention from a simple rescue into a major military operation.

There were deficiencies in the functions and procedures of civilian and military organizations carrying out the presidential decisions, particularly during the first days of the intervention. The Dominican Task Force set up at the State Department acted more as a clearinghouse for information and briefing center than as a functioning body to make decisions and coordinate the American response to the crisis. Neither did the country team in the Dominican Republic, especially in the early days of the rebellion, successfully provide the proper direction and coordination of the American political-military effort. State Department and embassy employees reacted overcautiously to events as they occurred and tended to put off hard decisions, thereby avoiding radical positive initiatives. The embassy's refusal to negotiate with the rebels during the crisis period reflected this caution. Military officials and Department of Defense personnel, on the other hand, eagerly accepted action, desired to use the force at their disposal, planned ahead, and took corrective action as soon as possible. McNamara and the Joint Chiefs eagerly volunteered the services of the military early in the crisis, alerted a large contingent of troops almost two days before the president authorized the first troop landings, and formed a joint task force whose commander departed for the Dominican Republic five hours before the president decided to land the first contingent of marines. These organizational problems added to the difficulties of synchronizing the political and military actions taken during the crisis period.

Washington officials found it difficult to define American goals and to state them clearly as missions to be accomplished in the Dominican Republic. In the first days of the intervention both the political and military goals were obscure. Although the goal of evacuation of threatened civilians was obvious to all, the military was not sure of any additional missions and even thought at one stage of equipping the intervening troops solely for riot control. Prior to the president's decision to intervene to prevent a communist takeover senior military officers already had stated the reason for the intervention as to prevent a communist takeover. This tendency by military officials to see the revolutionary faction as communist even while official American policy remained neutral reflected their training and indoctrination in anticommunism and counterinsurqency. Later in the intervention Washington officials formulated a set of goals, which they transmitted to their civilian and military personnel in Santo Domingo by fact sheets, press releases, and other communications. This action cleared up much of the earlier confusion.

The Atlantic Command and subordinate commands had issued contingency plans for operations in the Dominican Republic. These plans were outdated and in some cases inadequate for conditions in the Dominican Republic. The plans contained instructions to ready the military forces for action so that at the time of decision the decision-makers would have a full range of military options. Forces ready for action are more prone to be used, thus, contingency plans can be self-fulfilling. This factor probably played a part in military officials acting in anticipation of events. The Dominican contingency plans envisaged a much smaller intervening force of from 75-80 percent less than that actually used. This caused military authorities to make last-minute adjustments leading to major confusion and inefficiency. Hastily made changes caused air force and navy aircraft and ships to arrive in Santo Domingo improperly loaded with their hold capacity only partially utilized. Outdated troop lists and tables of organization and equipment led to inefficient army improvisation, and air force plans lacked important details of airlift operations such as communication frequencies.

Although Dominican contingency planning increased force readiness, outdated and poor quality plans decreased the efficiency of operations. Political considerations concerned with the uses of the intervention forces were missing from contingency plans. Although

Conclusions

McNamara briefed the president and others on the contingency plans, Washington officials apparently did not discuss their political implications. Disregard of these considerations led military authorities to airland the 82d Airborne Division troops at the San Isidro Air Base even though the base was the headquarters of the junta. As could be expected the American press interpreted this as an example of U.S. partiality for the loyalists. There apparently was little consideration given to the fact that the opposing forces might not be all communists but could consist of groups opposed to the government from a variety of backgrounds, many sincere in their goal of establishing a democratic government of the Left. The U.S. goal of separating the political factions impartially should have been one of the major considerations during both the planning and decision-making processes.

The United States had the necessary mobile forces available and moved them quickly and decisively to keep the conflict limited in time and scope and to prevent the perceived threat of "another Cuba." This type of quick preventive action did not resemble that associated with crisis management in which two opponents attempt to modify behavior through the use of force or the threat of force. Some requirements of crisis management did apply, however, to the initial days of the Dominican intervention. These included presidential control of military options, tailoring the size and composition of forces to specific objectives, restricting the use of force to limited objectives, and coordinating military with political and diplomatic actions. These requirements involved direction and control of the intervention forces, which was the most difficult part of the management problem.

During the crisis period President Johnson personally controlled American military options. He first authorized the use of a small marine force to safeguard and evacuate American citizens, then increased the size of the intervening force when it became apparent that more men were needed to secure an international safety zone. Finally, he authorized a full scale military intervention but retained control of the size of this force by authorizing its commitment in increments. To meet a deteriorating situation in Santo Domingo, he diverted the first contingent of 82d Airborne troops to hasten their arrival. The piecemeal commitment of forces fulfilled another principle of crisis management requiring pauses in military operations to allow opponents to assess the situation.

Another requirement of crisis management applicable to the Dominican action was tailoring the size and composition of the forces used to specific objectives. Many critics considered the size of the intervening force as far above what was required to restore stability in Santo Domingo. The president based the size of the force on what was to be accomplished. His senior military advisers agreed that to separate the hostile forces, isolate the area of operations, secure a large safety zone, and create a military situation for a negotiated peace a large intervening force was necessary. They also agreed that preventive action required sufficient armed forces to eliminate any doubt about the accomplishment of objectives. This demonstration of strength fulfilled another principle of crisis management requiring military options to provide a clear and appropriate demonstration of the manager's resolution and of his objectives.

Washington and embassy officials placed many restrictions on the use of military force during the Dominican operation. Such restrictions fulfilled another requirement of crisis management restricting the use of force to limited objectives. During the crisis period, Bennett restrained the navy from an aerial show of force over Santo Domingo and Washington officials restricted marine ground operations to securing the international safety zone. They would not permit Palmer's troops to carry out a frontal assault on rebel positions in the city. Washington also rejected York's complaints that compliance with a cease-fire would hinder American military operations. Because of the confusion generated by Martin's uncoordinated cease-fire negotiations with the rebels on 1 May, Washington tightened the troop rules of engagement. The troops could still fire and maneuver in self-defense but now must return to their original positions after any ground action. It also was necessary for them to request permission to fire even when under attack. This permission was rarely granted.

Restrictions and last minute changes to plans also affected air operations. The last-minute decision in Washington to increase the number of troops by a factor of four caused overcrowding at the Pope AFB staging area. Washington orders for diversion of the air assault force caused many problems in logistics and air traffic control. The decision in Washington to give combat troop airlift priority over support elements delayed deployment of fighter and reconnaissance aircraft and slowed the introduction of communications and radar equipment into the objective area. A Washington decision to prohibit the use of F-100s to deliver critical, photographic intelligence decreased the effectiveness of photographic reconnaissance. Washington officials also limited flight operations over the city of Santo Domingo to altitudes over 1,500 feet, which reduced the effectiveness of fighter and reconnaissance support. Such restrictions frustrated military officers and decreased the efficiency of operations. American officers had been brought up to fight wars under traditional doctrine, which required maximum use of firepower, concentration of force, and the use of surprise and mobility. The necessity to impose restrictions and control military operations directly from Washington limited the exercise of command by local commanders even though recognized by them as necessary. The decision to establish a corridor north of the rebel stronghold in Santo Domingo rather than confront the rebels directly, although a second choice for General Palmer, avoided "another Hungary" in which civilians and the city might have suffered more than the rebels.

The principle of crisis management requiring the coordination of military and diplomatic actions also applied to the Dominican action. Although political-military coordination at the Washington level was adequate, coordination between civilian peace negotiators and troop commanders in Santo Domingo broke down during the early crisis period. The breakdown was caused by lack of information available to negotiators and military officers on American troop positions. Martin had not been properly informed of American troop positions or plans when he met with Caamaño, the rebel leader, on 1 May, nor had the American troop commanders been properly informed of the cease-fire negotiations. Subsequent to the crisis period coordination between the embassy and the American troops improved largely due

Conclusions

to the personal, cooperative relationship between Ambassador Bennett and General Palmer, senior commander of the American ground forces. In summary, although the president and his advisers did not consciously follow the principles of crisis management and concentrated on a quick, decisive military strategy to accomplish their goals, many of these principles applied to the Dominican action.

Problems of control and coordination were not limited to the important area of political-military relationships but included interservice coordination, military-civilian coordination in areas such as psychological warfare, and control of operations within a single service between continental and Dominican commands. Interservice coordination became more difficult after military officials dissolved the joint task force on 7 May. It was not until the next December that American air and naval forces in the Dominican Republic again came under the control of a single commander. During psychological warfare operations, personnel air delivering leaflets and conducting airborne radio broadcasts found that they needed to coordinate their efforts more closely with United States Information Agency(USIA) personnel for successful psychological warfare operations. Army and air force officials also discovered that special arrangements for the coordination of airlift requests were necessary once the army corps headquarters had shifted from Fort Bragg to Santo Domingo. Ground troop commanders found that they needed tighter control of their troops because of the political and rapidly changing nature of urban warfare and a more responsive system for determining troop positions. All three military services operating aircraft in the Dominican area had problems in coordinating the activities of their air support because of the density of air traffic over Santo Domingo.

An important control measure used during the Dominican intervention was the system of communications and operational control centers established in the early 1960s for control of crisis situations and flexible response. President Johnson had expanded the White House communications network and the operational control centers established in Washington, at the unified command level and even at lower levels of command, improved the reception, processing, and dissemination of information. The communications system worked well during the crisis period especially at the Washington and unified command levels. The control centers centralized communications and helped in coordinating the actions of the White House, Department of Defense, and State Department with those of CINCLANT in Norfolk and the commander of the U.S. forces in the Dominican Republic.

The requirements of limited war and flexible response stressed control of military forces from the highest level of government. Although President Johnson communicated directly with his diplomatic representatives in the Dominican Republic, he controlled his military field commanders mostly through the Joint Chiefs of Staff. He did, however, talk directly with General Palmer when necessary. This system worked well during the intervention but in Santo Domingo lack of adequate communications created a major problem during the early days of the crisis. Initially an amateur radio served as the only communication link between the embassy and the ships of the amphibious group. Even communications equipment brought ashore by the marines did not have sufficient power to reach the flagship of the amphibious task force. Early in the crisis the <u>Boxer</u> furnished the only secure communications link from Santo Domingo to Washington, resulting in overload of this net. The early Washington decision to grant communications and radar equipment second priority to combat elements in the airlift necessitated improvisation of field communications with continental commands until 7 May when army, air force, and Defense Communications Agency communications equipment began operating in the Dominican Republic. Up to that time the army and air force relied on naval circuits and an airborne command post to provide long-range communications with the mainland.

In addition to analyzing management problems during the intervention this study has investigated the role of the participating American military forces. This role was characterized by diversity in the political uses of the intervening forces, in the types of military operations carried out during the crisis, and in the roles of the military personnel. As a military operation the intervention must be considered a complete success. American military and civilian authorities prevented a communist takeover of the revolt and introduced order into a chaotic situation by interposing U.S. troops between the belligerents and by using enough troops to ensure that police, evacuation, and disaster relief operations could be simultaneously accomplished. The size of the force used was a sufficient deterrent to convince both sides to the conflict that it was futile to continue to fight. It also convinced some of the communist leaders to disappear underground. The speed and form of military reaction indicated the capability, mobility, and flexibility of U.S. joint military forces deployed to distant distressed areas to stabilize critical situations. In order to accomplish the stabilization mission the intervening units had to be large enough and move into the objective area rapidly enough to overwhelm any possible opposition before it could organize. Air delivery of all the combat elements of the 82d Airborne Division and elements of the 4th Marine Expeditionary Brigade 1,200 miles in about four days satisfied these requirements. The rapid buildup to over 23,000 American troops and military personnel allowed the U.S. ground forces to carry out a wide variety of activities in the Dominican Republic.

Marines from the Amphibious Ready Group were the first ground forces to be used in the Dominican intervention. They conducted a vertical envelopment by helicopters to secure an evacuation zone, then an amphibious landing of additional troops and armored vehicles to establish an international safety zone. Marine aircraft furnished combat air patrol over fleet units, performed photographic reconnaissance, and evacuated civilians to ships waiting to transport them to Puerto Rico. American naval ships were prepared to deliver gunfire support if necessary, blockaded the Dominican Republic, and prevented loyalist naval ships from attacking the rebels. They assisted in surveillance missions, delivered food and medical supplies, and made port visits to gather information and establish a U.S. presence. They also helped in the towing and salvage of Dominican ships and furnished the ground forces with special support such as scuba diving.

Conclusions

Diversity also characterized air force operations. Ten major air commands participated in Dominican operations and support. The air force supplied air transports for the airlift of the 82d Airborne Division to the Dominican Republic and evacuated civilians via airlift from Santo Domingo. Air force transports airlifted troops and police from Latin American countries to the Dominican Republic to participate in the IAPF and evacuated patients to hospitals in the United States and Puerto Rico. Air force fighters performed combat air patrol and reconnaissance, supplying the ground troops with photographic intelligence, and cargo aircraft furnished logistical support to the ground troops.

Paratroopers from the 82d Airborne Division, in addition to their military duties, acted as police, took part in a civic action program including helping the Dominicans to restore power in the city, and participated in a Dominican disaster relief program supplying the needy with food and medical care. They also collected intelligence, interrogated rebel suspects, and carried out psychological warfare and jamming in coordination with air force and naval units. Army Special Force units in outlying Dominican communities collected intelligence and established a U.S. presence. The paratroopers also trained the Latin American troops and police participating in the IAPF, patrolled junta territory as members of teams enforcing the cease-fire, and assisted the provisional Dominican government in maintaining the peace.

This brief summary of the uses of American military forces in the intervention illustrates the importance of considerations other than those of a strictly military nature in the success of a stability operation. What is needed is the establishment of an orderly environment in which political, economic, sociological, psychological, and other forces operating in the country have a chance to work together in solving the country's problems. Establishing this orderly climate meant using American troops to supply and distribute food and medical services to the Dominicans. It meant carrying out civic action programs in the countryside such as the construction of schools and roads. It also meant supplying Dominican civilians with technical advice on a wide variety of subjects such as how to plant crops. In psychological terms it meant how to promote a positive image of the American soldier to the Dominican people.

Because the conflict developed from a localized coup rather than from a broad-based insurgency, mastery of the civil strife depended on control of Santo Domingo. U.S. troops gained control of the city by setting up defense positions at primary access roads, bridges, and the airfields near Santo Domingo. They accomplished this with a minimum of casualties and without any major disruption to the life of the city using surprise, concentration of forces, and rapid, mobile action during the confusion created by the urban guerilla warfare. This type of warfare was different from that practiced in counterinsurgency operations in the countryside. The troops learned of the importance of the early occupation of key facilities such as power plants, radio stations, and major industrial, financial, and civic buildings. They also learned or relearned such lessons as that sandbags provide the best defense against sniper fire in relatively unexposed areas.

The success of the military operation proved the soundness of joint American doctrine for airborne and amphibious landings followed by combined marine and army operations to secure strategic terrain and facilities. The operation also reaffirmed the necessity for the use of sufficient force, sophisticated communications in the objective area, and flexible troop organization so that sufficient numbers of signal troops, military police, and medical and logistical units will be on hand to cope with the particular problems associated with urban guerrilla warfare. The operation also indicated the necessity for a joint headquarters in the objective area with control of all the participating forces and proved the usefulness of relatively new military weapons such as assault helicopters, airborne command posts, and airborne communications relay.

The use of the IAPF was unique. Never before or since has the OAS established a combined military force to quell internal unrest in a member state. Use of such a force in the face of the long-standing opposition of the Latin nations to military intervention, especially by the United States, was a major achievement and could set a new direction for regional relationships.

One of the most distinguishing features of the 1965 Dominican intervention was its variation from the historic standard set by the small marine expeditionary forces used by the United States in interventions in the Caribbean and Central America early in the twentieth century. U.S. military intervention now became a major operation using army, navy, and air force forces in relatively large numbers. Operations reflected a high degree of mobility, a capability of isolating the area of operations from sea, land, or air interference by outside powers, a quick resolution of the conflict using overwhelming force, and a withdrawal of forces without the necessity for extended occupation of the country involved.

Another unique aspect of the Dominican intervention, which differed from other U.S. interventions of the cold war period including the Korean War, the Vietnam War and the 1958 Lebanon operation, was that this marked the first intervention in the Caribbean region close to the U.S. doorstep. The cold war suddenly seemed much closer to home. Seen as a possible Soviet-backed Castroite power-grab, the Dominican intervention proved that the United States would react quickly and decisively if required in what the nation historically has considered its own back yard.

A warning must be added to the above conclusions in order to prevent lessons learned during the Dominican intervention from being applied too readily to future situations. The intervention was unique in that the Dominican Republic is a small island country with a friendly population. This discouraged armed resistance to the intervening troops and aided in isolating the area of operations and in the supply and withdrawal of American troops. The rural people lacked a strong sense of nationalism, which made it relatively easy to localize the revolt. Had not these characteristics been present the intervention might have been much more difficult. Also, revolutionary movements have become more skillful in building public support for their causes in the United States. As the Dominican intervention proved, there is a necessity for a reliable public information program

Conclusions

to explain the need for a resort to the use of force in resolving a conflict.

Bibliography

BOOKS

Ambrose, Stephen E. Rise to Globalism. Baltimore: Penguin Books Inc., 1971.

Atkins, G. Pope and Larman C. Wilson. The United States and the Trujillo Regime. New Brunswick, N.J.: Rutgers University Press, 1972.

Ball, George W. The Past Has Another Pattern: Memoirs. New York: W.W. Norton, 1982.

Barber, Willard F. and C. Neale Ronning. Internal Security and Military Power: Counterinsurgency and Civil Action. Columbus, Ohio: Ohio State University Press, 1966.

Barnet, Richard J. Intervention and Revolution: America's Confrontation with Insurgent Movements around the World. New York: World Publishing Company, 1968.

Barry, Robert F., ed. Power Pack. Portsmouth, Va.: Messinger Printing Co., 1965.

Betts, Richard K. Soldiers, Statesmen, and Cold War Crises. Cambridge, Mass.: Harvard University Press, 1977.

Black, Jan. The Dominican Republic: Politics and Development in an Unsovereign State. New York: Unwin Hyman, 1986. Blackman, Raymond V. B., ed. Jane's Fighting Ships. New York: McGraw-Hill, 1964.

Blaiser, Cole. The Hovering Giant: U.S. Responses to Revolutionary Change in Latin America. Pittsburgh: University of Pittsburgh Press, 1976.

Blaufarb, Douglas. The Counterinsurgency Era: U.S. Doctrine and Performance, 1950 to the Present. New York: Free Press, 1977.

Blechman, Barry M. and Stephen S. Kaplan. Force Without War: U.S. Armed Forces as a Political Instrument. Washington, D.C.: Brookings Institute, 1978.

Borklund, C. W. The Department of Defense. New York: Frederick A. Praeger, 1968.

Bosch, Juan. The Unfinished Experiment: Democracy in the Dominican Republic. New York: Frederick A. Praeger, 1965.

Bracey, Audrey. Resolution of the Dominican Crisis, 1965: A Study in Mediation. Washington, D.C.: Institute for the Study of Diplomacy, 1980.

Caidin, Martin. The Long Arm of America. New York: E.P. Dutton & Co., 1963.

Carey, John, ed. Background Paper and Proceedings of the Ninth Hammerskjold Forum. New York: Oceana Publications, 1967.

Center for Strategic Studies. Dominican Action--1965: Intervention or Cooperation. Washington, D.C.: Center for Strategic Studies, 1966.

Clark, Keith C. and Lawrence J. Legere, eds. The President and Management of National Security. New York: Frederick A. Praeger, 1968.

Craig, Gordon A. and George, Alexander L. Force and Statecraft: Diplomatic Problems of our Time. New York: Oxford University Press, 1983.

Crossweller, Robert D. Trujillo: The Life and Times of a Caribbean Dictator. New York: The Macmillan Company, 1966.

Dinerstein, Herbert. Intervention against Communism. Baltimore: Johns Hopkins Press, 1967.

Draper, Theodore. The Dominican Revolt: A Case Study in American Policy. New York: Commentary, 1968.

Evans, Ernest. Wars Without Splendor: The U.S. Military and Low-Level Conflict. Westport, Conn.: Greenwood Press, 1987.

Evans, Rowland and Robert Novak. Lyndon B. Johnson: The Exercise of Power. New York: New American Library, 1966.

FitzSimons, Louise. The Kennedy Doctrine. New York: Random House, 1972.

Gleijeses, Piero. The Dominican Crisis: The 1965 Constitutionalist Revolt and American Intervention. Baltimore: Johns Hopkins Press, 1978.

Goldman, Eric F. The Tragedy of Lyndon Johnson. New York: Alfred A. Knopf, 1969.

Haffa, Robert P., Jr. The Half War: Planning U.S. Rapid Deployment Forces to Meet a Limited Contingency, 1960-1983. Boulder: Westview Press, 1984.

Halper, Thomas. Foreign Policy Crises: Appearance and Reality in Decision Making. Columbus, Ohio: Charles E. Merrill Publishing Company, 1971.

Halperin, Morton H. Bureaucratic Politics and Foreign Policy. Washington, D.C.: The Brookings Institution, 1974.

_____. Limited War in the Nuclear Age. New York: John Wiley and Sons, 1963.

Herbert, Anthony B. Soldier. New York: Holt, Rinehart and Winston, 1973. Hilsman, Roger. To Move a Nation: The Politics of Foreign Policy in the Administration of John F. Kennedy. Garden City, N.Y.: Doubleday and Co., 1967.

Hoopes, Townsend. The Limits of Intervention. New York: Wiley and Sons, 1969.

Hoxie, R. Gordon. Command Decision and the Presidency: A Study in Nationl Security Policy and Organization. New York: Reader's Digest Press, 1977.

Johnson, Lyndon B. The Vantage Point. New York: Holt, Rinehart and Winston, 1971.

Johnson, Richard T. Managing the White House. New York: Harper and Row, 1974.
Kennedy, John F. The Strategy of Peace. ed. Allan Nevins. New York: Harper and Row, 1960.
Kryzanek, Michael J. and Howard J. Wiarda. The Politics of External Influence in the Dominican Republic. New York: Frederick A. Praeger, 1988. Kurzman, Dan. Santo Domingo: Revolt of the Damned. New York: G. P. Putnam's Sons, 1965.
LaFeber, Walter. Inevitable Revolutions: The United States in Central America. New York: W.W. Norton, 1984. Langley, Lester D. The Banana Wars: An Inner History of American Empire 1900-1934. Lexington, Ky.: University Press of Kentucky, 1983.
_____. Struggle for the American Mediterranean: United States-European Rivalry in the Gulf-Caribbean, 1776-1904 Athens, Ga.: The University of Georgia Press, 1976.
Logan, Rayford W. Haiti and the Dominican Republic. London: Oxford University Press, 1968.
Lowenthal, Abraham F. The Dominican Intervention. Cambridge, Mass.: Harvard University Press, 1972.
MacCloskey, Munro. Alert the Fifth Force. New York: Richard Rosen Press, 1969.
McChristian, Joseph A. The Role of Military Intelligence. Washington: U.S. GPO, 1974.
McClintock, Robert. The Meaning of Limited War. Boston: Houghton Mifflin Company, 1967.
McLaurin, Ron D. Military Propaganda: Psychological Warfare and Operations. New York: Frederick A. Praeger, 1982.
Mahon, John K. and Romana Danysh. Infantry Part I: Regular Army. Washington: U.S. GPO, 1969.
Mallin, Jay. Terror and Urban Guerrillas. Coral Gables, Fla.: University of Miami Press, 1966.
Mansbach, Richard W., ed. Dominican Crisis 1965. New York: Facts on File Inc., 1971.
Martin, John B. Overtaken by Events: The Dominican Crisis from the Fall of Trujillo to the Civil War. New York: Doubleday and Co., 1966.
Martz, John D., ed. United States Policy in Latin America: A Quarter Century of Crisis and Challenge 1961-1986. Lincoln, Nebr.: University of Nebraska Press, 1988.
Mecham, John L. A Survey of United States Latin American Relations. New York: Houghton Mifflin Company, 1965.
Miller, Merle. Lyndon: An Oral Biography. New York: Ballantine Books, 1980.
Molineu, Harold. U.S. Policy toward Latin America: From Regionalism to Globalism. Boulder: Westview Press, 1986.
Moreno, Jose A. Barrios in Arms: Revolution in Santo Domingo. Pittsburgh: University of Pittsburgh Press, 1970.Munro, Dana G. Intervention and Dollar Diplomacy in the Caribbean, 1900-1921. Princeton, N.J.: Princeton University Press, 1964.
Osgood, Robert E. Limited War: The Challenge to American Strategy. Chicago: The University of Chicago Press, 1957.

Palmer, Bruce, Jr. Intervention in the Caribbean: The Dominican Crisis of 1965. Lexington, Ky.: The University Press of Kentucky, 1989.
Paterson, Thomas G. et al. American Foreign Policy: A History. 2d ed. Lexington, Mass.: D. C. Heath, 1983.
Perkins, Dexter. The Diplomacy of a New Age. Bloomington, Ind.: Indiana University Press, 1967.
_____. Hands Off: A History of the Monroe Doctrine. Boston: Little, Brown and Company, 1948.
_____. The Monroe Doctrine, 1867-1907. Gloucester, Mass.: Peter Smith, 1966.
Phillips, David A. The Night Watch: 25 Years of Peculiar Service. New York: Atheneum, 1977. Redford, Emmette and Richard T. McCulley. White House Operations: The Johnson Presidency. Austin: University of Texas Press, 1986.
Rippy, J. Fred. The Caribbean Danger Zone. New York: G. P. Putnam's Sons, 1940.
Roberts, Charles. LBJ's Inner Circle. New York: Delacorte Press, 1965.
Rodman, Selden. Quisqueva: A History of the Dominican Republic. Seattle: University of Washington Press, 1964.
Sapin, Burton M. The Making of United States Foreign Policy. Washington, D.C.: The Brookings Institution, 1966.
Schlesinger, Arthur M. Jr. A Thousand Days: John F. Kennedy in the White House. Boston: Houghton Mifflin Company, 1965.
Schoenbaum, Thomas J. Waging Peace and War: Dean Rusk in the Truman, Kennedy and Johnson Years. New York: Simon and Schuster, 1988.
Sidey, Hugh. A Very Personal Presidency. New York: Atheneum, 1968.
Slater, Jerome N. Intervention and Negotiation: The United States and the Dominican Revolution. New York: Harper and Row, 1970.
Stebbins, Richard P. The United States in World Affairs, 1965. New York: Harper and Row, 1966.
Szulc, Tad. Dominican Diary. New York: Delacorte Press, 1965.
Tansill, Charles C. The United States and Santo Domingo 1798-1873: A Chapter in Caribbean Diplomacy. Baltimore: Johns Hopkins Press, 1938.
Taylor, Maxwell D. Swords and Plowshares. New York: W. W. Norton, 1972.
_____. The Uncertain Trumpet. New York: Harper and Row, 1960.
Terry, George R. Principles of Management. Homewood, Ill.: Richard D. Irwin Inc., 1964.
Valenti, Jack. A Very Human President. New York: W. W. Norton, 1975.
Weil, Thomas E. et al. Area Handbook for the Dominican Republic. Washington, D.C.: U.S. GPO, 1973.
Welles, Sumner. Naboth's Vineyard. Boston: Paul P. Appel, 1966.
Westmoreland, William C. A Soldier Reports. New York: Doubleday and Co., 1976.
Wiarda, Howard J. The Dominican Republic: Nation in Transition. New York: Frederick A. Praeger, 1969.

Wiarda, Howard J. and Michael J. Kryzanek. The Dominican Republic: A Caribbean Crucible. Boulder: Westview Press, 1982.
Wicker, Tom. JFK and LBJ. New York: William Morrow and Company, Inc., 1968.
Williams, Phil. Crisis Management Confrontations and Diplomacy in the Nuclear Age. London: Martin Robertson and Co., Ltd., 1976.
Young, Oran R. The Politics of Force: Bargaining during International Crises. Princeton: Princeton University Press, 1968.

ARTICLES

"AID's Academy: Foreign Police Training Ends," Federal Times, 19 March 1975.
"Airborne Ready Forces," Airborne Quarterly (June-August 1965).
"The Air National Guard," Air Force and Space Digest (September 1965).
"All American Teamwork," Army Digest (January 1967).
"The Atlantic Area Command," Navy (May 1965), 26-27.
Box, Clyde. "United States Strike Command Stateside and Global," Air University Review (September-October 1964), 2-10.
"Chronology of Events, Dominican Republic Crisis of 1965," Congressional Digest (November 1965), 264-266.
Connett, William B., Jr. "Operations Center-Locus of Crisis Management," Department of State Newsletter (July 1964), 16-18.
Cuello, J. I. and N. Isa Conde. "Revolutionary Struggle in the Dominican Republic and Its Lessons," World Marxist Review (December 1965 and January 1966).
Dare, James A. "Dominican Diary," U.S. Naval Institute Proceedings (December 1965), 37-45.
Dean, Merrell E. "Managerial Styles," Air University Review (March-April 1967), 41-46.
"Debate over the Soundness of the U.S. Action in the Dominican Republic," Congressional Digest (November 1965), 269.
Delaney, Robert F. "The Psychological Dimension in National Security Planning," Naval War College Review (January-February 1973).
"Evaluation and Compatability: 1965's Key Words in Tactical C and C," Armed Forces Management (July 1965), 45-46.
Farris, Philip A. "USARSTRIKE: Ready to Go," Army Information Digest (October 1965), 12-16.
Ferguson, Yale H. "The Dominican Intervention of 1965: Recent Interpretations," International Organization (Autumn 1973).
Fullbright, J. William. "The Situation in the Dominican Republic," Congressional Record (15 September 1965).
Gilmore, Kenneth O. "The Truth About Santo Domingo," Reader's Digest (May 1966).
Goodsell, James N. "Are Dominican Rebels Reds?" Christian Science Monitor (18 May 1965).
Greening, W. E. "Why Political and Social Crisis in Latin America Raises Doubts Regarding Reliance on O.A.S.," Magazine of Wall Street (29 May 1965), 269-271, 291-292.
Hamilton, William A. "The Decline and Fall of the Joint Chiefs of Staff," Naval War College Review (April 1972).

"How Does STRICOM Get on the Move?" Armed Forces Management (July 1965).

Johnson, Harold K. "The Army's Role in Nation Building and Preserving Stability," Army Information Digest (November 1965), 6-13.

Klein, William E. "Stability Operations in Santo Domingo," Infantry (May-June 1966), 35-39.

"Logistics for Stability Operations," Military Review (September-October 1966).

Lowenthal, Abraham F. "The Dominican Intervention in Retrospect," Public Policy (Fall 1969).

_____. "Limits of American Power: The Lesson of the Dominican Republic," Harper's (June 1964).

Mayer, Laurel A. and Ronald J. Stupak. "The Evolution of Flexible Response in the Post-Vietnam Era," Air University Review (November-December 1975), 12-21.

Meeker, Leonard. "The Dominican Situation in the Perspective of International Law," Department of State Bulletin, (12 July 1965).

Miller, Linda B. "Regional Organization and the Regulation of Internal Conflict," World Politics (July 1967).

Moskos, Charles C. "Grace under Pressure," Army (September 1966).

Moulis, Wallis J. and Richard M. Brown. "Key to a Crisis," Military Review (February 1966).

"Operation Dom Rep," Airborne Quarterly (June-August 1965).

Palmer, Bruce, Jr. "The Army in the Dominican Republic," Army (November 1965): 43-44, 136, 138.

_____." XVIII Airborne Corps Leads the Way," Army Digest (January 1967): 12-18.

_____. "Lessons from the Dominican Stability Operations," Army (November 1966).

Poe, Donald T. "Command and Control--Changeless Yet Changing," U.S. Naval Institute Proceedings (October 1974).

Pyatt, Rudolph A. "Dominican Republic Airlift Just Routine for MATS," News and Courier, Charleston, S. C.(4 May 1965).

"Resolution Establishing Inter-American Force," Department of State Bulletin (31 May 1965), 862-863.

Rippy, J. Fred. "The Initiation of the Customs Receivership in the Dominican Republic," The Hispanic American Historical Review (November 1937), 419-457.

Rodman, Selden, "A Close View of Santo Domingo," Reporter (15 July 1965).

Roucek, Joseph S. "The Dominican Republic in Geopolitics," Contemporary Review (June 1965).

Russell, Richard. "The Situation in the Dominican Republic: Tribute to Ambassador William Tapley Bennett, Jr.," Congressional Record (21 September 1965).

Shoup, David M. "The New American Militarism," The Atlantic Monthly (January-June 1969).

"Statement by President Johnson, April 30." Department of State Bulletin (17 May 1965), 742, 743.

"Statement by President Johnson, May 2, 1965," Department of State Bulletin (17 May 1965), 744-748.

"Swift as Eagles," Army Information Digest (July 1965).

"A Systematic Approach to Command Control," DATA (January 1966).
"To Moorer, the Dom Rep Action Proved--CINCLANT Has Command and Control," Armed Forces Management (July 1965).
Tompkins, R. "Ubique," Marine Corps Gazette (September 1965), 32-39.
"2500 Have Lost Their Lives in Bitter Dominican Conflict," New York Times (31 August 1965), 9. Ware, Hugh. "New Tools for Crisis Management," U.S. Naval Institute Proceedings (August 1974).
Wells, Henry. "The Dominican Republic: Aftermath of Despotism," Current History (January 1966).
_____. "The Dominican Search for Stability," Current History (December 1966).
Wiarda, Howard J. "The Dominican Revolution in Perspective: A Research Note," Polity (Fall 1968).
_____. "The Politics of Civil-Military Relations in the Dominican Republic," Journal of Inter-American Studies (October 1965), 465-484.
_____. "The U.S. and the Dominican Crisis: Background to Chaos," Caribbean Monthly Bulletin (July 1965).
Worley, Robert. "Striking a Balance in Advanced Command and Control Gear," International (December 1965).
Wyckoff, Don P. "An American Peace Keeping Force," Marine Corps Gazette (September 1965), 27-31.

PUBLIC DOCUMENTS

U.S. Air Force. Aerospace Studies Institute, Air University. The Dominican Republic Crisis of 1965: The Air Force Role, AU-434-66, December 1966.
_____. Military Air Transport Service, 772d Troop Carrier Squadron. Final Report, Operation Press Ahead, 11 June 1965.
_____. 9th Air Force, Airlift Task Force. TACOP Final Report, Power Pack, 24 May 1965.
_____. TAC, 353d Tactical Fighter Squadron. TACOP Final Report for Power Pack, 3 June 1965.
_____. TAC, 354th Tactical Fighter Wing. History January-June 1965.
_____. TAC, 363d Tactical Reconnaissance Wing. TACOP Final Report, 17 June 1965.
U.S. Army. FM 57-10 Army Forces in Joint Airborne Operations. Washington, D.C., March 1962.
_____. FM 100-20 Low Intensity Conflict. Washington, D.C., January 1981.
U.S. Congress, House of Representatives. Hearings before Subcommittee of the House Committee on Appropriation. Statement of Secretary of Defense Robert S. McNamara, p. 1, 89th cong., 2d sess., 14 February 1966.
_____. House of Representatives. Selden Resolution, House Resolution no. 560, 89th cong., 1st sess., 20 September 1965.
U.S. Congress, Senate, Committee on Foreign Relations. Background Information Relating to the Dominican Republic, 89th cong., 2d sess., 1965.

_____. Senate, Committee on Judiciary. "Testimony of Brigadier General Elias Wessin y Wessin," <u>Hearings before the Internal Security Subcommittee of the Committee on the Judiciary</u>, 89th cong., 1st sess., 1 October 1965.

U.S. Department of Defense. Blue Ribbon Defense Panel. <u>Report to the President and the Secretary of Defense on the Department of Defense</u>, 1 July 1970.

_____. <u>Capsule Facts for the Armed Forces</u>. AO-1, 5 May 1965.

U.S. Department of State. "The Acting Secretary of State to the Minister in the Dominican Republic," 19 March 1930, <u>Foreign Relations of the United States</u> II, 1930.

_____. <u>The Dominican Crisis: The Hemisphere Acts</u>, 1965.

U.S. Forces, Dominican Republic "Report of Stability Operations in the Dominican Republic." 2 parts. Santo Domingo, 1965. U.S. Joint Chiefs of Staff. <u>Dictionary of Military and Associated Terms</u>, JCS Pub No. 1, 3 September 1974.

U.S. Marine Corps. <u>Operations Against Guerrilla Forces</u>, FMFM-21, August 1962.

U.S. National Security Council. <u>History of Dominican Intervention</u>. Austin: Lyndon B. Johnson Library.

U.S. Navy. Atlantic Fleet, Amphibious Force. <u>Report of Participation in Dominican Republic Operations for Period 25 April to 6 June 1965</u>, 11 June 1965.

_____. Atlantic Fleet, Amphibious Group 4. <u>Report of Participation in Dominican Republic Operations</u>, 29 June 1965.

U.S. President (Kennedy). <u>Public Papers of the Presidents of the United States: John Kennedy</u>, 1961.

U.S. President (Johnson). <u>Public Papers of the Presidents of the United States: Lyndon B. Johnson</u> I, 1965.

OTHER SOURCES

Costa, John J. "The Dominican Republic: Intervention in Perspective," Unpublished thesis, U.S. Army War College, 2 May 1968.

Greenberg, Lawrence M. <u>United States Army Unilateral and Coalition Operations in the 1965 Dominican Republic Intervention</u>. Washington, D.C.: Analysis Branch, U.S. Army Center of Military History, 1987

Kelso, Quinten A. "The Dominican Crisis of 1965: A New Appraisal." Ph.D. dissertation, University of Colorado, 1982.

Long, Eldredge R., Jr. "The Dominican Crisis 1965: An Experiment in International Peace Keeping." Unpublished thesis, U.S. Naval War College, April 1967.

Mann, Thomas C. "Correcting Some Misconceptions," <u>Speech Department of State Bulletin</u>, October 1965.

Mason, John T. Interview with Admiral Masterson, 9 April 1973, no. 7 in United States Naval Institute, <u>Oral History Interviews, 1973</u>.

Palmer, Bruce R., Jr. The Dominican Republic." Speech to Pan American Society of New England, November 1966.

_____. Papers. U.S. Army Military History Institute, Carlisle Barracks, Pa.

_____. "U.S. Stability Operations in the Dominican Republic." Speech to Association of the U.S. Army, Washington, D.C., 11 October 1966.

Ringler, Jack K. and Henry I. Shaw, Jr. U.S. Marine Corps Operations in the Dominican Republic, April-June 1965. Washington, D.C.: Historical Division, U.S. Marine Corps, 1970.

Schoonmaker, Herbert G. The Tactical Air Command in the Dominican Crisis 1965. Langley Air Force Base, Va.: Office of TAC History, May 1977.

Yates, Jules D. "The Dominican Crisis." Mitre Working Paper Bedford, Mass.: Mitre Corporation, 1973.

Yates, Lawrence A. Power-Pack: U.S. Intervention in the Dominican Republic, 1965-1966. Fort Leavenworth, Kans.: Combat Studies Institute, U.S. Army Command and General Staff College, 1988.

Index

Agency for International Development (AID), 6, 99
Airborne command post, 69, 73
Air Force, Dominican, 22, 25, 26, 70, 111
Air Force, U.S.. See U.S. Air Force
Alerting system, 25-26, 31 n.20, 38, 79
Alliance for Progress, 5-7, 12, 16 n.15, 50
Alvin, Hugo Panasco, 114
Armed Forces Training Center (CEFA), 13-14, 22, 116
Arms, distribution of, 22, 30 n.9
Army, U.S.. See U.S. Army
Attachés, military, 6, 21, 25-26, 30 n.4. See also Intelligence

Balaguer, Joaquín, 6, 13, 19, 118
Ball, George W., 36, 40, 78-79
Batista, Fulgencio, 5, 11
Benitez, Jaime, 77
Benoit, Pedro, 34-35, 78,82
Bennet, William Tapley, Jr., 20, 26, 28-29, 35, 37-38, 78, 80, 83, 89; cease-fire stance, 81, 84; meets with President Johnson, 25; relations with Palmer, 88, 110, 129; support of Reid, 13; telecon with Washington, 40-41; walkie-talkie request, 34; Warns of possible communist takeover, 33
Benoit, Pedro Bartolome, 34-35, 78, 82
Bosch, Juan, 77, 83, 118; exile, 14; opposition to, 10, 23, 26, 29, 34; overthrow, 10-11; presidency, 7
Boxer (U.S.S), 23, 28-29, 37, 56
Bundy, McGeorge, 35-36, 45 n.11, 55, 112-113
Bunker, Ellsworth, 90, 115-117

Caamaño Deno, Francisco, 33-34, 111-112, 115-118; arming of rebels, 30 n.9; arrests Reid, 22; considers U.S. friendly neutral, 113; incident at Hotel Matum, 117; installed as constitutionalist president, 110; meeting at U.S. Embassy, 29; refusal to negotiate with Imbert, 109
Caribbean region, 1-7, 41-42
Castro, Fidel, 5-6, 11, 29, 35, 50-51, 84
Cease-fires, 23, 25, 29, 37, 41-42, 78-79, 81-84, 111
CEFA. See Armed Forces Training Center
Central Intelligence Agency. See Intelligence

Chain of Command. See Crisis management
Choke points, 1
Cindad, Nueva, 34, 82, 89, 113
Civic action, 59, 99-100. See also Evacuation
Combat airlift support unit, 69
Commander in chief, Atlantic (CINCLANT), 21, 23, 35, 89
Communications, 28, 129; back channel, 64 n.16; CRITIC, 35-36, 45 n.11; Dominican level, 56; "Talking Bird," 73; unified command level, 55-56; Washington level, 55
Communists, 21, 25, 33, 83; communist threat, 7-8, 33-34, 37, 39, 42 n.1, 43, 87-88
Conde Héctor, 87
Congress, 3-4, 8, 37
Connett, William B., Jr., 20, 23-24, 26
Constitutionalists, 10-12, 20, 22, 105
Costs of intervention, 119
Council of State, 6
Counterinsurgency, 1, 6, 8
Country Team, 20, 30 n.4, 54, 64 n.18, 125
Crisis management, 17 n.21, 49, 66 n.33; chain of command, 52-54; command, control and communications 54-57; decision-making, 7, 33-36, 40-42, 45 n.11 and 45 n.13; goals and objectives, 8, 50-51; military doctrine and missions, 8, 58-60; military planning, 26, 37, 57-58, 65 n.29, 66 n.30; principles of, 8, 17 n.21, 51, 62 n.11
Cuba, 1, 3, 5-6, 11, 24, 35, 42, 84
Cuban air force, 70

Dare, James A., 23, 37-40, 98
Daughtry, George W., 24, 28, 37, 40
De los Santos Céspedes, Juan, 14, 21-22, 82
Defense conditions. See Alerting system
Delashaw, Robert H., 58, 69, 73

Department of Defense, 102
Despradel Brache, Hernán, 29. See also Dominican National Police
Detainees, 105
Dominican Air Force, 21-23, 25, 111
Dominican Army, 9-14, 19-22, 28, 34, 38, 40, 80, 82, 84, 98, 110-111, 113, 116-118
Dominican National Police, 5, 21, 29, 34, 36, 78, 85
Dominican Navy, 22, 25, 28, 98
Dominican Red Cross, 35, 82
Dominican Republic: annexation by United States, 3; civil-military relationship, 9-10; constitutions, 11, 115; custom houses, 4; location, 1; occupation by U.S. Marines, 5; strategic importance of, 1
Dominican Revolutionary Party (PRD), 11, 14, 19, 88
Dominican Task Force, 125
Duarte Bridge, 26, 28, 34, 78, 80

EC-135 air-borne command post, 68, 69, 73-74
Economy, Dominican, 10, 12, 118
Eisenhower, Dwight D., 5, 7, 46 n.17
Elections, Dominican, 7, 188
El Salvador, 115
Embajador Hotel, 25, 28, 36, 39-40, 80, 90, 99, 111
Embassy, U.S., Santo Domingo, 19-20, 22-26, 28-29, 33-37, 40, 78-79, 81, 84, 111. See also Bennett; Connett
Engagement, rules of. See Rules of engagement
ESSO map, 85
Evacuation, 19, 23-26, 28-29, 35-37

F-100 fighter aircraft, 71, 128
F-104 fighter-interceptor aircraft, 71
Fact sheets, 60
Federal Bureau of Investigation (FBI), 43 n.2, 106

Index

Fighter support. See U.S. Air Force; U.S. Marine Corps; U.S. Navy
Figueres, José, 77
Flexible response, 7-8, 129
"Focos," 11
Fortas, Abe, 77
Fort Bragg, 26, 68, 73, 102
Fort Monroe, 73
Fortress Ozama. See Ozama Fortress
Fort Snelling (U.S.S.), 23, 40
Freeman, Paul L., 53
France, disapproves U.S. action, 46 n.17
Fullbright, J. William, 46 n.17

García-Godoy, Héctor, 116-118
Goals, U.S., 49-51, 126
Goldwater, Barry M., 46 n.17
Good Neighbor Policy, 41, 113
Government of National Reconstruction. See Imbert government
Grant, Ulysses S., 3
Great Britain, support of U.S. action, 11, 46 n.17
Green Berets, See U.S. Army Special Forces
Green Chopper, 100
Greenville, North Carolina, 102
Guantanamo Bay, 98
Guatemala, 89
Guerrilla Warfare, 7-8, 11, 132
Guevara, Ernesto (Che), 11
Guzman, Antonio, 112-113

Haina, port of, 28-29, 40, 90, 97, 98, 111
Haiti, 1
Harriman, Averell, 79
Helicopters. See U.S. Armed Service concerned
Hernando, Ramírez, Miguel Angel, 14, 19-20
Heywood, Ralph, 22, 26
Hispaniola, 1, 98
Honduras, 11, 114
Hotel Embajador. See Embajador Hotel
Hotel Matum, 117
House of Representatives, 48 n.30

Humanitarian operations, 99-100. See also Evacuation and Medical assistance
HU-1B helicopter, 72
Hungary, 82-83, 87, 128

Imbert Barrera, Antonio, 22, 68, 83; Imbert government, 109-113, 116
Insurgency, 7-8, 131
Intelligence: attaché reporting, 21, 33, 43 n.2; CIA reporting, 19, 21, 33, 43 n.2, 100-101; collection, 43 n.2, 106, 124; detainee center, 105; human intelligence (HUMINT), 105; production, 105
International Red Cross, 113
Inter-American Peace Force, 113-119
International Security Zone (ISZ), 39-40, 78-81, 97
Intervention, military, 6, 8, 29, 35, 37-38, 47 n.28, 48 n.30, 84, 130-132

Jamming, communications, 103-104
Johnson, Harold, 94 n.33
Johnson, Lyndon B., 1, 8, 21, 23, 25, 29, 35, 81-82, 114; advisers, 12, 36, 39, 45 n.13, 46 n.14, 61 n.8, 79, 112, 125; decisions, 33-36, 39, 40-42, 45 n.11, 46 n.17, 79, 125; Latin American policy, 12-13, 50; management style, 19, 43 n.2, 51, 53, 61 n.8, 127; press relations, 37; speeches, 37, 51, 60, 82, 88, 90, 102, 124
Joint air control coordination center (JACCC), 73
Joint Chiefs of Staff, 9, 36, 53, 66 n.33, 70, 83, 89, 126, 129; and alerts, 25-26, 38, 52, 54, 56, 79; communications with JTF, 53, 57; contingency plan approval, 57; diversion of airlift, 68; priorities on airlift, 70, 73; size of commitment, 41
Joint Task Force, 35, 53, 56-57, 63 n.15, 97
Junta, military, 24, 34, 38, 80, 109. See also loyalists.

KC-135 jet tanker, 67
Kennedy, John F.: Alliance for Progress, 5, 11; concern for another Cuba, 6; Dominican policy, 6; and Khruschev, 7; Kennedy-Johnson national security policy, 7-9; Latin American Policy, 11-12, 50
Kennedy, Robert F., 46 n.17
Khrushchev, Nikita S., 7
Knapp, Harry S., 5

Langley Air Force Base, Virginia, 53, 73
Lann, Fred, 56
LaSalle (U.S.S.), 98
Latin American brigade. See Inter-American Peace Force
La Vega, 22
Leap-frogging by battalion, 89
Lebanon intervention of 1958, 47 n.28, 132
Lejeune, Camp, 26
Leoni, Raúl, 79
Limited war, 129
Line of communication (LOC), 42, 82, 87-90, 113
Logistical support, 38, 62 n.11, 74, 97, 130-131
Loyalists: and attaché influence, 21; request walkie-talkies, 34; and MAAG support, 40; retire to training center, 80. See also Dominican Army; Junta
Luce (U.S.S.), 98

McCain, John S., Jr., 53, 98
McCone, John, 29
McNamara, Robert S., 9, 36-37, 39, 41; centralized control of military, 8; importance of crisis management, 49; as manager, 61 n.8; relationship with Wheeler, 66 n.33; on size of troop commitment, 79; telephone conference with Bennett, 40
McNickle, Marvin L. 53, 73
Mann, Thomas C. 13, 21, 38, 79, 112; assumed key role in crisis response, 24, 61 n.8; implemented new U.S. Latin American policy, 12; met with President Johnson, 39; opposed landing marines, 45; telephoned by Bennett regarding cease-fire, 81
Marines. See U.S. Marine Corps
Marinho, Ilmar Penna
Martin, John Bartlow, 7, 11, 41, 61 n.8, 87; cease-fire arrangements; 77, 82-85; conclusion concerning Castro-communists, 87; Johnson's emissary 42, 77-79; press conference 88; relationship with Imbert, 109-113; on why rebels armed 30 n.9
Massive retaliation, 7
Masterson, Kleber S., 35, 38, 40, 53, 56-57, 63 n.15, 68, 78, 80-81, 83, 89, 97
Mayobre, José Antonio, 112
Medical assistance, 35, 98-100
Military Air Transport Service (MATS), 67
Military Assistance Advisory Group (MAAG), 6, 20, 30 n.4, 34, 39, 40, 62 n.11
Molina Ureña, José Rafael, 22, 25-26, 29, 34
Monroe Doctrine, 3-4, 48 n.30
Moorer, Thomas M., 21, 52-53, 56. See also commander in chief, Atlantic (CINCLANT)
Montás Guerrero, Salvador, 34
Mora, José A., 79, 82, 87, 112-113
Morales, Carlos, 4
Morehead City, North Carolina, 97
Morse, Wayne L., 46 n.17
Moscoso, Teodoro, 79
Moyers, Bill, 13:1 1, 36
MRC-98 communications, 74
Muñoz, Marin Louis, 10, 77

National Command Authorities (NCA), 52
National liberation, wars of, 7
National Military Control Center (NMCC), 21, 55
National Palace, 9, 115
National Security Council (NSC), 7

Index 149

Newport News (U.S.S.), 97
Nicaragua, 114
Nonintervention, 3, 6, 41, 113

Occupation of Dominican Republic, 5
OH-13 helicopter, 72
Okinawa (U.S.S.), 97
Operation Plan 310/2-65, 57-58, 65 n. 27, 65 n.29
Operations centers, 19, 24. See also Crisis Management
Operations, code names for: Barrel Bottom, 40; Green Chopper, 100; Power Pack, 68-69, 74 n.3, 80; Press Ahead, 114
Organization of American States (OAS), 5-6, 37-38, 77, 79, 82, 84, 89
Ozama Fortress, 78, 80
Ozama River, 78, 80, 98, 105, 113

Palmer, Bruce, Jr., 21, 53, 61 n.8, 83, 118-119, 128; commander of ground forces, 79; and Inter-American Peace Force, 114; planned troop linkup, 88-90; relations with Wessin y Wessin, 110-111; communicated directly with the president, 73
Panama, 89
Panama Canal, 1, 4, 62 n.11
Papal nuncio, 78, 81-82, 84
Paraguay, 114
Paratrooper-marine linkup, 87-90. See also line of communication
Peace commission, 89, 112
Peace corps, 7, 35
Peña Gómez, José Francisco, 14
Perimeter, marine, 80
Plans, contingency, 19, 25-26, 126. See also Operation Plan 310/2-65
Police, Dominican National, 21, 25, 29, 35, 39, 78
Polo grounds, 28, 37, 40, 80
Pope Air Force Base, North Carolina, 38, 68-70, 73

PRD. See Dominican Revolutionary Party
Provisional government, 116-118
Psychological warfare, 20, 25, 29, 33, 102-104, 129
Puerto Rican National Guard, 70
Puerto Rico, 1, 3-4, 10-11, 24, 39, 77, 98

Raborn, William, 21
Radio stations, Dominican, 20, 22, 25, 29, 82, 101. See also Psychological Warfare
Raleigh (U.S.S.), 23, 28, 40, 72
Ramey Air Force Base, Puerto Rico, 39, 67-69, 94 n.36
Rankin (U.S.S.), 23, 40
RB-66 aircraft, 71
Readiness, conditions of, 31 n.20. See also Alerting system
Ready Group, Amphibious, 23-26, 28-29, 35-40
Rebels. See Constitutionalists
Reform Party, 13
Reid Cabral, Donald, 12-14, 19-22
RF-101 aircraft, 71
Rikhye, Indura, 112
Rivera Caminero, Francisco, 22, 24
Rivera Cuesta, Marcos, 20
ROAD (Reorganization Objective Army Divisions), 65 n.29
Roosevelt Corollary, 4
Roosevelt, Franklin D., 113
Roosevelt Roads Naval Station, 26, 72, 94 n.36, 98
Roosevelt, Theodore, 4
Ruchamkin (U.S.S.), 23, 28
Rules of engagement, 39, 86-87, 128
Rusk, Dean, 6, 24, 36; adopted management style of Marshall, 61 n.8; instructed to seek OAS help, 79; Thursday Telecon with Bennett, 40-41; warned of Bosch weakness, 10
Russell, Richard, 36

San Christobal, 19, 111
San Isidro Airfield, 13, 26, 39-40, 68-69, 78, 80, 82, 111

Samana Bay, 3, 101
Sans Souci, 81
Santa Cruz Air Base, 114
Santa Maria Cathedral, 24
Santiago, 22, 117
Santo Domingo, 1, 6, 20, 22-24, 26, 29, 34, 38, 41
School of the Americas, 119
Security zone. See International Security Zone.
Selden Resolution, 48 n.30
Shlaudeman, Harry, 82, 84
Showcase of democracy, 6, 13
Size of military commitment, 79
Snipers, 81, 82
Social Christian Revolutionary Party (PRSC), 11
Soviet Union, 7, 84
Spanish-American War, 3
Special Forces, 8, 100-102. See also U.S. armed service concerned
Strategic Air Command, 67, 69
State Department, U.S., 8, 39, 54, 81; Bennett got resume of policy, 78; formulation of U.S. policy, 24-25; Mann appointment, 12; predicted Wessin victory, 29
Sweeney, Walter C., Jr., 53

Tactical Air Command, 25, 53, 67, 70. See also U.S. Air Force
Tactical air control center, 73
Times, 30 n.10
Triumvirate, 1, 10-12, 20
Trujillo, Rafael, 5-6, 9, 12-13

UH-1B helicopter, 72
UH-1D helicopter, 72
Unified commands: Alanntic Command, 21, 25, 52-54, 56, 64 n.16, 65 n.27; Southern Command, 62 n.11, 67, 114; Strike Command, 8, 25, 53, 62 n.11, 92 n.9
United Nations, 84, 111, 113
U.S. Air Force: airborne command post, 68, 73; air control, 57, 73; airlift, 25, 67-70, 114, 127, 130; communications, 57, 73-74; fighters and reconnaissance aircraft, 25, 70-71, 94 n.36; major commands, 67; planning, 58; psychological warfare, 103, 129; special forces, 8, 102-103
U.S. Air Force, aircraft: C-47, 103; C-119, 67; C-123, 101, 103; C-124, 67; C-130, 67-70; C-130 "Talking Bird," 73; C-130E, 69; EC-135, 68, 73; KC-135, 67; F-4C, 71; F-100, 71, 76 n.15, 128; F-104, 71; RB-66, 71; RF-101, 71; U-10, 103
U.S. Air Force, Air Defense Command, 67
--331st Fighter Interceptor Squadron, 71
U.S. Air Force, Air National Guard, 67, 73
U.S. Air Force, Communications Service, 74
U.S. Air Force, Continental Air Command, 67
U.S. Air Force, Military Air Transport Service, 67
U.S. Air Force, Tactical Air Command, 25, 53, 56, 67, 75 n.4
--9th Air Force, 75 n.4
--19th Air Force, 58
--1st Air Commando Wing, 101, 103
--Special Air Warfare Center, 103
--353d Tactical Fighter Squadron, 71
--463d Troop Carrier Wing, 114
U.S. Air Force, Strategic air command, 67, 69
U.S. Air Force, Southern command, 67, 114
U.S. Air Force, Task Forces: Air Force Task Force, 58, 75 n.4; Task Force 121, 53, 73
U.S. Army: alerts, 25-26, 31 n.20, 79; intelligence, 104-106; planning, 57-58; communications, 73; counterintelligence, 106; helicopters, 72, 102; planning 57-58; psychological warfare, 102; Task force 120, 53, 80

Index

U.S. Army, 18th Airborne Corps, 58, 79
--82d Airborne Division: check points, 99; civil affairs program, 99-100; Duarte bridgehead, 80, 89; Hotel Matum incident, 117; intelligence, 104-105; linkup with marines, 87-90; peace force, 113-114; reconnaissance patrol, 85; rebel zone reintegration, 117; renewed fighting, 15 June, 115-116; rules of engagement, 86-87; troops block runways, 111; troop withdrawal, 119; 2d Bridgade, 84; 3d Brigade, 79-80; 307th Engineering Battalion, 100; 307th Medical Gattalion, 100
--101st Airborne Division, 58, 79, 92 n.9
U.S. Army, Continental Army Command, 26, 53, 56
U.S. Army, 519 Military Intelligence Battalion, 105
U.S. Army, 1st Psychological Warfare Battalion, 102
U.S. Army, 7th Special Forces Group, 100; countryside detachments, 101-102; intelligence, 100-101; psychological warfare, 102; sewer war, 101
U.S. Army, Special Warfare Center, Fort Bragg, 102
U.S. Forces, Dominican Republic, 53
U.S. Information Agency, 102-103, 129
U.S. Marine Corps: amphibious landing, 40; beginning of withdrawal, 115; communications, 28; doctrine, 59; embassy guard augmented, 36; extension of security zone, 111; helicopters, 28-29, 36-38; humanitarian assistance, 99; International Security Zone (ISZ), 78-81; linkup with paratroopers, 85, 87-90; pathfinders, 28, 36; rules of engagement, 39, 86-87; tanks and armored vehicles, 40
U.S. Marine Corps, 2nd Marine Division, 23, 26, 97
--4th Marine Expeditionary Brigade, 84
--6th Marine Expeditionary Unit, 23, 37, 39; 1st Battalion/6th Marine Regiment, 84; 3rd Battalion/6th Marine Regiment, 23, 80
U.S. Navy: amphibious lift, 97; blockade of Hispaniola, 98; communications, 57; evacuation, 23-25, 29, 37-38; helicopters, 28, 72, 111; humanitarian aid, 35; logistics, 97; naval gunfire support, 38; planning, 37, 57-58, 65 n.29, 89, 126; sea surveillance, 98; special forces (SEALs), 101; Task Force 124, 40, 53; underwater demolition, 40
U.S. Navy, Commander in Chief, Atlantic (CINCLANT), 21, 23, 35, 42, 53-54, 56, 63 n.15, 89, 120 n.17
--Amphibious Ready Group, 23-24, 26, 28, 36, 38-39, 120 n.17
--Caribbean Sea Frontier, 38, 62 n.11
U.S. Navy, ships: Boxer, 23, 28-29, 36-38, 40, 56, 80, 97-98; Fort Snelling, 23, 40; LaSalle, 98; Luce, 98; Newport News, 97; Okinawa, 97; Raleigh, 23, 28-29, 40; Rankin, 23, 40; Ruchamkin, 23, 28, 40; Wood County, 28, 38, 40
U Thant, 112

Vance, Cyrus, R., 112-113
Vaughn, Jack H., 21-22, 112
Venezuela, 4, 79
Viegues, Puerto Rico, 23-24
Vietnam War, 1, 41, 132
Voice of America, 102

Wars of national liberation, 7
Webb Air Force Base, 71
Welch, William L., 68

Wessin y Wessin, Elías, 22, 24, 26, 28-29, 34, 40, 45 n.11, 104-105, 109-110; 1963 coup against Bosch, 10-11; cease-fire talks, 81-82; forced out of country, 116-117; power behind throne, 14; requests U.S. support, 25
Western Hemisphere, 4, 48 n.30

Wheeler, Earl, 36, 40-42, 64 n.16, 66 n.33, 79, 89
White House situation room, 55
Wilson, Woodrow, 4-5
Wood County (U.S.S.), 28, 38
Worley, Robert F., 75 n.4

York, Robert H., 26, 53, 79-83

About the Author

HERBERT G. SCHOONMAKER is Commander, U.S. Naval Reserve (Retired) and holds a Ph.D. from the University of Georgia. During his career as a military historian with the U.S. Army and Air Force, he authored a considerable number of classified studies.